COSMIC CONSPIRACY

Other books by Patricia McLaine

THE RECYCLING OF ROSALIE

THE WHEEL OF DESTINY

Plays by Patricia McLaine

LOVE IS CONTAGIOUS

SIDNEY

COSMIC
CONSPIRACY

PSYCHIC TO THE
RICH AND FAMOUS

A MEMOIR
BY

PATRICIA MCLAINE

This book is for my thousands of clients—the faithful and true—who believed in me and trusted my gifts.

And for my family and friends for loving and encouraging me with all the strangeness that is still in my life!

CONTENTS

METAPHYSICAL MAGIC

ACKNOWLEDGMENTS

The primary reason I wrote this memoir is because of the encouragement of my four eldest grandchildren: Oliver, Jonah, Lydia and Shaina Brassard, my daughter Tomi's children. As the youngsters grew older, one, two, or more, occasionally joined me for lunch or dinner, without their parents, in a restaurant. That was when I began to tell them stories about the amazing people I had met and of the many fascinating and unusual things that had happened to me. Before long, all four of them were telling me that I should write a book about my unique life experiences—so here it is.

With respect to this book, I need to express my sincere thanks to my long-time client-friend, Gwen Davis, for encouraging me to write this memoir and to name names (blame it on Gwen, celebs) and for being so generous in her praise. I also want to thank my good friend, Jeanne Avery, for becoming a successful astrologer (as predicted) and for writing her wonderful astrology books (as predicted), in addition to writing me a lovely foreword for this book.

I also want to thank my special friends, Sheila Weidenfeld and Maggie Linton, for reading the early drafts and providing me with quotes. In addition, I want to thank my very long-time client-friend, Pattye Horne, (with me since I charged $10) for reading several drafts and tactfully pointing out my errors. And I want to thank my efficient editor-client-friend, Diana Read, for catching my many flub-ups and making the welcome corrections.

The signed celebrity pictures in this book were gifts from my celebrity-clients. Most of the pictures were given to me around 30 years ago. The only photographer's name is for Gwen, which she provided. In a future edition, I will be happy to credit all other photographers, provided I am contacted about the picture(s) taken.

I also want to sincerely thank my stepsister, Ginger Guevara, who has always been there for me and shared my long journey since fourth grade. And I want to thank my special friend, Judy (Justine) Diamond, who has given me such tremendous support and encouragement with regard to my writing.

As a disclaimer on behalf of my offspring, neither my children, nor their spouses, nor any of my grandchildren necessarily believe in or embrace my complex belief system that includes astrology, psychic phenomena and reincarnation. My mother allowed me to follow the dictates of my heart in terms of beliefs, and I have granted my descendants the same privilege.

At this time, I also want to sincerely thank my two children, Tomi Gail Jacobs Ziobro and Mark Lawrence Jacobs, for growing up to be such fine individuals of whom I am exceedingly proud, for presenting me with so many attractive and interesting grandchildren, male and female, and for putting up with and loving a mother who works in a rather bizarre profession that includes a significant roster of famous, unusual, and talented clients—and an extraordinary number of invisible friends!

In Love and Light,

Patricia McLaine, September 2010

FOREWORD

If you are preparing to read *Cosmic Conspiracy*, be sure to allow the time to finish this page-turner in one sitting. The adventure you are about to encounter is sure to capture your attention and imagination. Reading the saga of Pattie's life from childhood onward is possibly going to change your life, as well as your consciousness.

Pattie's ability to take you through the earthly and profoundly exciting events of her life is skillfully interwoven with her inner journey. As life presented her with many challenges, her spiritual growth simultaneously took her into uncharted visions of what life is really all about.

I met Pattie in the early '70s after I moved to California to resume my work in film and television. As a New York actress trained by Sandy Meisner, I was able to land wonderful jobs in Los Angeles with such stars as Andy Griffith, Louis Jourdan and Peter Lawford, among others. I had backup from the best casting director in Hollywood, Eddie Foy III, and I was on my way.

About the same time, many friends told me I should consult Pattie for a reading. They said, "You'll just love her. She is another redheaded Scorpio and a very talented tarot card reader." Indeed, she is the best. With great anticipation, I went to her adorable house in the valley and had my first reading.

I was rapt with attention until Pattie said, "Forget about this acting business. You're going to be a very well known astrologer and will do something different with your approach to the age-old subject."

I remember being just so angry that she would say that. I had studied hard, sacrificed a great deal to do summer stock and taken voice lessons three times a week. In fact, I was hired to do my first opera in the role of Susanna in *The Marriage of Figaro* at the Amato Opera Theater in New York, when it was too late to postpone my move to Los Angeles. Pattie later described my reaction as "You bristled." No kidding! When my ex-husband died, very unexpectedly, I took a trip back to New York to be with my daughter. To my great surprise, I never worked in theater again.

To say that Pattie changed my life is putting it mildly. I'm sure she has had the same (only more gentle) reaction from many of her clients. Indeed, in spite of myself, I started doing astrological charts in Los Angeles and finally moved back to New York City. Eventually, I landed my first book contract with Doubleday, Inc. after being hired to write a daily astrological newspaper column for Fields Syndication.

Pattie and I were always in touch with each other as an eternal bond was re-created. We have the same past life memories as a Christian martyr in Rome, with death coming to each of us in a different way. Our connection with Susan Strasberg began early in our friendship, as Susan also spontaneously remembered that life. Pattie introduced me to Susan and valued Susie as one of her closest friends.

When I moved to the beautiful island of Ibiza, Spain, where I went to write three of my six books, I invited Pattie to participate in a healing conference in 1984 for the people living on the island. Pattie attracted the same following there as she had on all her other journeys. She was appreciated, loved and admired.

I could say so much more about Pattie's work and praise her to the skies, but I don't want to take time away from you as you begin your engrossing venture into the wonderful story of her life working in the realm of the paranormal.

With love and respect for her talent and her spirit,

Jeanne Avery, September 2010

This is me and my friend Jeanne Avery, January 1981

PROLOGUE

DREAMS AND VISUALIZATIONS

In considering the many decades of my present incarnation, I have often wondered how many people end up living the life initially dreamed of, or visualized—as we say in my trade. How many of us became what we dreamed of becoming throughout the years we have managed to survive on this sometimes dangerous, constantly changing, but magnificent planet called Earth? And, if we were one of the lucky ones who lived the dream—did everything turn out as planned, or were there constant rewrites along the way?

My first dream, or visualization, was to be another Shirley Temple. Her big box office success up on the silver screen commenced the year I was born. My dear mother started taking me to the movies as soon as I could sit up and sit still until intermission. The popcorn often kept me from talking, and yet, from the start I fell in love with the movies. The earliest films I can remember starred Shirley Temple. I was mesmerized by her curly hair, deep dimples, and the songs and dances performed so well at age six. My first tap dancing lessons were taken free at the park. I wanted to be just like Shirley even after I was six. And I'm willing to bet I was not alone in that dream during the early years of my young life.

My next dream was to be another Elizabeth Taylor. Perhaps you can imagine my thrill at age 11 when the woman seated next to me at the lunch counter in Woolworth's in downtown Kansas City, Kansas, said, "You have a profile just like Elizabeth Taylor's!"

My long, dark hair was similar. Later that day, I studied my profile in the mirror wondering if someday I might appear in films such as *Lassie Come Home* or *National Velvet*. Countless young girls dream of being movie stars. I fell in love with the movies and with actors because of my star-struck mother. Most Saturday afternoons were spent at the movies. Mother's favorite actresses were Bette Davis and Barbara Stanwyck, but it took me years to appreciate their talents. Going to the movies on a Saturday meant a double feature, news reel, cartoon, and a serial with cowboys and Indians or Buck Rogers—all of that and popcorn too for the price of a quarter—which was something to look forward to every weekend.

During my adolescence I had serious crushes on several male movie stars. I usually cut a picture out of a movie magazine and taped it to my headboard as young Darryl Hickman, Farley Granger, or Tony Curtis smiled at me. My current crush was faithfully kissed goodnight. At 14, I arose from a sick bed and convinced my stepfather, Raymond Shoaf, to drive my stepsister Ginger and me to the supermarket. Tony Curtis and Janet Leigh were making a public appearance. In my delirium, I broke through the police line, but Tony and Janet signed my autograph book anyway. The next day I was convinced that Tony Curtis had healed me just by looking into my eyes.

By then I no longer visualized simply being an actress. I had started writing stories in shorthand notebooks by sixth grade. My new dream was to be a writer. I wrote tales of Arabian princes, such as Douglas Fairbanks, Jr. or Errol Flynn, escaping from imminent danger on a flying carpet or galloping off on a horse to rescue some princess from a fate worse than boredom. The prince was always handsome and faithful to the princess forever, of course. Swashbuckling films were among my favorites. My dream had become to be another Maureen O'Hara. After all, I was Irish on both sides and mighty proud of it.

In high school, I took drama classes but was shy about getting up in front of people to pretend to be someone else. In English classes, where the grade was divided, my papers were marked B+ or A on content and C or C- on grammar. Sentence structure seemed unimportant compared to the stories in my head. My imagination was highly active.

My senior year in high school I had an idea for a play, which I wrote on a legal pad in longhand at the dining room table. With dialogue not all the characters speak perfect English. The characters and actions told the story of my three-act comedy, *Sidney*, with the main character a teenage girl with a boy's name. Sidney blossoms into quite the young miss and goes to the prom with the class heartthrob. It was "the ugly duckling that becomes a swan" with my twist, a popular theme often portrayed with slightly different characters and slightly different plots.

At 17, my dream was to be another Jean Kerr, or maybe Nora Ephron, except Nora was unknown to me at the time. She may not have even been visualizing herself as a writer yet. Who knows? Nora may have also written stories in spiral notebooks in junior high. But she was probably not nearly as funny as she was after her two failed marriages, something she probably never visualized. Eventually, laughing at our folly and heartbreak helps us to survive on the planet—more on Nora later.

In addition to being published by the Mormon Church, *Sidney* was published by Eldridge Publishing. I made a deal for royalties rather than selling the play outright for $200 (over the years more than $200 was received, but perhaps the royalties were the reason the play was eventually dropped). Nonetheless, I had become a professional playwright—and was no longer simply dreaming, visualizing, hoping and praying. At night while my first husband Tom (John Thomas Kallunki) performed in plays at the Glendale Centre Theater, and my adorable baby daughter Tomi (born August 28, 1958) was sound asleep, on my typewriter at the kitchen table I started to write another play that eventually became *Love Is Contagious*. When things were slow in my secretarial job at a construction company, I worked on my play. The funny characters and absurd situations turned into a three-act comedy. I no longer remember the original title.

The late Ruth Hale, a warm, lovely lady who ran the Glendale Centre Theater with her late husband Nate, said the play needed a title with the word "love" in it. Everyone falls in love and gets married during the three acts. I suggested *Love is Catching,* Ruth countered with, "*Love is Contagious.*" After a six-week run, during which the play was enthusiastically reviewed by reporters at the *Los Angeles Times* and *Glendale News Press*, my romantic comedy was submitted to the Dramatist Play Service in New York, a company that usually only published plays produced on or off Broadway. Glendale, California, is way off, off Broadway. Plus, my play was not submitted through a theatrical agent but by me—the aspiring playwright.

Several months later, Dramatist Play Service decided that my play had so much merit they were going to publish it. I was thrilled. The contract was signed in November of 1961, the same month my handsome young son, Mark Lawrence, was born (November 10, 1961). So there were two birthday presents for me that year. Mark's father was my second husband Bill (William Oliver Jacobs)—more on my two ex-husbands later.

Big dreams, purposeful visualizations and determined action—combined with a dash of talent—had resulted in two of my dreams coming true ("Faith without works is dead," it says in the Good Book)—in the publication of my two plays. This was years before I read *The Game of Life and How to Play It* by Florence Scovel Shinn (published in 1925), *Key to Yourself* by Venice Bloodworth (1960), or *The Magic of Believing* by Claude Bristol (published in the 1940s and forever in print). In the late 1970s I read Shakti Gawain's *Creative Visualization* (1967). I had basic instincts about "visualization" described in metaphysical books written before I was born, with the latest craze: *The Secret,* the book and DVD (nothing new). I had become a professional playwright and received royalties for plays performed by amateur groups around the country. For me—that was at least a minor miracle.

Having a play on or off Broadway is still my dream. I've written several other one-act and three-act plays. There were "almost productions" off, off, off Broadway in Hollywood, plus positive comments in rejection letters from theatrical agents in New York (my one-act play, *I Like Rainy Days*, was compared to the work of Tennessee Williams). It seemed my remarkable success with my first play, written at 17 and published at 19, and having two plays published and produced was no guarantee of nominations or of a lasting career as a playwright.

Another dream vanished when actor Jack Lemmon turned down starring in a film based on *Love Is Contagious*. He seemed perfect for Sam, the playboy artist who falls in love with young Sally, the naïve farm girl from Kansas. By then Jack Lemmon had tired of doing romantic comedy. He soon starred in the *Days of Wine and Roses*, which won Best Picture in 1962. Jack Lemmon was nominated for Best Actor, but he was passed over that time. Not all his dreams seemed to come true, either—and he was a really fine actor.

All at once, unforeseen obstacles seemed to block the fulfillment of my hopes and dreams and visualizations, even though I continued to write. What was going on?

Was it possible that all my dreams and visualizations were not intended to manifest? I was disheartened and utterly confused. At that time I had not even vaguely visualized the remote possibility that my eternal soul had perhaps made some kind of bargain before I was born, some sort of agreement that had not yet come to the full attention of my reincarnated personality. I had a few "inklings" about "other lives" and experienced strange patterns not considered the norm, but at that point in time those thoughts were hardly up front and center in my mind.

On the other hand, never once had I dreamed of, or visualized, myself as a card reader, astrologer, clairvoyant, or any type of psychic! I had no desire to be part of the weird and strange world of foretelling the future, tuning into past lives, gazing into crystal balls or any other suspect abracadabra. No metaphysical mentor had stepped up, tapped me on the shoulder, and said, "You're my pupil! Follow me into the strange world of the paranormal where even angels fear to tread." Even though, looking back years later, there were more than a few telltale signs along the way.

I was pushing 30 the first time I decided to try to read someone's cards. That Sunday afternoon I thought it was a game when I told my tall, lovely friend Carol Sutton (whose last name was later Spinoso and then Kruger), "I'm going to read your cards." I never thought I could really do it. Carol was just going along with the game to humor me.

Apparently, on that particular Sunday afternoon, I was being cleverly set up, by my mischievous though astute spirit guides, for one of the biggest surprises and the very beginning of the most magical and mysterious adventure of my life!

In my opinion, it was a clever, capricious and cunning scheme—if not an Absolute Cosmic Conspiracy!

THE TAROT PSYCHIC

By Henry Allen

Among the horde of favor-seekers, chip-cashiers, sages, exemplars, log-rollers, movers and shakers, shovers and makers, beautiful and bright young things, purveyors and survey-ors of the conventional wisdom and other eager folk riding into town last week on the rods of the Gravy Ex-press which always follows so closely the election of a new president was, look out Washington, Patricia McLaine, psychic to the stars, come all the way from Los Angeles.

She may be the first psychic to arrive for The Reagan Years in Wash-ington.

She got here Tuesday, on a tour whose last stop was actress Susan Strasberg's apartment in New York. Here, she set up shop in Georgetown on the dining room table (decorated with crystal panther) of Sheila and Ed Weidenfeld, Sheila being former press secretary to Betty Ford and member of the Reagan transition team, Ed being the Republican lawyer.

McLaine's been doing Tarot-card readings ever since for Sheila Weiden-feld's friends, and friends of friends, as the word spreads of eldritch in-sights.

"I have to have a friend, a sponsor, wherever I go," said McLaine over lunch at The Palm restaurant, where

The Once and Future Cards Of Patricia McLaine

XII

THE HANGED MAN.

the current Washington biggies gather for lunch under caricatures of themselves. Some caricature artist will be busy in the coming months, painting out the old, in the new.

These are uncertain times here, all the better for her trade.

"All predictions for me say I'm sup-posed to live in the East while Reagan is in office," she said. Then, shifting into the prophetic mode: "I see dra-matic changes in the next six months. Nancy and Ronald Reagan will bring class to Washington. I'm worried about the hostages, though, and I think the Middle Eastern war could go on for a long time."

This gift of prophecy does not cloud her face with extravagant drama, however.

"I'm the girl-next-door psychic," she says. "People come to my house in Woodland Hills and find me wearing curlers."

She's 44, a jolly redhead who looks like she could make friends almost anyplace. So far in Washington, she says her biggest catch as a client has been a senator she can't name, unless you count Takoma Park's own Goldie Hawn. Back home, where she started doing readings when she was a secre-tary at Twentieth Century-Fox, she has read the cards for Peter Sellers,

See TAROT, B7, Col. 3

Top, Tarot card from The Rider Tarot Deck; above, Patricia McLaine; by Margaret Thomas—The Washington Post

Monday, November 24, 1980, *The Washington Post,* Style, Photo top: Tarot cards from the Rider Waite Deck, and above: Patricia McLaine by Margaret Thomas—*The Washington Post*

1

TAROT PSYCHIC TO
THE RICH AND FAMOUS

Many of my clients still lead truly extraordinary lives. Numbered among the most celebrated still living on Earth— or now on the Other Side—are the following:

STAR PLAYERS

Bella Abzug	Don Adams	Rona Barrett
George W. Bush	Christina Crawford	Michael Crichton
Jamie Lee Curtis	Sarah Ferguson	Jack Ford
Sharon Gless	Goldie Hawn	Patricia Hearst
Tippi Hedren	Anjelica Huston	Judith Krantz
Alan Ladd, Jr.	Diane Ladd	Esther "Estee" Lauder
Shirley MacLaine	Ted Neeley	Yoko Ono
Sam Peckinpah	Millie Perkins	Jon Peters
Michelle Phillips	Victoria Principal	Sally Quinn
Kimberly Rockefeller	Peter Sellers	Jess Stearn
Alana Stewart	Susan Strasberg	Joan Tewkesbury
Brenda Vaccaro	Dr. Brian Weiss	Oprah Winfrey

Each Star Player had a reading at some time, if not too many for me to remember. In some instances, a sudden insight may have been expressed in person. For instance, in 1990 I was introduced to George W. and Laura Bush at a party in the Georgetown home of Sheila and Edward Weidenfeld in Washington, D.C. That party was held during my previously predicted one term of young George's father, President George H.W. Bush. It was some time before George W. was elected governor of Texas.

Soon after we met, I said to George, "You have a very bright future in politics."

"Why, thank you, ma'am," he replied, with Laura smiling at his side.

The rest is history, to use a cliché. On that day I had also sensed that George W. would one day be President of the United States.

At the time I was not giving our future 43rd president a private reading. Rather, we were at a party shoulder to shoulder with many of Washington's prime movers and shakers. The charming Ed Weidenfeld was a prominent Republican lawyer. Years before, during the Ford administration, petite, adorable Sheila was Betty Ford's press secretary. I had simply experienced a psychic flash that popped out of my mouth. I have often wondered if our 43rd president recalls my "spontaneous prediction" made to him on that festive occasion back in 1990.

SUPPORTING PLAYERS

Prince Andrew	Warren Beatty	Betsy Bloomingdale
Ben Bradlee	Leslie Bricusse	Lloyd Bridges
Ellen Burstyn	George H.W. Bush	Allen Case
John Cassavetes	Prince Charles	Bill Clinton
Joan Collins	Princess Diana	John DeLorean
Michael Douglas	Maureen Dowd	Harlan Ellison
Nora Ephron	Cary Grant	Melanie Griffith
Jerry Hall	Rex Harrison	Mick Jagger
Elton John	Christopher Jones	Kate Hudson
Noel Marshall	Steve McQueen	Paul Newman
Jack Nicholson	Nancy Reagan	Ronald Reagan
Kurt Russell	Frank Sinatra	Robert Stack
Lee Strasberg	Barbra Streisand	Rod Stewart
Sharon Tate	Robert Wagner	Natalie Wood

A Supporting Player may have appeared in a reading of one or more of the Star Players, in a reading for some other ordinary or extraordinary person, may have been part of a psychic flash, or even played a part in my life. Some appeared in my dreams or revelations of events destined to transpire during a specific year. Insights are typically received before an event, although hindsight is sometimes involved, which on occasion extends to past lives.

Since I never planned to be a psychic, I entered the realm of the supernatural with intense curiosity mixed with considerable reluctance. From the start, it seemed that my spirit guides were humoring me with a job at a major studio where rising stars performed in motion picture extravaganzas or on some hot new TV series. Plus, one of my new BFFS (best friends forever), Susan Strasberg, made her acting debut on Broadway in 1955 in *The Diary of Anne Frank,* in the first portrayal of Anne Frank, in addition to appearing in many films with legendary Hollywood stars: Hume Cronyn, Jessica Tandy, William Holden, and Henry Fonda, to name a few.

From the beginning, I possessed indisputable paranormal gifts. No one ever taught me what a reading involved or how to do one. A psychic in Tujunga, California, named Nita told me I was a natural psychic and could do what she did. That puzzled me.

As it turned out, my readings are done in an altered state only slightly removed from the norm, perhaps somewhat out of focus, but not in trance. The state of consciousness used to give a reading might be compared to the alpha wavelength of meditation, a state entered into not only by the mystic, medium or clairvoyant, but by the inventor, poet, writer and artist. In this "space" or place in awareness, direct inspiration is available to anyone willing to quiet the mind and be receptive.

The higher states of awareness are available to all who make a truly genuine effort.

From 1966 until 1980, I kept no records except for names and telephone numbers in appointment books, many already discarded. Since it is necessary for me to enter an altered state to do a reading, names and events are often forgotten unless something leaves a special imprint on my mind. Over the years, some clients have given me bogus names. Perhaps those with a high profile were afraid of being labeled a "kook" by the intrusive tabloids or feared disapproval from a powerful parent (king, queen, president or sheik) or even ridicule from a lover or spouse. Many religions frown on soothsayers. Nonetheless, for more than four decades I have given readings to all kinds of people, including nuns, monks, ministers, Scientologists and priests. It seems likely that more than 30,000 readings, perhaps even 40,000, were given to those of every faith, in person or on the telephone, to include Christians, Protestant and Catholic; Jews, Buddhists, Hindus, Muslims, Sikhs, agnostics and a variety of pagans, those of every nationality and race from most economic standards and nearly every political persuasion.

Prior to 1980, because of hesitation on my part, telephone readings were never given. However, on vacation with my son Mark during spring break at the Club Med in Cancun, a woman from Montreal begged me until I finally agreed to give her a telephone reading once we were all home. She wrote me a check, converting my fee from Canadian dollars on the spot. That was how I finally learned that *Consciousness is indeed everywhere.*

In addition to an in-depth study of astrology, my earliest metaphysical explorations included reading books on numerology, graphology, palmistry and psychometry (the vibrations in an object), and eventually, an all-embracing study of tarot. Upon learning that my Libra rising could turn me into a dilettante, I decided to attune to my Scorpio nature to master astrology and tarot, with the other equally viable methods for "psychically tuning in" relegated to the back of my mind.

It was the books by Rudolf Steiner and C.W. Leadbeater that made me decide to be a "voluntary clairvoyant." After first becoming fully aware of my psychic abilities, I had several disconcerting experiences in public. Shopping in a supermarket, I could see that a woman had terminal cancer and not long to live. I doubted she was aware of her condition, and I had no plan to let her know. Another time, it seemed that an abusive husband could very well kill the woman I saw putting oranges in a bag. If I said something, she could have thought I was nuts. What right did I have to butt in? These were issues I had no desire to know about, if there was no way for me to be of service. I rarely give unsolicited advice. Neither am I interested in placing myself in a position of ridicule or danger.

One day, it seemed that an "inner voice" told me that if I didn't focus on a person in a certain manner—I wouldn't *see* or *know* anything about them. Many natural psychics have little or no control over their psychic abilities. There are still times I receive spontaneous premonitions or warnings for myself or others, ominous or exciting, but I seldom pass on unsolicited information. I tend to be careful in recounting any of my flashes, even to close friends or family members. In my opinion, psychic information can be controlling or manipulative when unsolicited. In the case of some "so-called psychics," I have become fully aware of perhaps their unconscious attempts at controlling people. How about the ones who told my clients not to see me anymore where my clients let me know?

During the time I am "reading" for someone, I am officially clairvoyant, clairsentient, and sometimes clairaudient. Other psychics have told me that I have been doing this work for centuries. Did it all begin when I was an astrologer in Atlantis or even before? I have worked with many different intuitive systems. This time I was born with a highly sensitive body with my chakras (spiritual centers) fairly open. During a reading, my attention is directed toward the individual and may include the horoscope—the personal blueprint for a lifetime. As I begin to shuffle the cards, it is a signal to my unconscious to become a receiving station for that person. By scheduling an appointment, the individual has given me permission to interpret the horoscope and the cards in a spread, which often includes tracking the Akashic Record of the past, present and future. Readings usually include information or insights regarding other family members, in addition to friends, business associates, lovers, and perhaps enemies.

In terms of predicting the future, freewill must be taken into consideration. Most human beings tend to be governed by personal needs, whims, wants, passions and emotions, besides imperfections and character flaws. How much control do you have over your mind? Feelings? Body? Appetites? In religious or spiritual orders, one primary purpose for fasting is to gain mastery over the physical body, to learn to place mind over matter. Fasting enormously helps to develop the will.

Also, psychic predictions are not set in print or stone. Consciousness creates. Character determines destiny. Motivation and intent develop character. For years these concepts were shared with many clients, along with aspects of the ancient Hermetic Law of Attraction: How we create our own reality. You are creating your own bright future this minute—or not! Be positive and the best that you can be to create your own perfect destiny or reality.

When it comes to having an accurate psychic reading, more depends on the level of being and integrity of the reader than on the level of education or sophistication. There is a difference between a psychic impression and direct knowledge, or intuition. Psychic impressions involve an element of risk when it comes to interpretation. The querent may also change his or her mind in terms of a path to take or goal to pursue. I have never claimed to be *all-seeing* or *all-knowing.* That surprised some clients and that reaction always equally surprised me!

On occasion, *revelations,* also known as *direct knowledge,* something *destined* to happen, may be received during a reading. *Pure intuition* is superior to a purely psychic impression. The psychic realm is ruled by the element of water, which also rules emotion and assumes various consistencies and shapes: fluid, still, flowing, frozen or misty. An object or situation viewed with psychic vision might be compared to seeing something through water. Is the water still or flowing, clear or murky? Sometimes a psychic picks up a hope, dream, or desire in someone's aura without being able to differentiate between what is sure to manifest and what may simply remain an unfulfilled hope or dream. However, with pure intuition, an aspect of the intellect ruled by air, the likelihood of a relationship, event, or situation coming to pass is nearly 100 percent. Timing is another matter entirely. Five or 10 years might be required, but not always or often. Destiny manifests in Divine Time! Timing is the most difficult aspect of doing readings. At times I am right on target, other times years off. Things happen sooner than expected, such as in days instead of months or years.

At first, I thought I was telling a story from glancing at the cards. I had written plays. But the stories I was telling people about their future instantly started to come true. On the other hand, I have always been, and shall always be, in awe of my magical, mysterious ability to accurately discern the present, the past, and the future!

A word of warning: not everything any psychic says is necessarily going to happen, and that includes me: Seventy-five percent accuracy is respectable. Some claim my readings are

99 percent accurate, but not everyone. A psychic may not be able to tell you exactly what you want to hear about a situation, goal, or individual you desperately want at the time of a reading, or during your entire life, for that matter. Some things may not be meant for you in this lifetime. Or deep down, you may not really want what you think you want. Or your Higher Self is protecting you. Or you may be reluctant to take responsibility for being what you think you want to be—or having what you think you want to have.

Fame and fortune entail enormous responsibilities and deprive you of privacy. Perhaps the thing you think you want the most is not your karma this time around. You could be living out a dress rehearsal, which does not mean you should give up on your hopes or dreams. Sooner or later, everything you ever dreamed of being or having will be yours, so you may gain the wisdom and experience from being *that* or having *that* to add to your storehouse of knowledge, skill and awareness.

My spiritual teacher, Ann Davies, claimed that no one can read for another person unless the reader is on the same level of spiritual development or at a higher level than the seeker. The Qabalistic students were also warned to avoid the temptations of Christ: fame, fortune, and/or power, for they tend to corrupt. Some people are unable to handle adoration, since deep down they know how easy it is to fool people. We all enjoy being entertained by a clever stage magician. Great wealth may lead to complications, not limited to the abuse of drugs, alcohol, sex, or gambling away fortunes that might be put to better use. It is easier for most to live a simple life than to spend a lifetime in the spotlight, to wield great power or manage great riches. There are many sad tales of those who have risen to the heights only to fall from grace. It takes an evolved soul to deal wisely with fame, worldly power, or extreme wealth.

Another point that I need to make: the better I get to know a person—the less likely I am to be accurate in giving them a reading. Personal bias and awareness rob me of objectivity. I make a point to never read for family members. My objective in giving any reading is to tell the truth as far as my perception and judgment allow. My better readings are usually for perfect strangers or the clients who seldom call or talk to me. Clients who want to socialize are sometimes warned: I can be your friend or your psychic. It is difficult for me to be both. I am fond of most clients, pleased to hear of someone's success and saddened by their losses. The choice of some to simply be a client has been painful at times, but perhaps better for them in terms of the value they place on my perceptions.

Following the freaky fringe of society and living contrary to what might be considered the norm has been lonely for me at times, especially when someone calls me a "white witch" or "white magician." Fortunately, folks like me no longer have to live in fear of being hanged (as in Boston) or burned at the stake (as in Toledo, Spain) in the United States of America, although such karmic patterns persist in nations where ignorance and superstition prevail. I could never have walked my path these many years without the love and support of my dear friends and family members.

One of my rules: No information up front about anyone planning to have a reading, except for birth data. Foreknowledge can cloud my judgment and steal my thunder. No one should ever be coerced into going to a psychic. My readings are for those open to the experience. Another thing, psychic ability in no way guarantees spiritual development. Some have been known to become acutely "psychic" after a bump on the head or an accident, which is hardly prescription for the possession of profound wisdom and understanding. A psychic gift is the same as many other talents and skills: singing, composing, dance, artistry, writing, mathematic, or an ability to discover or invent. Since I seldom walk around tuned in or turned on, if a client calls with a quick question I am usually at a total loss. I have to quiet my mind and meditate on a troubling situation to come up with an answer or any real insight.

Occasionally, I have intruded into the lives of public figures. During the late 1970s and early 1980s, my predictions featured in the tabloid, *The Star,* were sometimes altered, which was upsetting. My heart goes out to celebrities whose lives become fodder to sell tabloids. When someone schedules a reading, it is my task and privilege to shed light, to primarily withhold judgment, to point the way, listen with an open heart and mind, and nearly never to tell anyone what to do. I try to encourage my clients, not only regarding the development and refinement of talents and skills, but in the cultivation of self-respect and self-confidence. These qualities enable anyone to live a more meaningful life.

Since my readings are conducted in an altered state, the majority of predictions are immediately forgotten. Detailed discussion about a past prediction that manifested may be remembered. Predictions made for others are not part of my life experience. When the client leaves, or the telephone call ends, within about 20 minutes I return to my normal state of mind or may get ready to give another reading.

In 1972, I started to tape readings because of a young woman who returned for another session. She mentioned the suicide of a friend. I remembered mentioning that as a possibility. She denied I had said anything. Therefore, the next day I bought a tape recorder and tapes. From then on, most readings have been taped, with the tape given to the client. At times, a client may not want physical evidence of having a reading: No tape is then made. There is no way for me to remember what was predicted or discussed during 50 to 80 readings in a month 12 months a year. At that time, I felt the need to go on record. My clients tend to replay their tapes weeks, months, or years later, with some surprised by the predictions that did come true. There are psychics who refuse to be taped, or even to allow note-taking. Some clients tell me that they fall asleep to the sound of my voice. Considering the thousands of predictions I have made during thousands and thousands of recorded sessions, there are few things vividly remembered at this late date.

Within the pages of this book, I have no intention of revealing your deepest, darkest secrets—only a few unlikely to embarrass you. Neither do I plan to disclose the seamier sides of life that entered into the visions of my mind through the colorful tarot cards on the table or the various aspects of the planets in your horoscope. I have no plan to name all names—to fully disclose certain unsavory situations regarding the suspicious characters that entered the lives of some of you from time to time.

On the other hand, I may reveal, in perhaps vague terms, or even with absolute candor, a few of the lesser intrigues in the lives of some clients revealed to me through the mysterious tarot cards or the clairvoyant visions of my mind—especially those that involved political mistresses, extramarital affairs, call girls, con men, and Washington's premiere dominatrix— just to make this book an interesting read!

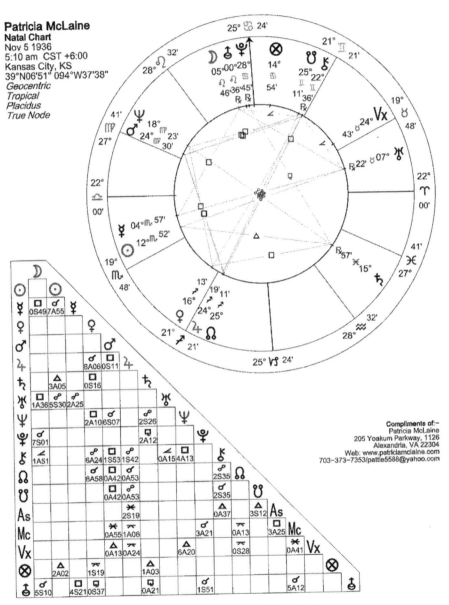

Patricia McLaine
Natal Chart
Nov 5 1936
5:10 am CST +6:00
Kansas City, KS
39°N06'51" 094°W37'38"
Geocentric
Tropical
Placidus
True Node

Compliments of:-
Patricia McLaine
205 Yoakum Parkway, 1126
Alexandria, VA 22304
Web: www.patriciamclaine.com
703-373-7353/pattie5588@yahoo.com

My Astrology Chart – Caution!

2

DESTINY CALLING

According to the wisdom of known and forgotten centuries, our destiny is written in the stars. That is how it started out with me. I was named Gail Patricia McLain on November 5, 1936, 5:10 a.m., born the daughter of Lona Corian Schaible and Lewis Edward McLain. My parents were married the day I was conceived in Los Angeles, California, sometime in February, but divorced before my birth in November in Kansas City, Kansas. For reasons unknown to me, my mother left my father when she was three months pregnant to return to her parent's home in Kansas, divorce my father, and have me.

I weighed in at 8 pounds 8 ounces. Since my mother was only 4 foot 11 inches, it was not easy for her to give birth to such a big baby. In those days, the doctors let a woman rip. I was an instrument baby. For that reason, my mother and I spent my first month in the hospital. She was unable to have more children. I was an only child until age 12, but that's getting ahead of the story.

In the hospital was a nurse studying astrology. As a gift to my mother, she drew my horoscope in my baby book. It was one of those "divine coincidences" arranged by the Lords of Karma that set me up from the start. A horoscope, a natal astrological chart, is a blueprint of the heavens with the positions and degrees of the luminaries (sun and moon) and sacred planets at the time, longitude and latitude, city and state or country of birth. A natal chart indicates potentialities and possibilities, talents and skills, heartaches and triumphs, awaiting the soul on its return journey through time and space in three dimensions. With an accurate birth chart, the knowledgeable astrologer has the information necessary to discern personal karma, family karma, national karma, and world karma with regard to the destiny of a reincarnating soul: in this instance: me.

When I was three months old, my mother took me for a walk in my baby carriage. She stopped in front of a church, probably not Catholic since a priest had once told her not to read the Bible. Nonetheless, with me in her arms, my mother knelt before a Christian altar and dedicated my life to God— without my permission. Mothers do those things in what they consider as the best interests of the child. Perhaps my spirit guides, along with hers and my father's, invaded her mind on that cold, wintry day—with a very strong suggestion.

Both my parents were zealously religious. They met in Los Angeles as young Foursquare Gospel missionaries caught up in the charismatic preaching of the Reverend Aimee Semple McPherson. On occasion, Sister Aimee was known to fly through the air like Peter Pan before delivering a rousing Christian sermon. She must have been something with her five planets in Libra and moon in Sagittarius. Billy Graham is Scorpio with Mars and the moon in Sagittarius. There are many Scorpio–Sagittarius preachers trying to help the world. Scorpio is the sign of transformation and reformation. Sagittarius can be filled to the brim with enthusiasm and righteous indignation!

Mother was Sagittarius with her moon in Scorpio. Dad was Scorpio with his moon in Libra and Sagittarius rising. My father was a part-time Pentecostal minister during his life, but never the Billy Graham of his dreams. It was fate, though fleeting, that combined the genes to produce me. My parent's love of the Lord fervently brought them together, but was unable to keep them together for my sake. Looking back, it was for the best. Hindsight is often clearer than foresight, since it is only much later when all the pieces in the puzzle of any life begin to make real sense.

The first time I remember staying with my father in California I was 10. He and his third (or fourth) wife, Edith, were members of the Rosicrucian Order, AMORC, with its offices in San Jose. As a girl, I had no knowledge of the teachings of the Ancient Mystical Order of the Rosae Crucis (Rose Cross) associated with the mystical teachings of Jesus and the Mysteries of the Universe. And yet, during my brief stay, my father and Edith spoke to me about becoming a Vestal Virgin for the Rosicruician Order. That sounded pretty weird to me at age 10.

The ancient Vestal Virgins were virgin holy female priests of Vesta, Goddess of the Hearth, the only women allowed to be *Priests* in ancient Rome—not *Priestesses*! My father's fourth (or fifth) and last wife, Sylvia, was also a Rosicrucian. It was years before Sylvia and I discussed the similarities between the Rosicrucian doctrines and my eventual complex belief system. Most of our beliefs were pretty much the same.

My horoscope is not an easy one. Over the years, some clients studying astrology wanted my birth data. In horror, Aries Pattye once exclaimed, "How did you ever survive with *this chart?*" According to late Washington astrologer-columnist Svetlana Godillo, who had one reading from me, two T-squares in a natal chart may indicate insanity. With seven T-squares, you have either a fascinating psychotic or a very interesting individual. The jury is still out on that one.

Horoscopes reveal karma: good, bad and indifferent, which a person is likely to face, patterns determined well before birth, perhaps at the time of conception. All those books read from various schools of psychology and psychiatry compiled by esteemed observers of madness and other abnormal states of mind (Freud, Jung, Reich, Lowen) always made me wonder if I was really psychic or simply insane.

Symptoms associated with neurosis or psychosis, especially schizophrenia, are experienced by most psychics, clairvoyants, or mediums, perhaps daily: hearing voices, having visions, seeing discarnate entities, angels or demons; sensing the unseen or unknown, experiencing premonitions of the future, receiving revelations of the past, and having unusual dreams that sometimes come true. Everyone is a little psychic (if not slightly insane). Or, as my mother used to say, "You don't have to be crazy to live in this world, but it helps!"

Most "normal" persons tend to ignore the subtle promptings of the subconscious or unconscious that usually express in terms of feelings or sensations. Domestic animals are often psychic, especially dogs and cats, perhaps farm animals and wild animals as well. Members of the animal kingdom tend to be empathetic and telepathic. However, the various and occasional grand *hallucinations* of a clairvoyant or medium tend to be fully coherent—though at times troubling or unpredictable—even for those of us up for the experience.

After reading numerous psychology books, from the beginning of my psychic work I thought it was best to keep my mouth shut around certain people with respect to what I might be able to do, see, hear, or otherwise discern. I had no desire to end up on some funny farm with electrical shock treatments. I had seen the movie, *One Flew Over the Cuckoo's Nest,* when I was already a working psychic and had already met Jack Nicholson and Michael Douglas at the home of my friend Susan Strasberg. No lobotomies for me, thank you very much. I hope to keep my wits about me until Gabriel blows his horn!

In 1966, when I started to read cards I was working as a secretary at 20th Century Fox Studios and served my apprenticeship giving free readings to many willing and fascinated individuals. At the time, I was unsure if it was even right for me to give readings. Some gave me phony names, perhaps feeling uncomfortable about letting anyone know they had seen a *fortuneteller*—a word with carnival connotations that still seriously irritates me. In my opinion, everyone should stay away from the neon signs downtown and those giant palms out on the highway. Every business has its charlatans: medicine, banking, law, and, naturally, politics. A few of my clients paid as much as $5,000 to have a supposed "curse" removed. The fact is: we all have karmic lessons to learn or we would have reincarnated in a more highly evolved system. Read the newspapers or watch the news on television—the majority of individual souls on this planet still seem rather primitive and spiritually unconscious!

During my early childhood on State Street in Kansas City, Kansas, my mother and I lived with my two uncles (mother's older brothers: Harold and John Jr.) and my maternal grandfather, John Louis Schaible. Through my seventh summer we lived in the house behind Grandpa's gas station and auto mechanic garage. We were the only white folks on the block. All the other neighbors were mostly poor blacks for several blocks in each direction. Next door was an abandoned house. Behind our house was a large vacant lot with broken slabs of concrete, piles of sand and gravel, and discarded rubber tires among the weeds. There were days I wandered there alone looking for the fairies that rarely appeared in daylight, only at dusk or after dark.

My mother said my sighting of "tiny winged creatures flying around" was a product of my *overactive imagination,* which really hurt my feelings. They were not fireflies, though I had seen those too. Every now and then, I caught sight of tiny, beautiful beings with rapidly moving wings darting around the weeds and wildflowers. J.M. Barrie had already written *Peter Pan* before my birth. Nearly every Saturday morning I listened to *Let's Pretend* on the radio. Regardless, what I was able to see on some evenings were tiny, beautiful, flying fairies!

Children under the age of eight are often highly sensitive to the patterns of the inner (especially the astral) plane. Young children often see fairies, elves, dwarves, angels, mythical beings, and the spirits of the departed. Honest! Cross my heart and hope to die—stick a needle in my eye!

When I was five, my mother and I boarded a bus to Kansas City, Missouri, to see a new Walt Disney animated feature film: *Snow White and the Seven Dwarfs.* That wicked witch scared me so much that I cried and screamed until the manager asked us to leave. Mother muttered on that bus all the way home. It was years before that witch could be viewed dispassionately—and she still doesn't happen to amuse me!

A highly active imagination is as necessary in psychic work as it is for any creative process. My spiritual teacher, Ann Davies of Builders of the Adytum, the Temple of Holy Qabalah and Sacred Tarot in Los Angeles, said, "There is no such thing as *imagination.*" What we label as *imagination* is simply part of *the field* that physicists and consciousness researchers talk and write about—scary, considering horror movies and gruesome thrillers. Frankenstein's monster is probably still stalking the unaware and innocent on the Astral Plane.

While I was still a child I would sometimes peer into the window of the abandoned house next door and wonder why no one ever swept the floor or picked up all the newspapers. All my playmates up and down the red brick street, with red brick sidewalks, were colored children. I was unaware of racial differences even at the time I entered my segregated elementary school. The cut-off age for kindergarten was age five by October. That year I was turning six early November. My mother had already taught me how to read and count. After two weeks, I was advanced to first grade.

I invited my new white girlfriend to come home and play after school. When her mother picked her up, she was appalled to see that we lived in the poor industrial section of town in a black neighborhood. That confused me. Some of my black playmates had an uncle in Hollywood who was Rochester (Eddie Anderson) on the *Jack Benny Show* on the radio. Their aunt sent old lingerie with ostrich plumes and long dresses with sequins and sparkle we used for dress-up. We would strut around in their house pretending to be movie stars. That never happened in the white neighborhood, so I only went to her house once.

My German grandfather, born in Missouri, was much loved and respected by everyone in the neighborhood. Sometimes Grandpa gave away gas or worked on some old jalopy for free. Before the automobile retired the horse, my grandfather was a blacksmith. ("Horse shoer" was the "occupation of father" written on my mother's birth certificate.) In fact, as a young man, Grandpa once shod Jesse James' horse at gunpoint without getting paid! Cheap outlaw! Grandpa's horseshoes were displayed in the museum in Kansas City, Missouri. He designed distinctive horseshoes for each of the prominent families. It was the shining moment of his young life. Before it became a garage to repair automobiles, the building was Grandpa's blacksmith shop. Those pictures are on my living room wall with other pictures of the "dearly departed."

"Your grandfather would give the shirt off his back to a poor man in need, regardless of color," my mother said. My grandfather was special. I'm proud to have his genes. He was a good and honest man.

During the hot Kansas summers, my uncle sometimes gave me a quarter to walk down to the beer parlor to buy him a quart of beer. "To wet his whistle," Uncle Johnny used to say.

He would usually add an extra nickel or dime by the time I was five. It made me feel important to be trusted with the quarter and the beer, which I only dropped once, much to my chagrin. A nickel or dime bought a whole lot of candy at the little store around the corner. My favorites: chocolate covered malt balls, bubble gum, and Tootsie Pops.

Inside the beer parlor was a jukebox and dance floor. Late at night you could hear the music playing and Grandpa would smile and say, "The darkies are dancing."

I liked to dance too, especially while waiting for the beer. One time this young black man put a dime in the jukebox and picked me up and put me on top of a table. Then he started clapping his hands and calling out, "Dance, baby! Dance!"

And did I dance!

I remember one Sunday morning out by the gas pumps when my grandfather and uncles were talking about how, "The Japs bombed Pearl Harbor!"

"What are Japs?" I inquired.

"Shut up," Uncle Harold said.

"What's Pearl Harbor," I inquired.

"Be quiet," Uncle Johnny said.

After that, my mother marched me into the house where the radio was blaring with the news of a horrible attack on our naval fleet in the South Pacific.

The next day, President Roosevelt made his famous radio address: "Yesterday, December 7, 1941—a date that will live in infamy—the United States of America was suddenly and deliberately attacked by the naval and air forces of the Empire of Japan…"

In 1942, my cousin Harold Jr., 16, and his girl Vivian, 15, eloped and got married. They ended up with six kids and a happy marriage, the only happy marriage in my family except for Grandma and Grandpa Schaible. Uncle Johnny and my cousin Harold Jr. joined the Navy to avoid the draft. My cousin Bob lied about his age and joined the Navy, too. Uncle Harold, their father, joined the Air Force. My first stepfather, Wiley Hoffman, joined the Army, as did my father, Lewis McLain. All the men went off to fight Hitler and the Nazis in Europe, or Hirohito and the Japanese in the South Pacific. It was a strange yet exciting time.

Back on State Street my grandfather often took me to see Aunt Lottie. He promised me a dime, "If you can sit still and be quiet for 30 minutes." That required maximum effort on my part, so I usually bargained for a quarter. Maybe that is one reason I ended up giving readings: I talk and people listen—since I'm talking about them!

As a child, I sometimes prayed to never grow up to be "normal" or "ordinary." Those words sounded boring to me. My prayers were answered. My life has not been anywhere near ordinary and not even close to normal.

Once when I was seven, Grandpa gave me the money to get on a streetcar alone to go and see Aunt Lottie. In those days, that was safe for a little girl. Doors were not locked. Newspapers rarely reported horrors regarding children. So I got on the back of the streetcar and sat, all excited. It was my first trip alone on a streetcar. Wow!

An old, gray-haired black man came over and poked me hard on the shoulder. "You go sit up front with the white folk," he said in a mean tone.

I was always taught to respect my elders, so I got up and sat up front. And I cried all the way to the where Aunt Lottie was waiting. I didn't know about segregated streetcars. Black and white was not important to me. I couldn't understand why that old man had made me move. He hurt my feelings.

Thankfully, for the most part, segregation is no longer a big deal in the United States. As they sang in *South Pacific*, "You've got to be carefully taught," which is still true regarding prejudice toward religion, politics, or race—*You've got to be carefully taught*. Left to their own devices, children would grow up free of prejudice.

In the 1940s, my mother and I often drove from Kansas City to Los Angeles and sometimes back again. We often crossed the country on Route 66, the southern route, especially in the winter. My uncles would tease me, since my response to driving to California again was usually, "Where's the suitcase?"

On one trip, with WWII waging on both fronts, our green Chevy coupe, Betsy, suffered two flat tires at the same time outside of Bluewater, New Mexico. Tires were hard to come by during the war. Without much money, for several nights my mother and I slept on a mattress on the living room floor in the home of a generous Mexican family. It was fun to play with their five kids. When we finally went into town to get the tires Grandpa had shipped by train from Kansas City, we rode on the flatbed of a truck piled high with carrots. Soon after that, my mother and I left New Mexico. One morning, I woke up in time to see the sunrise over the Painted Desert in Arizona—a magical sight I shall never forget.

My Aunt Kathryn, my mother's older and only sister (my mother was the baby of four children) and my Uncle Paul Turnbow lived in Alhambra, California, with Gloria, my only girl cousin and my aunt's only child. One year during the war, Mother was "Rosie the Riveter" at a defense plant in Southern California. During that time, my mother and I played poker and gin rummy with discarded rivets in the house trailer with an outhouse in the middle of five acres somewhere near Five Points. Other times, we played with the Ouija board.

My Irish grandmother, Lona Corian Courtney Schaible, born in Kansas, whom I resemble, died of a heart attack at age 59 when I was five. Her mother, my great-grandmother, was born in Morgantown, West Virginia, and my great-great-grandparents came over on the boat from County Cork, Ireland. When I was a girl I always blamed Grandma Schaible for not letting me sleep on the top bunk in that house trailer.

Late one evening, using the Ouija board, Mother inquired, "Is it safe to let Gail (she always called me by my first name) sleep on the top bunk?"

The Ouija Board thingy swiftly slid to NO!

And even though I made her ask again and again, my grandmother kept saying NO from the spirit world—and that upset me.

In Redondo Beach, California, lived my great Aunt Sade, right across the street from the Pacific Ocean. I don't remember how we were related. Still, Aunt Sade was a spiritualist and held séances around a big oak table in her dining room. I thought it was great fun. All of us sat around the table with our hands on top, and the adults asked questions. Then, there was a lot of knocking from the spirits. I forget how many knocks meant YES or NO. At times, the heavy oak table used to rise up off the floor and settle down again. There were mostly women; only a few men attended the séances.

Being naturally suspicious, one day I crawled around under the table to see if I could find something to make it rise, but I could find nothing. It had to be the spirits. I was convinced.

Once, when I was nine, my mother and Aunt Sade were talking about my aunt's dead husband, Uncle Harry, when Aunt Sade said my great uncle was always hanging around, making lights flicker, turning the radio on or off, slamming doors, shutting or opening windows. He always made it a point to let her know he was there. Sometimes she saw him in the house.

"Where is he today?" I inquired.

"He's sitting over in the parlor in his favorite rocking chair."

I started staring hard at the rocking chair, narrowing my eyes and concentrating for all I was worth, and then all of a sudden, I could make out a shadowy outline of a man in the chair. The chair started to rock back and forth, which surprised my mother and my aunt. But it didn't surprise me.

"I can see him!" I boldly announced.

My aunt turned to my mother and said, "She's going to be a medium when she grows up."

I had no idea what a "medium" was. And my mother wasn't interested in explaining it to me on that day. She had attempted to communicate with my dead Irish grandmother again and was not at all pleased with her answer.

At this point, it is important to explain that just because my grandmother was dead does not essentially mean that she was all-knowing or wise. Dead is not necessarily better. Dead is not perfection. The refinement of character and talents takes place in this dimension on the physical plane. Therefore, if your Aunt Gertrude was a busybody here, she is most likely still a busybody on the Other Side. Keep that in mind if she won't let you sleep on the top bunk because you might fall and break something.

There was another time I had an interesting experience with a dead person in Kansas City. The family went to an Irish wake about the time I was seven. All these people were talking, smoking and drinking, and an extremely wrinkled old lady was laid out in a blue dress with a white lace collar in a white satin-lined casket. Flowers were everywhere. I thought she must be 100. I had never seen her alive. She was my first dead person. Death seemed very mysterious to me at that wake.

I stared at the woman in the casket, expecting her to open her eyes and say something. The strange part was—I could swear she did open her eyes and close them again right after looking at me. On the way home I told my mother, but she said it was just my "overactive imagination" again. In those days, grownups seemed confused about many things, things like fairies, snowflake patterns, and dead people who are not actually dead.

My mother never believed me when I told her about the pretty patterns of snowflakes in our porch light one evening. It seemed to me that grownups missed out on a whole lot of what was going on in the world. This is still true with many adults. Children are more open to the fourth and higher dimensions. They see dead people that are not really dead and have invisible playmates not the least invisible to them. Much later in life, I realized that I never saw those snowflakes with my physical eyes. I had to have seen the beautiful six-pointed lacy patterns with my third eye, clairvoyant vision. The hexagon, or six-pointed Star of David, esoterically represents the perfect blending of the masculine and feminine principles of Creation, the conscious and unconscious aspects of mind. All snowflakes are hexagons, the same as most flowers. Numbers actually run the gamut throughout Creation. Sound and number create the Cosmos.

At 12, I was baptized into the Church of Jesus Christ of Latter Day Saints, the Mormon Church. In junior high my good friend Mona invited me to church and youth events. It was fun being a Mormon in my adolescence. The church has a fantastic youth program. At 18, I sang with the Mormon Youth Choir in the Hollywood Bowl, and I attended many dances with live bands. At 14, I read the New Testament from cover to cover. In grammar school in Kansas, I attended church school after regular school and heard stories from the Old and New Testaments. There was so much drama and excitement. Since my mother and I lived with Uncle Johnny, and both worked long hours, it was more fun to go to church school than to be home alone.

While attending Alhambra High School, I started to tune in to my classmates and friends, especially those at church. I never realized that I was particularly psychic or that my perceptions were any different from those of anyone else. At times I could sense which girl would marry which guy and how many kids they might have, what profession might be pursued. I was right about 95 percent of the time.

My Patriarchal Blessing administered by an Elder of the Church said I was from the Lost Tribe of Levi, the original tribe of the priesthood. A boy from that tribe could be a Bishop in the Church without attending council. I was devout during my 10 years in the Mormon Church, often bearing testimony to the truthfulness of the Gospel of Joseph Smith. I believed he was a true prophet in interpreting the golden plates from the Angel Moroni that became the *Book of Mormon,* which I also read in my teens—the supposed biblical history of the tribes on the North and South American continents.

Sometimes I was asked to give talks in Sunday school or at evening services. Afterward, some adults told me that I was an "inspired speaker filled with the Holy Spirit." At 17, as a Stake missionary I went from door-to-door trying to convert people to the Church, the same as Mormon missionaries still do in different states and countries. I was fully sincere in my beliefs.

One beautiful Sunday after church, I went for a walk alone to circle the convent on the hill in our neighborhood. Walking along, suddenly I had a remarkable realization that I had always been and would always be—there never was a time when I was not. It was exhilarating and uplifting, an experience to confirm my belief in eternal life. I have never forgotten the moment.

During my teens I started to wonder about reincarnation. The Mormon Church teaches of a pre-existence and an afterlife on three different levels to be determined on Judgment Day. Where someone ends up depends on his or her faithfulness to the teachings of the church—the same as with any religion. The Mormons believe you can become a god, rather than realizing that you are a god incarnate who has simply forgotten your divinity (a metaphysical concept). Personal beliefs tend to change.

After two marriages of two years each, which ended in divorce, plus a child with each husband, my beliefs changed considerably: beliefs about God, beliefs about life, and particularly beliefs about "happily ever after." My youthful dream to marry for time and all eternity and iron my own sheets, bake my own bread, and be the all-American housewife with at least six children had been unrealistic at best.

My first marriage at age 20 to another Mormon was a poor choice on my part. After my disappointment with Tom, I tried to be an atheist or at least agnostic. I started to smoke and drink coffee and alcohol: habits frowned upon by Mormons. If you smoke cigarettes, you will never end up in the Celestial Kingdom. I figured if I was going to end up in the lowest kingdom, I might as well have some fun in the process. My second husband Bill was agnostic—a conscious choice on my part.

One Sunday afternoon between marriages, I had a strange experience. I was looking for something and had forgotten where I put it. My daughter Tomi was with her father for the weekend as I frantically searched my one-bedroom apartment looking in every cupboard and drawer to find the item. I no longer remember what I was looking for at the time.

Finally, frustrated and nearly exhausted, I decided to lie down and take a nap. Then perhaps when I woke up I would know where the thing was. That had happened to me before. However, shortly after lying down, I was suddenly up again walking from room to room in my apartment. I was searching every cupboard and every drawer for whatever it was I wanted to find. It was very bright in all the rooms, the same as it had been when I lay down. Then, I walked into the bedroom and started to look through a small dresser, when all at once, out of the corner of my eye I noticed a girl lying on my bed with her back to me.

I was shocked. Who was she? When had she entered my apartment? How could something like that have happened without my knowing it?

Then, in an instant, I was on the bed wide awake in a very dark room—and I was terrified. I just knew that someone was standing behind me at my dresser. Who was she? How had she gotten into my apartment? Had I forgotten to lock my doors?

Breathing rapidly, heart pounding, my whole being filled with terror, I finally got up the courage to roll over onto my back. To my astonishment, no one was standing at the dresser. Then, I remembered standing at the dresser and noticing a girl on my bed with her back to me. Was I going crazy? It was the strangest dream I ever had in my life as I tried to figure out exactly what had happened. I couldn't have been in two places at once, could I? How could I have been the girl on the bed and the girl at the dresser? Strange!

Sometime later, my friend Jenna McMahon, the owner of the Cameo Playhouse in Hollywood, suggested that I read *The Projection of the Astral Body* by Sylvan Muldoon and Hereward Carrington. My weird, unnerving experience on that Sunday afternoon was fully explained in the book. I had had an out-of-body experience. Holy Guacamole! The self-proclaimed agnostic was changing her mind again. And how many bodies did I actually have? An astral body? Wow!

In 1964, not long after my second divorce, my two children and I moved into an apartment in Burbank the size of our former Glendale living room. That was the house my wealthy second husband, Bill Jacobs, promised me before he changed his mind. However, karma is karma.

As fate would have it, the owner of my new apartment building had been to see an astrologer in Canoga Park named Franka Moore. She also had a reading from some psychic in Venice Beach by the name of George Darius. The stage was set for my Destiny to unfold.

For years I had wondered, "What do all those scribbles and numbers in my baby book mean?" I scheduled a reading with Franka Moore: $10 to have my horoscope interpreted, which blew my mind in less than an hour. In amazing detail, Franka described my parents and my two husbands. My chart indicated divorced parents. Plus, I had a difficult chart for marriage. No kidding! However, to my tremendous delight, I had the chart of a writer! I had published two plays and received modest royalty checks. I had written more plays. I was thrilled. I had also started to read books on the power of visualization.

Since Franka had given me such good news about the future, I made an appointment with psychic George Darius in Venice Beach. By this time I fully expected George to tell me that the audience would soon be calling out, "Author! Author!" as I accepted a Tony or an Oscar.

"You're going to be a famous psychic and travel the world to read for the rich and the famous," George cheerfully exclaimed. "You're going to be on the radio and television, be written up in newspapers, magazines and in people's biographies."

George had false teeth that clicked while he talked, which made it hard for me to understand him as he said, "You're going to travel all over the world, so never be afraid to fly, because you have a whole tribe of American Indians looking after you."

"A whole tribe?" I faintly responded, without a clue about Indian or spirit guides even after all those séances at Aunt Sade's place.

"I can see you in London, Paris, Rome; India, Hong Kong and Singapore. You're going to travel the world and read for the rich and the famous, for royalty! You'll be making public appearances on radio and television. You'll lecture and teach."

Me, lecture? *About what?*

"But what about my plays and stories?" I inquired, having already decided that the man must be crackers.

"You're going to write philosophical and metaphysical books, ten to twelve."

In all honesty, I wasn't even sure what the word "metaphysical" meant. I went home feeling disappointed and fully mystified.

When I started to work at Fox the next year, most secretaries were running from one psychic to another and that included me. Some "so-called psychics" were so far off base I found them pathetic. Then I went to see Lucille Joy in Hollywood.

"You were born *knowing*," Lucille said. "You're going to see a lot of people like me, but you let it go in one ear and out the other. You know what's best for you. You could do what I do and you could do it a whole lot better than I do. You'll always have at least 10 extra years of youth and look much younger than you are. And when you tell people things, they had damn well better listen!"

Psychic after psychic was starting to tell me that I could do what they did, which still had me completely mystified. I was a playwright. *I had the chart of a writer!* Metaphysical books?

Then, in 1966, on a hot August Saturday, while the children were with Bill for the weekend, I was suddenly possessed by what can be best described as "cabin fever." After exhausting every possibility in my address book to go out, since I didn't want to go out alone, I was antsy to the point of distraction. Finally, I walked to the liquor store and purchased a deck of regular playing cards, two packs of cigarettes (I still smoked), and a cheap bottle of Chablis. Numerous cigarettes burned up in the ashtray on that night.

By then, I had already taken several astrology classes with Franka and was starting to interpret charts. However, on that particular evening I called Nita in Tujunga and asked, "What do I do with the cards? Is there a book I can read to learn how to read cards?" Nita had given me several readings with regular playing cards.

"Don't read anything. Sit down with the deck and decide what each card means to you."

From nine o'clock Saturday night until around three early Sunday morning, I drank wine and smoked one Virginia Slim after another, laying out cards this way and that. Before long, I had devised a system and decided on a planetary meaning for every number and suit in the deck of cards. Diamonds were earth. Hearts were the water of emotion, spades air, and clubs fire. Six months later, I read a book on numerology that assigned the same planets and elements to the numbers and suits that I had. I seemed to be on the right track!

My friend, Carol Sutton, was one of those I had called on Saturday during my panic attack. She had a date that night, but agreed to see me on Sunday. The moment Carol arrived I said, "Sit down. I'm going to read your cards."

Seated at the dining room table, I shuffled the cards and "pretended" to give Carol a reading. "You have to tell Howard to be careful. He could be chasing a speeding motorist on his motorcycle and hit an oil slick. His bike could go out from under him and he could break his arm and dislocate his shoulder," was one thing I said as the vision filled my mind.

At the time, Carol's boyfriend was a motorcycle policeman in the San Fernando Valley. After her "reading," I fixed us some dinner and we talked.

The next Thursday Carol called me. To our mutual amazement, my vision of Howard and his motorcycle had unfortunately come to pass. Howard was in the hospital with cuts and abrasions, a broken arm and a fractured collarbone.

At my suggestion, the following weekend Carol went to see Nita for a reading ($5). When Carol arrived at my place, she said, "Nita told me pretty much the same things that you did, but you were more specific."

I was dumbfounded.

Suddenly, the things that George and the other psychics had said about my being able to do what they did seemed to be true. I told Franka. She discouraged me from doing psychic work because of my T-square of Saturn opposite Neptune square Venus. But she also said, "Trust your instincts."

Soon I was reading cards for other friends and co-workers at the studio. More and more people were hearing about my accuracy. A first, I thought I might save money reading for myself. Wrong! No psychic can read for himself or herself, except on rare occasions. Even then, I pick up on my family and friends to the point of its being almost impossible to see anything for me. The element of objectivity is missing! The cards become just cards.

One day I read for actress Jenna McMahon and could see doctors, hospitals, and even cancer in her cards. In 1958, my mother had died from cancer, primarily because she had refused surgery on a tumor in her uterus 10 years earlier. The doctor said it was the type of tumor to turn malignant. Three years earlier, Jenna had had surgery to remove fibroid tumors from her uterus and she had never gone back to see the doctor. Jenna was unhappy with my predictions for her career. She had worked as an actress in New York and had gone on the road with plays. She wanted to be a successful actress. I could see her as a successful writer, winning various awards and ending up with lots of real estate.

During the next month, Jenna's health preyed on my mind. I called her weekly to see if she had seen her doctor. I even volunteered to pay for her visit. Finally, after all my nagging, even though she had no symptoms, Jenna went to her doctor. Her pap smear came back with three out of four-types of cancer cells. She was scheduled for an immediate hysterectomy. During surgery, the doctor also removed scar tissue wrapped around her appendix as well as her appendix, which could have burst in time.

For several months I had been searching my heart and my soul as to whether or not I should continue to do readings. Was it right for me? Could I hurt someone? Many religions frowned on such practices. Witches were burned, hanged, or drowned. Soothsayers were stoned to death in the Old Testament. An astrologer I respected had warned me. I was in a quandary about "my gift" and whether or not to use it

"I think you have your answer now," Jenna said from her hospital bed.

Who knows how long it might have taken for the cancer to claim her life as it had my mother at 47? Jenna was in her 40s.

I have other tales to tell about the miracles and magic that happened during the journey of my life, about other fascinating and amazing individuals who have kept me on my path in the weird and wonderful realm of the paranormal. After all, I'm just warming up!

Stay tuned!

3

TRANCE AND OTHER HAPPY MEDIUMS

Without knowledge of the incredible and inspirational life of trance-medium Edgar Cayce, also known as "the sleeping prophet," I never would have become a psychic. Cayce died when I was eight. I learned of him through my Mormon friends, Bobbie and Ray Wood. They had read his biography, *There is a River,* by Thomas Sugrue. The three of us also read Gina Cerminara's *Many Lives Many Mansions* about Cayce and reincarnation. I was amazed by his medical readings, how Cayce had helped so many in such amazing ways. But what fascinated me more were his readings of past lives, especially those in ancient Egypt and Atlantis. Those readings were a wake-up call that changed my belief system forever—with God firmly back in the equation.

While Edgar Cayce read the Bible every year, I only read the New Testament through once and never finished the Old Testament. All the "begetting" really got to me. I knew about David and Goliath, Samson and Delilah, Moses and the children of Israel, and the Ten Commandments. After all, I had seen every Cecil B. De Mille motion picture extravaganza— great stories with poignant lessons about how you had better be good or pay the consequences. I had become aware of how religion (and politics) uses fear to keep their followers in line. We do reap what we sow—with karma the working out of the Universal Law of Cause and Effect.

Initially, Edgar Cayce was uncomfortable with the concept of reincarnation. The subject is not clearly defined in the Good Book, unless the mind remains open in interpreting some scriptures. Throughout the centuries, scriptures have been altered with the recopying and editing of scrolls. Eventually, Cayce accepted reincarnation as the evolution of the soul. It never seemed right to me to have only one shot to express talents and skills. Hindus and Buddhists believe in reincarnation, as did those in many ancient mystical orders.

In my opinion, the truth behind a prodigy: the soul has been practicing for lifetimes to now express excellence. Lasting success only comes when the time is right for the soul and humanity is ready to benefit from a work of art, discovery, or invention such as the wheel, electricity, or the printing press. With most new inventions, the Patent Office can receive applications for nearly the same invention within days or weeks. Therefore, if an amazing idea strikes, make haste to have your day in the sun—for it may be your time to shine.

Not long after my belief system expanded, with my psychic abilities in full operation, I learned to track the Akashic Record (part of "the field" physicists have discovered) to tune into my past lives. Before long, I was also glimpsing aspects of the past lives of clients in a slightly altered state, not in trance. I have often been surprised when a client says that another psychic has "already told them about that life," sometimes a psychic in another country. My life's journey is still filled with constant surprises and amazing revelations.

My Pisces friend Bobbie, born Barbara Pennington, has a beautiful singing voice. We met in our late teens and were roommates in Alhambra. Bobbie often sang in church and was rather popular with the men. One suitor, Ray Wood, had been married before. Divorce is frowned upon by Mormons. However, Cancer Ray, the older man, was bonkers over Bobbie. Ray had a magnificent baritone singing voice. He often soloed with the Southern California Mormon Choir in Handel's *Messiah* at Christmas at the Los Angeles Music Center. Ray lost the role of Curly in the film version of *Oklahoma* to Gordon MacRae, who possessed the dark good looks preferred by the studio. (Little did I know I would one day read for Sheila MacRae!) Ray Wood was a strawberry blond with a ruddy complexion, not the perfect leading man type.

On the day that Ray proposed to Bobbie in Modesto, California, he took her for a walk in the park and sang—"I Only Have Eyes for You"—just like in the movies! I loved to hear Ray sing. He and Bobbie sang at my first wedding reception and often sang at church events, together and separately. I have many fond memories of holiday gatherings in their home, which included family and friends at Thanksgiving or Christmas with all the singing and music.

Early on, I envied Bobbie because of all her handsome suitors! We lived across the street from the Alhambra Ward of the LDS Church in an apartment owned by Aunt Myn Priestley. Everyone called her "Aunt Myn," even though she was just a grand old lady with red hair confined to a wheelchair because of a heart condition. At one time, she sang opera in an impressive coloratura. Aunt Myn lived a long and productive life and was loved by many.

I attended Brigham Young University in Provo, Utah, for two quarters. I had to work for a year to save enough money to go. Some members of my family thought I was "uppity" for wanting to go to college. No one offered assistance, even though I desperately wanted a college degree. My mother had an eighth-grade education. The fathers of my church friends were doctors, dentists, or lawyers. My stepfather was a UPS driver and repaired watches at night, which ruined his posture. Later, I attended classes in philosophy at Pasadena City College as well as acting and playwriting classes at the Pasadena Playhouse. Those were my favorites. However, the philosophy classes opened my mind and stretched my concepts in amazing new directions never before considered.

My mother was a full-time housewife for the first time after she married Raymond Shoaf. Mother and Raymond never attended the Mormon Church, although my mother was baptized as a Mormon to please me. My stepsister Ginger (Virginia Lee) and stepbrother Gene (Elliot Eugene) became members of the Mormon Church. Strangely enough, back in fourth grade, Ginger and I had pretended to be sisters. That was what we told our classmates. Ginger's mother died when she was 10. When we were 12, her father used to take us kids on long Sunday afternoon drives to the beach, mountains or Griffith Park—an outing for the price of a tank of gas.

One Sunday afternoon, since my mother was going to be home alone again, I asked Raymond if she could come along. After all, my mother worked six days a week as a grocery checker. I never considered I might be playing matchmaker.

One afternoon, Ginger's younger brother Gene asked my mother if she would be his mother too. Not long after that, from where we kids were in the old Chevy's rumble seat, through the back car window we saw my mother and Ginger's father kissing. As a result, in the seventh grade at Fremont Elementary, the kids refused to believe us when we told them that we really were sisters. Had our "pretending" been a form of premonition? Sometimes you pretend, and later, things happen.

Our living conditions in Alhambra, California, were modest. My biological father never paid child support, which upset my mother and altered my opinion of him, considerably. My father never offered to help with college. Nevertheless, at last I was part of a family, even though life was not perfect. At least I was no longer an only child.

Serious discussions about ESP, Edgar Cayce, and reincarnation took place between me and Bobbie and Ray Wood during the years of their marriage and the birth of their three sons: Michael, Kevin and Bart. By the time I divorced Bill, my second husband, Bobbie had told me of Harold Sherman's books, *How to Make ESP Work for You* and *TNT – The Miraculous Power Within You*. Those books seriously changed my life and further opened my mind. Soon, I was experimenting with altered states and self-hypnosis. Startling experiences became the norm, some out-of-body, others out-of-mind, including what we now may call "remote viewing."

In 1964, in an astrology class with Franka, I heard of a trance-medium in Canoga Park. This reminded me of Aunt Sade saying that I would "grow up to be a medium." The spiritualist "church" was located in a rundown strip mall next to a pizza parlor. And, although he worked in a deep trance, Edgar Cayce rarely allowed other entities to enter his body. On the other hand, the Reverend Plume from London, England, was a genuine trance-medium, a spiritualist in the old tradition. He was a small, personable, white-haired man, perhaps in his 60s. His plump British wife, Bertha, had her braided white hair pinned up on her head and played the organ with enthusiasm: "Rock of Ages" and "Onward Christian Soldiers" reminded me of my mother playing on her organ.

By that time I had divorced my second husband and was dating a Gemini man named Stewart. He attended the spiritualist church with me the first time. Initially, the reverend delivered messages from the spirit world on his own. In fact, he looked at Stewart and said, "You can see all the spirits gathered here tonight the same as I can, can't you?"

Stewart glanced around the dimly lit room and said, "Yes." That surprised me!

"Your third eye is wide open," the Reverend said.

Later that night, Stewart confessed he had seen my dead mother hanging around. He assumed her posture and blew me away. Stewart had given me a Ouija board, which we used together to contact the spirits. It seemed Stewart had considerable experience with dead people. Years before, in the Midwest, he was driving down a highway one night and picked up a hitchhiker. The man turned out to be a high school friend who had been killed in an automobile accident the year before. How would that grab you?

To my knowledge, Stewart is the only medium I ever dated. It seemed he entered my life just to go to that spiritualist church and get in touch with his destiny. I wonder if he still sees and talks to spirits and whether he has used his gift to help people. His Oriental spirit guide nearly materialized in my bathroom one night, which scared me. He vanished when I screamed, "Don't do that!" Spirits have feelings too. They don't want to scare you! It is not a Hollywood horror show on the Other Side, in spite of all these ghost hunters and spooky horror films!

Several different entities (spirits) alternately entered the reverend's body. One named George had been a Cockney fishmonger in London before his "transition." One evening George went to the pub he had frequented for years for his usual pint, and lo and behold, the bartender fully ignored him, even after he shouted at the bloke. Needless to say, George was more than a little miffed after giving that pub his business for over 30 years.

In exasperation, George decided to take his business elsewhere. Once again, he received the same rude treatment. The bartender fully ignored him. George went from pub to pub until he ran into a Catholic priest on the street who introduced himself as Father John. "George, you've passed over," the priest explained. "They can't see or hear you anymore. You're dead."

George thought the priest had totally lost it.

Nonetheless, Father John marched George back to the boarding house where the fishmonger had lived for the better part of the past 30 years. Lo and behold, there George was sitting in the rocking chair near the window in the parlor. As fate would have it, he was as dead as one of those mackerels he had peddled on the streets of London.

Soon, George was on assignment as an astral worker, the same as Father John. Their task was to locate discarnate souls walking around in their astral bodies fully unaware that their physical bodies had expired. The delicate situation was gently explained to the newly departed, and then, they were led to their rightful place on the Other Side. Since he was a friendly sort of chap, George enjoyed his assignment, which included communicating with relatives still on this side of the veil by temporarily taking over the body of the Reverend Plume.

George said my mother hadn't realized she was dead when she first crossed over. My memories of the day of her passing are still vivid in my mind. I was 21 and more than seven months pregnant with my daughter when I learned of my mother's advanced terminal cancer. My father and stepmother Sylvia drove me from California to Renton, Washington, to be with my mother. Back in Los Angeles, Tom was out of work for the fourth time in a year and our situation was desperate. The Mormon Church Relief Society was even helping to feed us and pay the bills.

When my mother's doctor said it was only a matter of time, that night I knelt beside the bed and prayed that she would either be miraculously healed or released from her cancer-ridden body soon, with the final decision up to God. I didn't want to be selfish and keep her on earth, even though I sincerely wanted my unborn child to have her as a grandmother. She would have been a wonderful grandmother and my two children would have loved her to pieces.

Around 12 hours later, on the next day, my mother went into chain-stoking, an odd form of breathing common with those about to die. Soon, she left her body. The doctor was surprised, but I wasn't. God had heard the prayer of her only child and had taken her *home*. She didn't have to suffer anymore.

Hours later, after visiting the mortuary with my stepfather to select a casket, I was sitting on the same bed feeling numbed by the unexpectedly sad events of the day. It was a perfectly still July evening when I clearly heard my mother say, "Pattie," from the end of the bed. It was the place where she had stood two days earlier and called my name. That day, I had been equally surprised to find her standing there.

On the night of her passing, I turned, fully expecting to see my mother at the foot of the bed, as a warm, caressing breeze brushed right past me. I couldn't see her, but I got chills from head to toe. My mother had called my name from beyond the veil and confirmed her survival from his physical body. Perhaps I wasn't much of a medium, but I had definitely heard her call my name.

Another time when George was speaking through the Reverend, he turned to Stewart and me and said, "I tried to get to through to you two the other night when you were mucking around with the Ouija board, but you had attracted so many spirits into the room that I couldn't get through."

Until that moment, I had had serious doubts about the Ouija board. But not after George made that remark. Frequently, I had sensed the presence of spirits without seeing them. There was speculation that my apartment building was constructed on a Native American burial ground—not a good thing. In fact, one day when I went out to pick up my mail, I noticed a group of see-through people standing together on the other side of the patio. That was unnerving. In my humble opinion, spirit mediumship is one spooky business—a profession of which I would rather not be a part!

In those days, Stewart and I "mucked around with the Ouija board" more often than was perhaps prudent. One night during supper my two children started to act nervous. I sensed the presence of spirits and mentally asked them to leave. They were upsetting my sensitive children. Youngsters seven and younger can be extremely open to the fourth and higher dimensions, much more than older children who tend to shut down to pay attention to the present incarnation. Some aspects of the finer dimensions tend to distract a person from a present mission or purpose. Not everyone is developed enough to consciously and sanely dwell in two worlds (or more than one dimension). The less spiritually developed are unable to handle the odd experience and may be likely to end up in a mental institution with doctors fully ignorant of what may be happening, with a tendency to misdiagnose. This can be a sad, even tragic situation, but may be karmic for everyone concerned. In my opinion, psychiatrists need to study the chakras and the different bodies to better treat mentally and emotionally disturbed individuals. Those involved with Transpersonal Psychology should be sought out and consulted.

Around the time that my son Mark was four, one evening he had a high fever and crawled into my king-sized bed. Since I was concerned, I knelt beside my bed and prayed, asking ministering angels to heal him. Then I went to bed and slept through the night. Early the next morning, my initial instinct was to reach out and touch his forehead, which was surprisingly cool.

At my touch, Mark awoke and he smiled. Then he started to look around the room in an odd manner as though he was making eye contact with different persons. His expression was quizzical as he turned to me and inquired, "Where did all the people come from, Mommy? Did they come out of the TV?"

Stunned, I sensed the presence of spirits without seeing them. My spirit guides were clearly honoring my trepidation and protecting me in terms of my third eye, since I was not ready to work in that area. Nonetheless, I mentally thanked our invisible helpers for healing my son and asked them to please leave, since they were making Mark uneasy.

Slowly but surely, Mark's eyes followed one spirit after another as each apparently left my bedroom by the door. Then he smiled and said, "I guess they're going back into the TV," and he turned over and went back to sleep.

I didn't sleep. I was flabbergasted.

My young Scorpio son with Neptune (the planet of mediumship) conjunct his Sun had just seen a room filled with spirits who had healed him. He had clearly watched several different spirits walk out of my room. I was astonished. I wished I had had enough courage to see them, too. Mark no longer remembers what happened to him that day when he was a little guy, but his mother will never forget. And it was *not* his "overactive imagination"!

Not long after that, Stewart and I parted company. He had asked me to marry him, but my feelings for him were not the same as his for me. No more "mucking around with the Ouija board"! In fact, it is not wise to try to contact those in the spirit world unless you plan to help them communicate with their loved ones here. You are attracting uninvited guests into your home who are eager to make contact with those in the physical world. Keep that in mind and show respect to the Ouija board. It is not a game for the faint of heart. You could end up with much more than you may have bargained for!

I truly enjoyed the movie *Ghost* with Patrick Swayze, Demi Moore, and Whoopi Goldberg. I loved it when Whoopi's character becomes a real medium after faking it—one of those "be careful of what you wish for" moments! One client saw that film 18 times before its release on video. While young, she had lost siblings and her mother. It is still a favorite of mine, as well as Patrick's *Dirty Dancing.*" He must be doing just fine on the Other Side.

Each of my children saw Bill after his death. Mark was seven and Tomi 10 in June 1969. Weeks later, Mark said he saw his father standing at the foot of his bed one morning when he woke up. I told him his father was checking in on him from the Other Side and he shouldn't be frightened. On Tomi's 11th birthday in August, she saw Bill standing behind the waiter as the Mexican food was served. Their widowed stepmother, Peggy, had taken them out to celebrate her birthday.

"Your father just wanted you to know it was really him paying the check," I remarked.

Another spirit entity that used the Reverend Plume was Dr. Hu, a 2,000-year-old Chinese doctor who continued to heal those in this dimension. It was totally strange when the doctor took over the Reverend's body, because his face assumed Oriental characteristics and his movements fully changed. It was remarkable.

For years I had a kidney condition (Libra rising) that involved blocked ureters. I had seen an urologist for painful cystoscopies on a regular basis. For that reason, my friends encouraged me to go up front for a healing. During my childhood I had frequent bladder infections (Scorpio rules the bladder) when my mother would say, "You just have a cold in your kidneys." The chronic infections should have been treated and had caused serious scarring in the ureters that attach the bladder to each kidney. The treatments were beyond painful. Nowadays, they are usually done in a hospital. It upset my urologist when I called the treatment room the "Chinese Torture Chamber."

Perhaps it was only fitting that I be healed by a 2,000-year-old Chinese doctor using the body of a slight though charming British medium.

That evening I sat in a folding chair as Dr. Hu peered into my body. He mentioned my two pregnancies, my two children, and then, his eyes moved down. "You should have come to me sooner and you wouldn't have had to have these surgeries," he said.

The treatments had always felt like "surgeries" to me.

He placed his hands on my shoulders and heat coursed through my body. Then he summoned two women, not spirits but incarnate females. One woman placed her hands and arms across the front of my abdomen, the other placed her hands and arms across the small of my back. Heat was generated by the laying on of hands, as it says in the Good Book. After several minutes, the women moved on to assist others.

"You can go back to your doctor, but you won't need those treatments anymore," Dr. Hu said, smiling and bowing in Oriental fashion.

That night my donation was $5.

Months later, after my urologist retired, I went to see a new doctor in Hollywood for my yearly kidney X-rays. The new doctor had my previous records and my old X-rays, and yet, when I entered his office after the procedure, he had an odd look on his face. "Your urinary tract is perfectly normal. I see no reason for further treatment at this time," the doctor said.

Trust me—I was not about to say a word about a 2,000-year-old Chinese spirit doctor healing me through an English medium. Instead, I walked out onto Hollywood Boulevard feeling grateful and fully astonished. For $5, I had been cured of a condition that had caused me pain and considerable expense for years. But then, my spirit guides had to do something spectacular to get me to work in the realm of the paranormal on the freaky fringe of society. I have done my work kicking and screaming most of the way.

Another English medium who lectured at the Hollywood Press Club said I was psychically gifted because of my Celtic blood: Scot, Irish, English, and German. He also called me "self-effacing." However, it is necessary to keep my ego in check to be effective in psychic work or my readings would be inaccurate. Early on, anytime I tended to get the least bit cocky I was wrong. The personality must be set aside to do the work of Spirit. It is the Higher Self that needs to shine. If you *have to be right,* you will usually be wrong. We are all channels. Each of us is a godlet on the path to Higher Consciousness and freedom from the Wheel of Rebirth.

I think medium John Edward is terrific. I know his mother is pleased. He is a gifted medium with his ego in check, regardless of his fame. John is still young enough to do his work for many years, although mediumship and psychic work are draining. I was pleased when a California client said she originally heard about me from John Edward. I feature him on my website.

During the mid '70s, I had a session with a young male medium in the San Fernando Valley also named John. He said Edgar Cayce and Arthur Ford were helping me from the Other Side. I thought that was far-out! There is no way for me to do my work alone. Without knowing either man, I am grateful if they still find me worthy. The best help comes from the Higher Self. Not every medium is gifted as a psychic and not every psychic is a medium. Some possess one gift or the other. I have mediumistic moments, but I'm not even close to John Edward. By making a sincere effort, you too can communicate with your dearly departed friends and relatives who communicate mainly through thoughts, feelings and dreams. Pay attention! If you send a thought to a departed loved one, you will receive a "thought-filled" answer.

In the early 1970s, in a reading for a young woman there were strange voices on the tape other than hers or mine. Other clients had mentioned strange voices on their tapes too, but I never paid attention. This woman's husband, in his mid-20s, had tragically died in an industrial fire. Right before I started to speak of him, a faint voice on the tape whispered, *"Fire,"* and I immediately started to talk about the accident and his subsequent death.

Later, someone whispered, "Mother," and I started speaking about her mother. Was it Edgar Cayce? Arthur Ford? It was *someone*. I used inexpensive tapes. She had played the tape in a sound booth with friends trying to prove life after death. She thought it might be her dead husband or mother. The voices were indistinguishable. Perhaps I am more of a medium than I realize. The life of the tape sadly ended that otherworldly experiment.

I mentioned the mysterious voices to another client who said, "Oh, sure! I have other voices and strange sounds on my tapes, too. You're one spooky lady."

During one reading I had mentioned her past life as a nun in France, and on the tape was the distinct sound of loud church bells GONGING back and forth. There was no church anywhere near me. It was a spirit church in some other century in France. How far out is that?

I am often amazed by the remarkable stories told by my clients—as well as being amused. The spirits seem to be having a ball with them—waking them up to other realities beyond this one, teaching them about higher, finer dimensions considered paranormal and highly suspect by many.

God is still answering my prayers—by making my life nowhere near normal and absolutely extraordinary—as the cosmic conspiracy continues!

4

THE STUDIO

From summer 1965 until fall 1968 I worked as a secretary at 20th Century Fox Studios in West Los Angeles. After the alimony from my divorce from Bill ran out, I had no other choice but to get a job. I had always wanted to work for a film studio or television network. I was still crazy about the movies and still writing plays—with my heart still set on being a writer.

Strangely enough, in 1964 I had a dream about working at 20th Century Fox. To my way of thinking, that studio was too far from Burbank. In the early 1960s, my stepsister Ginger invited me on a VIP tour of the Fox lot arranged by her fiancé's father. Her future father-in-law was in charge of circulation at the *Los Angeles Examiner* where she worked. Our private tour of movie-making included lunch in the commissary with a young actor named Jerry Orbach, who went on to make a name for himself in Hollywood and on Broadway. I really enjoyed his version of *Law and Order.* He also played Jennifer Grey's father in a favorite film: *Dirty Dancing.*

Choosing to ignore my dream, I applied to every studio near Burbank: NBC, Warner Brothers, Disney and Universal. After no luck at all, I checked out studios in Hollywood before signing on with an employment agency. And where did they send me—but to 20th Century Fox! Since I could take shorthand at 120 wpm and type 100 wpm, the woman in personnel said, "You could have walked in off the street with your skills. Then you wouldn't have had to pay the fee." A third of my first month's salary paid for the job. After that, my dreams received serious consideration—as with other lessons in my life learned the hard way!

At first, new secretaries were assigned to the Script department, where teleplays and screenplays were typed onto mimeograph sheets: no computers or laser printers then. At home I had an electric Smith Corona typewriter on which I typed my plays with carbon copies. Mistakes and erasers were aggravating and time-consuming—no spell check or automatic corrections. May the Lord of the Universe forever bless the inventor of the home computer! Many major motion pictures and TV series were being shot on the Fox lot then: *Lost in Space* and *Voyage to the Bottom of the Sea* were two that my children enjoyed.

After two weeks of typing scripts, my first assignment was as secretary to Claude Traverse, Associate Producer on the television series, *The Legend of Jesse James*. The offices and indoor segments were shot at the Culver Studios in Culver City where many famous old Hollywood movies were made, including *Gone With the Wind*. I fell in love with Rhett Butler at age 10. I was a happy camper when our first episode aired on September 13, 1965, with me on the couch with my kids. Christopher Jones (Jesse James) and Allen Case (Frank James) were handsome, talented, flirtatious actors—and I was working for one of the most renowned motion picture studios in the world. Hot damn!

One strange but fateful event that happened on that show took place on Mark's fourth birthday: November 10, 1965. The story editor insisted that I leave early to be home with my son for his birthday. Deep down inside I had this nagging feeling that I should *not* leave early. After her third and final "order" to clear my desk and go, with marked reluctance I headed for my car. Soon, I was edging into the rush hour traffic on the freeway. Los Angeles traffic has gotten worse since then—and it was already bad in 1965.

Finally, things started to move along in the outside lane when there was a break in the traffic in the inside lane next to me. I accelerated to change lanes. Then, all of a sudden, the cars directly in front of me abruptly stopped. I stepped on the brakes, and yet, I had already started to turn my car into the next lane—thus, suddenly, my car swerved sideways right in front of the oncoming traffic. My first thought, on the left side of my brain—with me fully seeing the oncoming traffic: *This is it! I'm going to die on Mark's fourth birthday*—expecting to hear CRASH, THUD, BANG, as I was crushed to death inside my car. And yet, at the exact same moment, on the right side of my brain, I had this crystal-clear conviction: *Everything is going to be just fine!*

Tires screeched from brakes applied by alarmed motorists—with me swerving sideways in front of the oncoming traffic—as my car ended up facing all the other cars head-on slammed into the center divider. There was a terrible traffic jam. And yet, strangely enough, there was a tow truck returning to none other than Burbank in the outside lane. Clever spirit guides, I say!

The man hooked up my car, while a policeman directed traffic and asked me questions without writing a ticket. After finally reaching the auto repair shop in Burbank, I called home. No cell phones and few pay phones in those days! Progress is a good thing! Instead of getting home early for Mark's fourth birthday, I was very late. Thankfully, only one car had skidded into the front of mine. The situation made me realize that I should have trusted my instincts and not left work early. I had yet to fully realize that the Higher Self communicates through thoughts and feelings more than in words. And, in my humble opinion, that story editor had totally untrustworthy spirit guides. Or did I need to have the experience, maybe?

Actors John Cassavetes and Dennis Hopper guest starred in *The Legend of Jesse James*. By the time those two arrived on the scene, I was passionately involved with married Libra actor Allen Case (Frank James). Some at the studio were aware of our romance. (More on handsome, charming Allen in another chapter.)

One day I was busy at my desk when Christopher Jones, John Cassavetes and Dennis Hopper surrounded me. Then, roguish Cassavetes, watching me with a suggestive expression on his ruggedly handsome face, smugly inquired, "Would you like to fuck?"

By then, I was friends with Christopher's wife, actress Susan Strasberg. I knew Cassavetes was married to actress Gena Rowlands. All eyes in the office were upon me, including those of producer Don Siegel, whom I had already rejected.

"No, thank you," I coolly replied.

And all three of the frisky actors burst out laughing. Then the bad boys walked away! I wondered if Allen had been bragging on the set—not a particularly amusing idea to me at the time.

While working on that lot, I helped out with public relations on a soundstage where affiliate television station managers from all over the country were viewing the new Fox TV series

up for syndication. My picture was taken with actor James Brolin, who had appeared in episodes on various shows. On another evening, I was asked to dress up and mingle at a Fox promotional party in a Hollywood nightclub. Mr. and Mrs. Edward G. Robinson, Jr. were at a table watching people dance when I walked over and asked Mrs. Robinson, "Would it be all right if I danced with your husband?"

Edward G. was in his 70s, but polite enough to dance with a star-struck young secretary to a slow number. After all, he was a major star when my parents were young. My father was impressed. Robinson had played a lot of tough guys.

The Legend of Jesse James was not picked up for a second season, so I was soon back in the Script department on the main lot in Century City. One day I was assigned to take notes during an interview of legendary actress Barbara Stanwyck then portraying Victoria Barkley in *The Big Valley*. That series also starred Richard Long, Peter Breck, Lee Majors and Linda Evans. I was intimidated by Miss Stanwyck, a favorite of my mother's, and only a few years older than my mother would have been had she lived.

At the studio, I was interviewed by actress Marlo Thomas while she was making her popular series *That Girl* to be her personal assistant. Actually, I had no interest in working for one actor, one writer, or producer, even though those jobs paid much better. I enjoyed being around different creative types, visiting sets, make-up and costume. That seemed more exciting than being a secretary to one individual. And I was still writing.

My next assignment was secretary to songwriter-lyricist Leslie Bricusse during the filming of *Doctor Dolittle*, which starred Rex Harrison, Samantha Eggar, Anthony Newley and Richard Attenborough. Finally, I was working for a star player. Leslie had enjoyed tremendous success with his scores from the London and Broadway musical sensation, co-written with Anthony Newley, *Stop the World: I Want to Get Off*. I loved the hit song, "What Kind of Fool Am I?" I felt like I was finally living!

My newly acquired friend, Scorpio Pat Hawkings (now married to Alan Warner), worked for Lillian Gallo, the first female executive in charge of television at a film studio. On our floor was an unknown, Frances Ford Coppola, in an office at the end of the hall polishing some script. Pat and I became friends during my brief assignment to Tony Hope, son of Bob Hope. Pat was among the first to have a reading. In fact, she gave me my first deck of tarot cards for my birthday in 1968. Pat's birthday is the day and year before mine. That was the summer she introduced me to a hippie who used tarot cards to give readings. When we exchanged readings, the cards fascinated me—another one of those divine coincidences, perhaps!

Another good friend acquired at the studio was Aquarius Susan Kelly. Her roommate had a thing for Leslie and no doubt showed up to check me out. Susan was a working actress in the 1960s, Playmate in May 1961. We formed a bond that is still going strong. With both of us from the Midwest (Susan from Oklahoma), we were also both divorced single moms. Susan's son Ken has had a fabulous law career. When Ken was 18, I gave him a reading and predicted his marriage at age 21. He has enjoyed a long, happy marriage that produced two fine sons.

One evening early in our friendship, Susan invited me to dinner to meet her "uncle" from Oklahoma, not a blood relative, but she called him "Papa." Susan had readings from me and we had also discussed life after death and reincarnation. These subjects were of interest to Papa.

While married to Bill, I had written an existential one-act play called *The Interim – Or Place Between,* my attempt to emulate Samuel Beckett: HE lives in a tree. The 50 pages of the one act were written in two four-hour sessions, eight hours during two consecutive days. While flying in a plane above the clouds the idea hit me and developed over a year. When I finally sat down at my typewriter, the characters and plot rapidly flowed from my mind onto the paper.

Three inmates in a mental institution (unbeknownst to the audience until the end) assemble on a lonely precipice to talk to HE and vent their grievances about a wayward humanity. The cast includes the Optimist, the Pessimist, and the Child, besides He who lives in the tree and is reluctant to descend even a few rungs down the ladder. The Sorrowing Mother is invisible to the attendants who arrive to escort the three inmates back to "safety" in the asylum. At the end, the attendants remove the ladder from the Tree to protect the inmates—so the lunatics may no longer communicate with the Divine. No more wrestling with the Angel. No further opportunity to glean wisdom from the Tree of Knowledge!

Bill, my agnostic husband, never understood the play. Tom, the actor, would have enjoyed playing the Optimist—I could see him in the role. In 1964, a little theater group in Hollywood showed an interest in the play and assembled a cast. I was invited to attend a read-through of the one act. Afterwards, I formed a brief friendship with Faith, the actress who was to play Mara, the sorrowing mother of the world. As it turned out, the producer wanted me to raise the money for the production. Newly divorced without money, I passed. At the same time, I was thrilled that the aspiring producer, who also wanted to direct, had found merit in my philosophical message.

Years later, having dinner with Susan and Papa, I brought up the subject of my one-act play, *The Interim,* how it was "almost produced" in Hollywood.

"I know that play. I've read it," Papa said.

Surprise!

My play had never been published or produced. As it turned out, Faith was a good friend of Papa's and had asked him to read the play to help her with the part of Mara. It was amazing to me how the threads in our Collective Destinies keep weaving a bigger, more colorful picture.

While working for Leslie Bricusse, many of the famous and talented stopped by our office. Actress Mia Farrow, then married to Frank Sinatra and appearing in the Fox series *Peyton Place,* often came by. Actress Ina Balin also showed up from time to time.

One afternoon, composer Henry Mancini was waiting for Leslie and watching me ever so closely when he inquired, "Haven't we met somewhere before?"

Before then, I had only seen him on television accepting Academy Awards with Johnny Mercer for their songs: "Moon River" from *Breakfast at Tiffany's* and "Days of Wine and Roses" from the film of the same name.

Vocal supervisor and music arranger, Ian Fraser, was often around to play one of the latest renditions of Leslie's many songs for *Doctor Dolittle* on the piano. One day, Leslie buzzed and said, "Miss McLaine, get your classy ass in here!"

Then he had me sit in this overstuffed chair as Ian played piano and Leslie sang to me the latest lyrics for "Talk to the Animals." Perhaps you can understand why I really loved my job!

At times, Leslie's beautiful wife Evie brought their young son Adam to the office. Adam looked like a miniature Leslie. I have a picture of them together. Anthony Newley, Samantha Eggar and Rex Harrison were often around, or else I ran into them in the commissary having lunch.

One day, I found it really disconcerting when Harrison's fourth wife, Rachel Roberts, was waiting for Rex in the outer office and kept staring at me in the most intense, bizarre fashion. She made me feel really uncomfortable. Rex had acted nervous around me a few times when we were both in line to pay our bills in the commissary. He smiled and was always very nice. In those days, my short red hair was in a bouffant hairdo and I wore false eyelashes—all the rage at the studio. After all, we were in the glamour business of creating dazzling illusions.

One day not long after that, Ian Fraser stopped at my desk and said, "I guess you've noticed how much you unnerve Rex Harrison?" He was smiling.

"I have," I confessed, aware that Rex was older than my father. I had always enjoyed his performances, especially as

Professor Higgins on the stage and screen in *My Fair Lady* and as Julius Caesar in the film *Cleopatra*.

"You remind Rex of his third wife, Kay Kendall," Ian said, "and that doesn't please Rachel one little bit!"

Kay Kendall had died young from leukemia. So I finally realized why the Welsh actress had given me the evil eye waiting for Rex to finish his song session with Leslie! Within years, Rex Harrison divorced Rachel Roberts and married two other women in turn before his death in 1990. Sadly, Rachel Roberts committed suicide in 1980.

One day the commissary was about to close and Leslie announced that he was hungry. I ordered him a club sandwich and hurried off in my miniskirt and high heels. It was late for lunch, so the lot was nearly empty, when whom should I pass but actor Steve McQueen. Steve smiled. In moments, I heard a loud cat whistle. Turning around, I found Steve walking backwards with a Cheshire grin on his handsome face.

That whistle made my month!

Little did I know that years later I would read for several ladies bedded by actor Steve McQueen! One woman met the actor in a bar and he approached her with, "I'm Steve McQueen, do you want to fuck?" Did Cassevetes take his cue from Steve?

Cheeky, but apparently, she did! Women often found McQueen's fame and rugged good looks irresistible. After his death, I read for his ex-wife, Neile McQueen, which added more colorful threads to the tapestry of my life.

Another time, I pushed the elevator button on the second floor to return to my office on the third floor, and when the door opened, Paul Newman was the only one on the elevator. Like a million other women, I had a crush on the actor who occasionally showed up in my dreams. To wit: I made every effort to remain calm as I entered the elevator, but my heart was racing as the door closed. After getting off, of all things—Paul seemed to be following me!

My heart raced even faster as I entered my office and turned at my desk, with as much poise as I could muster, to face Paul's handsome face and sparkling blue eyes.

With an amused grin on that nicely-chiseled face, Paul inquired, "Is Leslie in?"

My boss was buzzed. "Paul Newman is here to see you."

Leslie enthusiastically rushed out to greet Mr. Blue-Eyes Superstar, as I made every effort to still the beating of my heart and stop the shaking of my knees.

My children spent that Fourth of July weekend with Bill. Therefore, my Virgo friend Sheryl invited me to spend the day with her and her friends. Late in the morning we watched a baseball game in a Beverly Hills park between teams from two private clubs. One team was from The Daisy, a private disco popular with the Hollywood crowd. I don't remember why I chose to wear black pants and a black scoop-neck top to sit on the bleachers in the hot July sun. Sitting there in my sunglasses, I felt sticky in the heat.

Several children were seated on the bottom bench, one near me. Standing at the chain link fence in his blue jeans and a white T-shirt was none other than Paul Newman, sunglasses hiding his baby blues. Paul was smoking a cigarette and kept glancing my way. I was the redhead in black next to the blonde bombshell and exotic brunette watching the famous play baseball on a national holiday.

All of a sudden, Paul swaggered over and wedged his behind into the space on the bench between my behind and that of a young child. When one said, "Daddy," I realized the children were his. Meanwhile, there I was, shoulder to shoulder, with Mr. Blue-Eyes Superstar on a hot July day—and suddenly I was feeling warm in more ways than one!

In minutes, Sheryl suggested that we girls head for Malibu where some of the local hotshots were playing poker. That group included Stan Herman, prominent real estate developer in Beverly Hills, and Christopher Lemmon, son of Jack Lemmon—his father's spitting image. I experienced only brief angst remembering how his father had turned down starring in *Love is Contagious* as a film. At the time, maybe I should have asked Chris?

In those years, actress Natalie Wood was married to Leslie's screenwriter-business manager friend Richard Gregson. One afternoon, Leslie invited me to go along to deliver papers to their home. I politely sat and listened while Leslie and Natalie talked. That was months before the lavish gala Leslie hosted at the Coconut Grove for singer Shirley Bassey's opening. That night Shirley Bassey sang "Goldfinger," the title song Leslie had written with John Barry and Anthony Newley for the James Bond thriller that starred Sean Connery in 1964.

The gala was black tie. My date was Sagittarius lawyer Melvin Miller (who represented me in my divorce from Bill). Briefly, we spoke with Natalie Wood and Richard Gregson not long before the sumptuous banquet. My chiffon spaghetti strap gown was pale chartreuse and my crystal earrings dangled. We sat across the table from Ryan O'Neal and his first wife, along with others from the *Peyton Place* cast. Beautiful Micheline Lerner, recently divorced from Broadway lyricist Alan Jay Lerner (*Camelot, On a Clear Day*), was on my right. It was a star-studded, glitzy affair attended by everyone important in Hollywood. Unfortunately, that nightclub, once so popular, no longer exists.

It was the summer of 1966 when I was working for Leslie that my career as a psychic began. Besides my friends and family members, my new clients held various jobs at the studio. My apprenticeship was served by giving free readings on morning and afternoon breaks, at lunchtime and after work. Soon I was giving free readings on weekends as well to actors, writers, directors, producers, those in makeup and costume, in addition to scores of secretaries.

After Leslie, my next assignment was secretary to Nina Lammaele, story editor of the *Peyton Place* series. (I had one date at The Daisy with series actor Chris Connelly.) In that office I became friends with Aries Carol Mitchell. She worked for Irwin Allen (*Lost in Space, Voyage to the Bottom of the Sea, Time Tunnel, Land of the Giants*, and so forth) and readings for her included predictions of her marriage and the birth of her two daughters.

Nina Lammaele let me go. She said my skills were fine, but she doubted that anyone could be as nice as I seemed to be. I didn't find her to be the least bit nice. It was back to the Script department. Her vibes actually offended me.

One evening at The Daisy, I ran into Ann Miller in the ladies room. Peter Lawford was at the bar. I loved their old movies and was still star-struck after being at the studio for years. Movie stars are movie stars, after all, with most on Turner Classic Movies or some other cable channel these days!

At the studio, many secretaries wanted to be in show business: to act, write, produce, direct, design costumes or sets. You name it! I worked on a screen treatment. In one reading it seemed the pretty brunette secretary was going to be constantly getting off and on airplanes. She ended doing the traffic report for a local TV station and constantly boarded helicopters. She came back to the studio to let me know of the accuracy of my prediction.

It is not always good news in readings. Another girl came into my office and said, "You were right. My brother-in-law had a heart attack. He nearly died and he's only 44."

With so many predictions coming true, positive and negative, I became convinced of my accurate psychic abilities. Dear old George, with his ill-fitting teeth, and sweet Lucille had both been right. I could do what they did. And I had started to read for the relatively rich and famous.

In February 1967, my decision was to no longer spend all my spare time giving free readings to strangers. My salary at the studio was $135 a week before taxes. Most readers charged $5. I charged $5. My alimony was only for 18 months, and the $300 a month in child support never covered everything my children needed or deserved.

At the studio, I ran into actress Connie Stevens on a soundstage with actor Jerry Lewis. Connie and I had met at the Glendale Center Theater in 1959 when my play was produced. Early in her career, Connie had also performed in plays at the Glendale Center Theater.

Another assignment was assistant secretary to Owen McLean in Casting. When Jacqueline Susann's sensational novel, *Valley of the Dolls,* was becoming a film, legendary actress-singer Judy Garland was fired for not showing up on time—or sober. My instructions that morning: "Tell Miss Garland that Mr. McLean is not in the office if she calls. He doesn't want to talk to her."

"Mr. McLean is not in the office," I said to Miss Garland, even though it was a lie.

"If you don't put me through to Owen this very minute, I'll have your job!" Judy Garland screamed at me over the phone— and her words and tone made me feel really sorry for her.

After all, Judy was Dorothy in the *Wizard of Oz.* I had always loved all her musicals at those Saturday matinees, her old movies with Mickey Rooney. Sadly, Judy Garland died from an accidental overdose only two years later.

In the summer of 1967, Arthur P. Jacobs' *Planet of the Apes* was being shot while I was secretary to the writer of a WWII screenplay that never made it to the soundstage. My boss was seldom around as actor Charlton Heston (Moses) jogged on the lot in shorts, and upright apes dined in the commissary the same as regular humans. It was surreal when I saw a yellow convertible with the top down driven by an ape that waved!

Roddy McDowall and Kim Hunter were unrecognizable in makeup. It was a far-out fun time at the studio.

I invited Bill's nephew, Robbie Yapp from Atlanta, to the studio that June, since most of the time on that job I had nearly nothing to do. We spent some time in makeup watching a man being turned into an ape. And we visited the set of *Lost in Space*. My job allowed my friends and family members to see how movies are made, although not every job meant free time to play.

In 1968, my last assignment was in Publicity during the time of the Reverend Dr. Martin Luther King, Jr. and Robert Kennedy's assassinations. It was a sad time for our country with the anti-war demonstrations. Many young men were crossing into Canada to avoid the draft and Vietnam. My first husband spent three tours of duty in the army in Vietnam. In 1975 before retiring after his 20 years, Lt. Colonel John Thomas Kallunki (Virgo sun and moon) was in charge of bringing Americans back into the U.S. from Canada after the Vietnam War ended.

In Publicity, unintentionally I generated animosity by catching up on all the clippings and articles from newspapers and magazines on films and TV shows the other secretaries had let slide. It was boring work, but I felt it had to be done. That department was in another building across the street, not on the main lot. And then, there was the day I walked in on my boss passionately kissing the other secretary. He was married and I liked his wife. It was uncomfortable being placed in that position.

For that reason, it was no imposition when the psychologist working with Mark said that it would be best if I stayed home as a full-time mother. You could say Fate stepped in and took me by the hand—forcing me to become a full-time psychic.

Before long, my fee for readings was $10. Soon I was making more than the $135 a week gross earned at the studio. My reputation had spread and those at the studio still called for regular psychic checkups. By the 1970s, my fee was $75 when friends of Alan Ladd, Jr. gave him a reading for his birthday. I drove to his home in Beverly Hills and did the reading in his den. I had a serious crush on his father after seeing *Two Years Before the Mast*. And yet, in my teens I'd had a crush on a new actor nearly every month.

Among my predictions for Alan Ladd Jr.: "Tremendous success with a science fiction film," and that turned out to be *Star Wars*. Unbeknownst to me at the time, Ladd was one of the head honchos at 20th Century Fox Studios. The success of another film also seemed likely.

"What's the name of the film?" I inquired.

"The Right Stuff."

That star-studded motion picture produced by The Ladd Company garnered four Academy Awards. And yet, after the film's release in 1983, the award for Best Picture went to *Terms of Endearment* and earned my Taurus client actress Shirley MacLaine another Oscar. Another prediction!

I have many fond memories of my time at 20th Century Fox Studios. I still maintain close friendships with several who entered my life then—more on them later!

My dear friend, actor, author Susan Strasberg: "Dear Patty: Lady of potential possibilities and dreams to follow as yours are coming true. We'll call you 'Twinkle McLaine' so bright will your star shine. Love and Light, Susan. PS. One of your 1st but not oldest! S.S."

5

SUSAN STRASBERG AND CAST

There is no way for me to write about my initial experiences as a psychic without including my dear friend Susan Strasberg. Susie played an important part in my journey. Considering our close bond, on the morning after her death on January 21, 1999, my clock radio set for National Public Radio in Alexandria, Virginia, awakened me with the announcement: "Actress Susan Strasberg is dead of cancer in New York at the age of 60..."

I was stunned. Was I dreaming?

No friend or family member had called me on the day of her death to let me know. My children, Tomi and Mark, were Susan's Qabalistic godchildren. She had been one of my closest friends for more than 33 years. While we were talking on the telephone only 10 days earlier, Susan had insisted that my story, *The Recycling of Rosalie*, a romantic love story about life after death and reincarnation be made available to the reading public. Recently, she had read an account of a near-death experience (NDE) similar to my description of the afterlife. My concern was immediate when Susan mentioned losing 25 pounds without any effort. I knew her cancer had returned.

In 1994, Susan was diagnosed with breast cancer. The doctor apparently gave her six months to live at the time. Later, she was supposed to have been cured by a Russian healer in San Francisco who turned out to be a charlatan. Susan said that a doctor had claimed she was cancer-free. Since I was once healed by a 2,000-year-old Chinese spirit doctor through an English medium, I had no reason to doubt her. But when our time is up—you know the cliché. I never wanted Susan to leave this earth, but it seemed to have been her time.

In days, my daughter Tomi, her second husband Gary, and my two granddaughters, Lydia and Shaina, picked me up outside Pennsylvania Station in New York City to attend Susan's funeral. At the solemn occasion were Jennifer, Susan's daughter; Anna, her stepmother; her half-brothers, Adam and David, and many friends who loved her. All of us had gathered to say farewell to a bright star with a clever wit and special knack for friendship. Her beautiful face still smiles down at me from her signed 8 x 10 glossy over my computer table—her Gemini inscription covering all available space (as seen in this book). From time to time, when things seem bleak, I hear her saying "everything is going to be fine."

Our mutual friend, Aries Barry Ross Parnell, sent me a lovely framed picture of Susan in period costume from her role in the AFI film, *The Stronger,* directed by another Scorpio friend of Susan's, Lee Grant. In elegant profile, Susan is on my living room wall surrounded by other relatives in period attire, including Great-Grandfather Franklin, my German grandfather's maternal grandfather in his Masonic regalia— all of them together in my memorial corner for those on the Other Side.

In 1965, Gemini Susan and I met at 20th Century Fox when Susan was married to Leo actor Christopher Jones and expecting her only child, Pisces Jennifer. It was my first assignment on *The Legend of Jesse James.* Christopher was Jesse James. Libra Allen Case was Frank. Don Siegel (later to produce *Two Mules for Sister Sara* and *Dirty Harry*, both with Clint Eastwood) was the producer. Executive producer David Weisbart, who had discovered James Dean and produced *Rebel Without a Cause* also discovered Christopher Jones. Chris had striking good looks and a style similar to Dean's. The two actors were born in opposite signs. Aquarius James Dean was Leo Christopher's idol.

Among the regular actors on the series: Robert J. Wilke, Tim McIntire, Ann Doran, and John Milford. Others, long since famous, guest-starred. I remember the young Kurt Russell coming into the office to ask for my boss. Others were John Cassevetes, Dennis Hopper, and John Carradine, who graciously signed a picture for me.

The reason I got to know Susan was because I had been placed in charge of fan mail. Since I was new at the studio, I believed in authenticity and refused to sign Susan or Christopher's names to their pictures. The signature is usually that of the secretary. I composed typewritten letters to thank each fan for his or her interest as I pretended to be Susan or Christopher or both.

One afternoon, with a pile of 8 x 10 glossies of Christopher, Susan, and both together, and my typewritten letters, I drove to their home on official studio business. I wanted them to sign the letters and the pictures. Susan and Christopher were amused by my insistence upon their signatures. After all, Susan had grown up in show business and appeared on Broadway at 16 in *The Diary of Anne Frank*. At 15, Susan appeared as Kim Novak's younger sister in *Picnic,* which also starred Bill Holden. She has appeared in films and TV shows too numerous to mention. Google Susan Strasberg! Christopher has his own website. Unfortunately, Chris developed more than a few bad habits that got in the way of his acting career. I hope he has changed. He was a fine artist besides being an excellent actor.

That first time I was in their home I happened to notice some books on a shelf. Perhaps not so coincidentally, Susan and I were then reading Gina Cerminara's *Many Lives Many Mansions.* It turned out that we were both fascinated with reincarnation, Edgar Cayce, and anything paranormal. It was near Thanksgiving when Susan asked about my plans. Since

Bill was taking my children on a ski trip, Susan invited me to join them for Thanksgiving dinner. I was utterly delighted.

Susan Strasberg was born May 22, 1938. Geminis tend to collect people. Gemini rules the intellect, with most interested in and able to discuss a wide range of subjects. If you're planning a party, invite a Gemini to keep things interesting. Susan had Leo rising, perfect for her acting and her sunny disposition. My moon is Leo, so there was instant rapport. It was obvious to me that we had a personal karmic connection. Her Pisces moon conjunct Jupiter trined my Sun and Mercury. The two of us could talk and talk: about men, friends, children, her career, our aspirations, and anything to do with psychic phenomena. Our charts had many connections, which is what happens in developing any close bond.

I was always crazy about the theater and movies. Besides writing plays, I had tried to act. My first husband Tom and I each had supporting roles in the premiere production of *Love is Contagious*. Nevertheless, when the review in the *Glendale News Press* claimed that I had "done an injustice to my play by appearing in it"—that was the end of my acting career! I don't know how actors endure the criticism. On the other hand, the critic of the *Los Angeles Times* gave me a decent review, but that was after the actors had rehearsed and rehearsed me. I was more interested in the audience's reaction than in my performance. No more acting in this lifetime!

Susan Strasberg was my first movie star friend. However, I quickly learned that actors are just people with the same needs and hang-ups as anyone else. I loved her stories about her younger years with her parents, Lee and Paula Strasberg of Actor's Studio fame, the fabulous parties and famous actors that were a part of her life. At 19, Susan had a torrid love affair with Scorpio actor Richard Burton, who was married to his first wife at the time.

Susie was among the first to have readings from me. I never charged her, but she did great PR for me with her friends in the theater, film, television and the media. Occasionally, I had psychic flashes about Susan while talking to her on the telephone or driving her to LAX to fly off to make a film, do public relations, or attend some type of film festival.

Once, seated in the airport VIP lounge, a good-looking man walked through the door and I turned to her and said, "He's on your flight and you're going to have dinner with him in New York."

That happened. Nothing further. Apparently, he wasn't her type.

Another time, Susan was leaving for Hong Kong and I said, "I see a tall, dark and handsome Oriental, probably Chinese, with a moustache and goatee. You're going to have an affair with him, and he's going to give you jewelry."

She made a face and said, "I don't like beards or moustaches."

"Well, you're going to like this one!"

And we both burst out laughing.

The handsome Chinese man turned out to be in the jewelry business. Since Susan was born the Year of the Earth Tiger, his gift to her was Tiger's Eyes in a necklace and bracelet. Classy! He came to see her in Beverly Hills, but by then she was already involved with someone else. Susan could be fickle in terms of men.

Before Susan flew off to Australia, I said to her, "You're going to meet a man who will sweep you off your feet."

He did, except that he was drunk. The man picked her up in the hotel lobby and twirled her around, which embarrassed her. When Susan came home, she said, "I didn't know he was literally going to sweep me off my feet!"

Not every man was going to be her prince or hold her interest.

I have countless fond memories of Susan. I shall never forget when Jenny was small and I was with them around Christmas.

Christopher put a Nazi helmet on top of the Christmas tree! Her brother Johnny was there. Chris had several accidents with expensive cars purchased with Susan's money. All was not happy with the Joneses.

I was well aware of the trail of beauties that traipsed in and out of Chris's dressing room at the studio. His growing fame in film had done nothing to stifle his colossal libido. I never mentioned his shenanigans to Susan until after the divorce. I never wanted to hurt her or to separate Jenny from her father, with my own fatherless childhood a painful reminder. My mother died six weeks before my only daughter, Tomi Gail, was born, and Susan's mother died six weeks after her only daughter and child, Jennifer, was born. We shared that bond.

When my two children were young, Tomi used to dress up as Raggedy Ann and Mark as a clown to perform puppet shows for Jenny and her friends. The puppet shows were also given for Jennifer's young uncles, Adam and David Strasberg, when Lee Strasberg lived in Hancock Park in Los Angeles with his second wife, Anna. Tomi also babysat the young Strasberg boys. My two children earned money doing puppet shows at birthday parties for the children of Lainie Kazan. Later, Tomi entertained the children of Tina Louise by herself. The children of other famous actors attended these parties, with me simply the transportation. My children enjoyed those times. Mark and his three children still collect puppets.

Jennifer Jones Strasberg was born with a heart defect, something that had always concerned me in terms of giving her mother a reading. I never knew what might show up in Susan's cards. After a while, I stopped doing readings for all close friends. The strain is sufficient with strangers.

My second husband Bill adopted Tomi. Prior to his death, Bill usually had the children on the weekend, which I often spent in the Malibu Colony with Susan. Her house was across the street from those on the beach. At one time or another, Paul Newman and Joanne Woodward, Cary Grant or Robert Wagner lived across or down the street.

One Sunday I brought my children to Malibu with me, along with our shaggy black cock-a-poo, Irving. Paul Newman was playing tennis on Susan's court and had left his brandy snifter of cognac near the net. What did our adorable dog do but lap up some of Paul's cognac! Let's face it, Irving had *taste!* But Paul was upset. What was Blue Eyes doing drinking and playing tennis at the same time? In those days, Newman drove a VW with a Porsche engine onto the Fox lot while starring in films such as *Hombre, Cool Hand Luke* and *Butch Cassidy and the Sundance Kid.* I'll forever have fond memories of that gorgeous actor! He made a significant contribution in film, in addition to continuing to posthumously support those in serious need in large sums with his fine line of food products: Newman's Own. All profits are still donated to charities.

One day at the beach, Mark ran into Susan's house and said, "I just saw the Sundance Kid jogging on the beach." I was sorry to have missed Redford. From the time I first saw him in *Inside Daily Clover,* with Natalie Wood, I just knew that Robert Redford would be a superstar—and I just love Leo men!

After Bill's death in June 1969, my children were usually with me at the beach at Susan's, although just for the day. One Saturday afternoon, Susan wanted a reading, so we went upstairs while the children played a board game. A beautiful red silk Spanish shawl with a long fringe was being used as her bedspread. I shuffled the cards and spread them out on the embroidered Spanish shawl.

In the reading it seemed that Susan would be flying somewhere in the South to make a film, and on the plane she was going to meet a blue-eyed, blond Scorpio man who would grant her fondest wish. My vision of Jenny was of her running on the beach in a year. Because of her defective heart, Jenny had never been able to run.

Right before Susan's flight south, our mutual friend Barry Ross Parnell, handed her a book: *The Seth Material* by Jane Roberts. Susan didn't want to take such a big book on the plane, but Barry insisted, "Take it. I feel it's very important to you."

Susan has written about this in her autobiography, *Bittersweet,* with an excerpt in *People* magazine in 1980. The blue-eyed, blond Scorpio man turned out to be Louis Dorfman from Texas, a friend of Dr. Denton Cooley, a leading heart surgeon. The main reason Louis approached Susan in first class was because of *The Seth Material.* He wanted to discuss the revolutionary spiritual concepts expressed in the book.

Months later, Susan and Jennifer, then six, traveled to Houston, Texas, where Dr. Cooley would operate on Jennifer's heart. The day of surgery, I was up early in Sherman Oaks, California, to meditate. Susan had asked me to help out during Jenny's operation.

When Dr. Cooley came up to Susan soon after completing the surgery, he said, "Jenny should be fine by the first of the year."

In my meditation during Jenny's surgery, angelic beings surrounded her. When she awoke in recovery, Susan told her about the angels I had seen. Jennifer said she had seen them too. I was thrilled with the success of the operation, and equally thrilled that we had shared a vision of ministering angels during a highly important moment in young Jennifer's life.

By 1974, Susan and I lived about a mile apart in Encino, California. In 1975, for the Memorial Day weekend we had decided to take a trip to the mountains. Tomi had her driver's license and wanted to take her new car. Susan and Jennifer and Jenny's friend, Susan Traylor, went in Susan's car, Tomi and her friend, Anna Garduno, were in Tomi's car, and Mark and his friend, Scott Kirschner, were in my car in a caravan up the highway to Sequoia National Park in Northern California. This was also a late birthday celebration for Susan, who brought along her favorite lemon mousse. Susie loved dessert and she was also an excellent gourmet cook. I tried to emulate her Sunday champagne brunches in our homes in Encino and Woodland Hills.

We had reserved two bare-bones, non-insulated cabins in the campgrounds of Sequoia National Park. These days the accommodations are much more luxurious. Our cabin had two wood-burning stoves: one inside for heat, the other on the porch for cooking. A bare light bulb cast strange shadows on the cobwebs. The public restrooms with showers were a block away. I'm hardly the outdoors type and neither was Susan. We were single moms with our children and their friends on a great adventure among the giant redwoods, unaware until much later of the brown bears that raided the trash cans. It was scary when we wanted to brush our teeth or use the toilet. We ran from what must have been bears, squealing all the way to the cabins. Miss Movie Star was braving the dangers of the wild with her spineless psychic friend.

The bacon, eggs, and pancakes tasted great cooked outdoors the next morning. The coffee was a disaster, but we had brought along instant. We had barbecue lighting fluid and stick matches, and those park rangers enjoyed assisting two ladies in distress. The air was clean so far away from the Los Angeles smog. Squirrels chattered. Hawks and eagles soared. We explored the giant redwoods and the gift shop with its Native American jewelry. I still have my copper medallion on a chain that reminds me of the twelve signs on the zodiac.

The next day we drove to Kings Canyon National Park. I had already been a student with Builders of the Adytum, a mystery school in Los Angeles with Ann Davies as my teacher, for nearly five years. Susan had attended lectures. In 1974, Tomi and Mark were Qabalistically baptized by Ann: their feet dedicated to tread the path of God and their hands to perform God's handiwork. The symbol of the Qabalah Temple is the Star of David with a cross in the center, combining mystic Judaism with mystic Christianity. Susan was Mark's godmother and my friend Tish Leroy was Tomi's godmother. It seemed that if anything happened to me, my friends would look after the spiritual needs of my children. I never dreamed I would outlive them both.

At the time I meditated each morning, sometimes on the symbolism of a specific Tarot Key. I have always loved the grandeur of our national parks. My children have been to Yosemite National Park, Yellowstone and Grand Teton National Park, Glacier National Park, Lake Louise and Banff National Park in Canada. Mountains, waterfalls and lakes lift my spirits and give me peace, even though I'm not the type to sleep outdoors. I prefer solid walls, windows and doors that lock.

In Kings Canyon National Park, the Kings River flows through the middle of the forest, with high granite mountains towering in the distance. Clever beavers had built a significant dam across the river. The children wanted to climb out onto the dam and explore. They had seen bear, moose, elk, squirrel, chipmunk and deer. Beaver was next. I decided to forego the precarious climb and to sit alone on the bank. Susan joined the children. Up until then, Susan had always been forced to be overly protective of Jennifer. In spite of that, all those crisscrossed sticks and branches with mud holding everything together, made it nearly impossible for her to hold onto Jenny for more than a minute. Susan was anxious. But God and His Heavenly Host were in charge that day.

Sitting alone beside the murmuring river with the stark granite cliffs before me, I was reminded of Tarot Key 4, The Emperor, with the same granite cliffs behind the Ancient of Days. That key partly represents the elevated, orderly aspects of the self-conscious mind. Key 4 is Aries ruled by Mars, the universal symbol for the masculine principle. Fire signs are considered masculine in astrology. Aries rules the head and eyes, thus vision, the ability to see and create images.

The lush green pine and cedar forest all around me reminded me of Tarot Key 3, The Empress: Venus, goddess of love and beauty, Mother Nature. The trees on Key 3 are cedars, the tree of Venus. At that moment, it seemed to me that The Emperor and The Empress, male and female, conscious and subconscious were in perfect harmony in that serenely beautiful place.

All at once, I heard what can be best described as a heavenly choir sounding a superb note, accompanied by myriad musical instruments and voices blended in an exquisite transcendent harmony. To say the experience was uplifting is indeed an understatement. And, the moment I started to question what I was hearing and I started to glance around in search of a radio or some other source for the music, the exquisite sound instantly vanished. All that remained was the soft murmuring of the river on a sunny spring day.

That was when it hit me—for one brief moment—I had been blessed to hear the Music of the Spheres. I also realized that I had the experience because of my recognition of the perfect blending of the masculine and feminine principles in that time and space. I was blessed with a major spiritual experience as young Jenny climbed out on a beaver dam for the first time in her young life. She was perfectly capable of maintaining her balance the same as all the others had to on that unstable edifice built by God's clever creatures to stop the flow of a mighty river in a magnificent mountain setting.

After their adventure on the dam, Susan was in tears. She was overcome by the fact that her daughter could be in the mountains at a high elevation, in the first place, and climb unaided onto a beaver dam. The children were all on their own in maintaining balance from the time of climbing out onto the dam, across the flowing river, until returning to shore. Finally, Jennifer was just another normal child. She no longer turned blue around her mouth because of a defective heart, but had a healthy glow as she ran. She was filled with energy and eager to explore all of nature's wonders that weekend. I hope Jenny's memory of the mountains when she was still a young girl is as meaningful to her as it still is to me.

In the 1970s, Lee and Anna Strasberg and their sons, Adam and David, lived in a lovely house in Hancock Park. I attended many parties in that house, mostly Sunday champagne brunches with famous actors, writers, directors, producers, and singers who also enjoyed the hospitality of our illustrious host of Actors Studio fame. Parties in the evening were more formal by design with fine food and wine, in addition to music for dancing. At one party I wore a long, off-white tailored empire gown with gold Egyptian-type hieroglyphics embroidered on the V-neck and cuffs of my long sleeves (see picture in this book with Susan and Barry). That evening, I danced in the patio with my date, Leo Ray Taylor, to a Strauss waltz beneath a bright full moon. It was utterly and splendidly romantic.

The only Passover Seders I ever attended were with Lee and Anna Strasberg, with Susan and Jenny and some others present as Lee read those special passages from the Torah.

I met Sagittarius actress Diane Ladd through Susan. Diane had several readings. It seems that I predicted her role in *Alice Doesn't Live Here Anymore.* For Diane's portrayal of Flo, she was nominated by the Academy for Best Supporting Actress. She received the Golden Globe and the British Academy Award

(BAFTA). I thought she might win the Oscar, but it turned out to be the British equivalent. Diane's daughter, actress Laura Dern, was one of Tomi and Mark's playmates at parties in Susan's home. In fact, Laura inherited Tomi's white canopy bedroom set, since my daughter was nine years older, she decided on antiques for her bedroom that year.

One Sunday brunch, I met actress Ellen Burstyn, who starred as Alice in *Alice Doesn't Live Here Anymore* and won the Oscar for Best Actress. At the time we met I had a secret from the time that Ellen was in New York playing the mother in the sensational horror film, *The Exorcist*. Off and on from 1969 until 1973, I had a love affair with my landlord in Sherman Oaks. Aries Noel Marshall was then married to actress Tippi Hedren, who also had several readings. Noel was the executive producer on *The Exorcist*. He had made the deal with Warner Brothers for William Blatty to receive $2,500,000, which Noel claimed was the largest sum paid for film rights at the time. Blatty wrote the novel and the screenplay. Ellen played the mother of Linda Blair, who portrayed the demonically possessed child. Supposedly, the idea for the book and film was based on a true story. There is more on Noel in other chapters.

During my conversation with Ellen, she related stories of the many strange and bizarre happenings on the set of *The Exorcist,* which happened during filming. Several involved with the picture had died under peculiar or unusual circumstances. There were accidents and fires on the set. When evil is the focus, people are asking for trouble, since aspects of evil are highly likely to manifest.

My first trip to New York City was during the filming of *The Exorcist*. Noel invited me as his guest and said, "Tell the person at the desk that you're my wife." I didn't resemble Tippi that much. But supposedly, I did resemble his first wife, although I was much younger.

During my few days in New York City, I took Noel with me to Sunday brunch at Lee and Ann Strasberg's apartment near Central Park. After brunch, the four of us lingered at the dining room table talking for hours. On the way back to our hotel in the taxi, Noel said, "You need to tell Anna and Lee not to let Ellen Burstyn know that I was there with you today." His lame reason: Ellen was after him. He said she had a drinking problem, the same as his mother. Noel never drank. That was the trip when I realized it was finally "the end." Noel was not a man to be trusted.

In compliance with Noel's request, I asked Anna not to say anything to Ellen. Still, I had to wonder if Anna had said something to her about me bringing the executive producer of her film to Sunday brunch. Ellen had been one of Lee's students at the Actors Studio.

Ellen Burstyn never had a reading. However, that Sunday she reached into her purse and took out a small box. "When I came here today I knew I was going to meet someone I was supposed to give this to. It's you," she said and handed me the box.

Inside was a clay artifact, the face of perhaps a priest from the Valley of Mexico from 900 AD, possibly Toltec. I used to keep the tablet on a shelf or table until it disappeared one day in November 2008. I have my suspicions about who may have taken it. Ellen said she had bought the tablet in Arizona during the filming of *Alice Doesn't Live Here Anymore.* I never saw her again after that day, except in films or on TV. Ellen is a fine actress. We spoke on the telephone only once after that. I never questioned her gift and still wonder if she knew about Noel and me. Were they having an affair too? Perhaps one day Ellen will tell me?

While Susan was still in the Malibu Colony, I reconnected with an old friend from Alhambra High and grammar school. Joan Tewkesbury arrived at my door in Sherman Oaks for a reading, but the last name in my appointment book was "Maguire." Joan had married an architect.

"You're *that* Pattie McLaine?" Joan exclaimed.

In high school, we had often run into each other on campus. At 11, Joan danced in the motion picture, *The Unfinished Dance*. One Mormon friend, Barbara Stanton, studied ballet and seemed impressed that I had gone to elementary and high school with Joan Tewkesbury. During the 1950s, Joan also danced in Broadway shows. But by the early 1970s, in addition to acting, Joan was writing and intensely interested in directing films.

I could see a bright future for Aries Joan. By 1975, there was the release of *Nashville*, which Joan had also written. The film produced by Robert Altman received a Golden Globe and a nomination for Best Picture from the Motion Picture Academy.

In 1982, after attending a conference in Bombay, India, I crossed paths with Joan again. My roommate of three weeks while I was touring India was Leo psychologist Fanya Carter of Santa Monica, one of Joan's dear friends. The first reading I did in India was for Fanya in our hotel room in Bombay. The threads in the tapestries of our lives were becoming even more colorful.

Actress Millie Perkins, who portrayed Anne Frank in the film version of *The Diary of Anne Frank*, was another client-friend met through Susan, who originally played Anne Frank on Broadway. Susan and Millie were born the same year and same month, with Millie weeks older as a Taurus. Susan had been deeply disappointed not to be cast in the film. In 1968, after Millie starred with Christopher Jones in *Wild in the Streets*, Susan and Millie became good friends.

Susan was looking for a house to rent during one reading and I said, "I can hear running water," thinking there might be a fountain or waterfall to go with the house.

On the day of her move, the rain was coming down in torrents. "You said you heard running water!" Susan quipped.

Her new mattresses arrived soaked through, because the truck had a leak. I drove my station wagon back to Sherman Oaks to pick up the twin mattresses in our den, which Susan and Jennifer used until their new, dry mattresses arrived in a week.

Susan hosted many fun parties in that house, which had once been owned by actor Errol Flynn. Some were intimate dinner parties, such as the one held for my birthday when Susan surprised me with two special guests: Goldie Hawn and Gus Trikonis, Goldie's first husband. Their birthday present was a handwoven Native American Eye of God that is still in my kitchen.

In 1967, when Susan and I first read Jess Stearn's *Edgar Cayce—The Sleeping Prophet,* we never dreamed we might one day end up in a book by the popular psychic researcher! In 1972, Jess featured Susan and me in his book, *The Miracle Workers.* Jess asked me to appear with him on radio and television to promote the book, but I was still opposed to having a public reputation as a psychic. Jess also asked me to be part of his research for his next book, *The Search for a Soul: Taylor Caldwell's Psychic Lives.*

Jess wanted me to give Taylor Caldwell a reading using my Master Spread with him present. At the time, it was a new reading that had come to me in deep meditation. I felt uneasy about tuning into Taylor Caldwell's past lives with Jess sitting there. The vibrations could easily get confused where I could start picking up his past lives instead. However, in 1973, I was so fascinated reading the book that I could hardly put it down. I severely chastised myself for not having been a part of it.

In the 1970s and 1980s, Jess Stearn attended many of Susan's parties. In turn, we attended smaller gatherings at Jess's home in Malibu. Jess and I had dinner together several times, usually in Malibu. On one occasion, Hugh Lynn Cayce, Edgar Cayce's son, joined us for dinner. That pleased me. Then, in 1984, when I was living in Arlington, Virginia, Jess again included Susan and me in his book, *Soulmates, Perfect Partners Past, Present, and Beyond.* My new East Coast clients were impressed.

In April 1975, I started my first novel, eventually called *The Recycling of Rosalie.* Susan was highly instrumental in the completion of the book. At first, I thought I was writing a short story, then a novella, but a small novel was completed in five months. Susan only lived a mile away, so after finishing the rough draft of the first chapter I called and drove over so she could read the first 10 pages. I needed reassurance.

"This is highly commercial. I love it," Susan said.

I was thrilled.

From that day on, Susan called almost daily to see if I had finished another chapter. If I had, she would drive over, make herself a cup of tea, and curl up on my bed with whatever came next in my story. Then, she laughed or cried, as appropriate. Susan really enjoyed my story. Rosalie falls off the roof in the first chapter and ends up on the Other Side. A Catholic priest is her astral guide. Rosalie and her experience in the afterlife was fun to write. Perhaps I should thank the Reverend Plume, George the fishmonger, and Father John for the inspiration!

That October I learned that psychic George Darius was still alive and had moved to San Bernardino. I made an appointment and drove out to see him for my second reading after 11 years. By then, George had fully discarded his ill-fitting teeth and gummed the reading. Actually, I preferred the clicking. Nonetheless, I felt the need to apologize for thinking of him as a crackpot in 1964.

I told George, "You were right about me being psychic— since 1966 I've done readings for the rich and famous just as you said I would."

"You haven't seen anything yet," George gleefully gummed. "There's more to come, many more of the famous and rich will seek you out. There'll be publicity because of predictions you make. You'll be on the radio and television. You'll travel the world."

"How long am I going to live?" George suddenly inquired.

"You'll probably live to 92," popped out of my mouth.

"I'll be 92 in December!" He looked crestfallen.

I mumbled something about him probably living to 102 and asked, "What about my novel?" I felt the need to change the subject. I was interested in my book, not about how famous I was going to be as a psychic, and not how long I might live.

"It's going to be a major motion picture!" George exclaimed. "I see Universal Studios!"

"What about the book?"

"That will be later after the film is a major success."

A major success with a film seemed exciting on the long drive back to Encino. George had also described three men he saw in my future, none whom I knew at the time. At this late date, I have only met two. I am still waiting to meet the man who flies a plane and deals in "motion"—and I'm still waiting for the success of that "major motion picture!"

Regrettably, George died at age 92 the following summer. I wished he had never asked me that question.

On Thanksgiving 1975, Susan gave my completed novel to actress Diane Ladd, who called early the next morning and wanted to star in a film based on my story. Diane took an option as I wrote the screenplay. However, Diane didn't want the nature spirits—you know—the fairies! Too expensive! In these days of digital art those fairies would be a snap!

The nature spirits returned in a later draft, with two more options and interest from an independent film company in 1997. I'm still counting on George! After all, in 1964 he saw me in Hong Kong and Singapore. In 1994, in a restaurant in Kowloon, China, across the bay from Hong Kong, I toasted George—still wondering about my "major motion picture."

In 1999, after Susan left her earthly body behind, I decided to take her advice about making my story available to the reading public. Editors, cover designers, an artist, and book printers were hired. That very summer, *The Recycling of Rosalie* was published as a trade paperback book. The story may still make it to the screen one day. And yet, writers, the same as actors, require the hide of an elephant to survive in this world— in spite of having an entire tribe of spirit Native Americans looking after them.

FAMILY ALBUM

My mother, Lona Corian Schaible, seated on her father's lap, my grandfather John Louis Schaible, my grandmother Lona Corian Courtney Schaible, my Uncle Harold C. Schaible, my Aunt Kathryn Schaible Turnbow, my Uncle John Louis Schaible, Jr., Kansas City, Kansas, circa 1912.

My mother and me, age 2-1/2,
Kansas City, Kansas, 1939.

Me, age 3-1/2, Kansas City, 1940

My stepfather Raymond Shoaf and my mother after their marriage in Alhambra, California, 1949.

My stepsister Ginger (Virginia Lee), my mother and me in Alhambra, 1954. I made Ginger's dress and my suit during my sewing days.

My stepbrother Gene (Elliott Eugene) Shoaf (1940-1999) graduation picture from Alhambra High, 1958. The kid who wrecked my 1950 Studebaker (first car) soon after it was paid off when he backed around a corner.

My adorable daughter Tomi Gail, age 3, 1961.

My son, Mark Lawrence, on my lap and my daughter, Tomi Gail, beside me in the house in Glendale, California, at Christmas, 1962, before the divorce. This picture is included because of the "spirit globes" hovering above us that showed up after the picture was developed.

My son Mark, me, and my daughter Tomi near the holidays, 1970.

My brother-in-law Hector Guevara, stepsister Ginger, me, my father Lewis McLain, stepmother Sylvia, and Susan Strasberg, 1974. The feather necklace was a birthday gift from Susan before I discovered my allergy to feathers!

My stepsister Ginger and her husband Hector with their son (my nephew) Phillip in Glendale, California, 1975. Phillip was born during Ginger's near-death-experience (NDE) on the delivery table in 1970.

My father and stepmother with my son, 2nd Lt. Mark L. Jacobs, and me in San Antonio, Texas, after Mark graduated from Officers Training with the U.S. Air Force, 1985.

Me and Mark at the Beverly Hills party of Leonard and Emese Green when Em signed a film option on *The Recycling of Rosalie*, November 1986.

My son Captain Mark Lawrence Jacobs,
U.S. Air Force, 1991.

My daughter Tomi Jacobs, 1990.

My son Mark and his wife Chelle on their
Maui honeymoon, May 1991.

My daughter Tomi and her children:
Oliver, Jonah, Shaina and Lydia Brassard
in 1993.

My stepsister Ginger with Mark's children: Chase, Autumn, me, Justin and her husband Hector at my birthday party in Woodland Hills, California, 2000.

My son Mark holding his daughter Autumn, son Justin, my daughter-in-law Chelle holding Chase at my birthday party in Woodland Hills in 2000.

My daughter Tomi and Jim Ziobro engaged in New York City, 2009

My grandson Chase holding Billy Bird (the macaw), Mark with Carmel the cat, granddaughter Autumn with Sneaky the cat, Chelle with the late goose Diamond, and Justin. In front the dogs: Bagel, Bianca and Cindy the Basset hound, 2009.

My grandson Oliver, daughter Tomi, granddaughters Shaina and Lydia and grandson Jonah celebrating Oliver's MBA from NYU in New York City, May 2010.

My new step granddaughters with their father, Jim Ziobro, and my daughter Tomi at their wedding on July 2, 2010: Audra and Janelle Ziobro, my son-in-law Jim and Tomi, grandson Oliver Brassard, Bryna Ziobro and Sreydy Ziobro in front on a boat on a lake in upstate New York.

LOVE AND MARRIAGE

6

HAPPILY EVER AFTER – OR NOT!

When I was young I always thought that love and marriage "go together like a horse and carriage" as in storybooks and all the movies with happy endings. I was going to marry a man forever, wash and iron his shirts, scrub his floors, cook his meals, and bear him at least half a dozen healthy children. I never learned how to hitch a horse to a carriage, either. Another dream was dashed.

My first husband and I both joined the Mormon Church without our families being members. Neither of us had families that practiced what was preached from those pulpits. My mother married four times, twice to one man, and my father married four times (maybe five). My Scot-Irish grandfather was put in prison in Oregon for being married to four women at once. He was not Mormon but a Presbyterian bigamist and stagecoach driver in the Old West, with perhaps a wife at every stop? My grandfather was probably a good liar, but perhaps rather dashing with his Scottish brogue. I wonder how many women he eventually married. Colorful, my ancestry!

Virgo Tom's parents were married only once and frequented the local bars. The Mormon Church condemns the evils of tobacco, alcohol, coffee, cola drinks, and sex outside marriage. Chastity was a big deal in the church! When Tom and I married in the Los Angeles Temple it was supposed to be for time and all eternity—which is a very long time. Thankfully, we were married for just over two years. I should have listened to Mildred when she analyzed his handwriting on Olvera Street in old downtown Los Angeles!

All through high school our group of teenagers had often gone to Olvera Street on Saturday night or Sunday afternoon on group dates. The taquitos with the green sauce were tasty for 50 cents. You could watch glass blowers create fanciful figures and smell the candles in the shops. The gift stalls sold all things 'Made in Mexico,' including finely crafted silver jewelry with lots of turquoise. Mariachis played. It was festive, clean fun in my youth. And, you could also have your handwriting analyzed by Mildred for 50 cents. What a deal!

I had grown up with Mildred analyzing my handwriting. One boy after another was dragged to see her, so I could find out more about him. Mildred had worked with the FBI analyzing the handwriting of criminals, solving forgeries and other crimes. I was impressed! For that reason, with Tom and I engaged and both of us 20—it was time for him to see Mildred.

When Mildred noticed my diamond engagement ring, she surprised me by saying, "You shouldn't marry this man! He's immature and doesn't know what he wants out of life. You're mature for your age. You can accept responsibility, but he can't. You'll be making a terrible mistake if you marry him. He has an atrocious temper and I seriously doubt that you'll be able to put up with him for long."

Tom had paid the dollar for the two of us to have our handwriting analyzed. Tom also turned beet red and looked like he was ready to blast into orbit. The next day I broke off our engagement. Tom was beside himself. For three days, he cried and begged me to marry him. But Mildred had been right about so many boys I had dated. Some of the things she said about Tom made sense. It was our Mormon caterer, Maureen Startup, who talked me into going through with the wedding. After all, the reception was to take place in her lovely home in San Marino. Plus, she was getting my hard-earned $500 for the cake and punch served on her fancy dishes. No champagne or alcohol at Mormon wedding receptions.

When we never received our wedding pictures, it seemed like a sign, besides the horrendous car trouble returning from our honeymoon in Carmel and Monterey. In fact, on the day I entered the Temple in Santa Monica to become Tom's wife—my whole body was screaming at me to try to let me know I was making a horrible mistake by marrying him. I have no regrets about having Tomi as a result of our union. But I do regret the hardships Tomi endured as a toddler from not having a responsible father, and from the fact I had to go back to work when she was five weeks old to pay the doctor for delivering her. Tom had trouble keeping a job. He was fired from about two or three different jobs a year.

After our divorce, Tom only paid two months' child support: $50 a month. He spent little time with Tomi. Even his mother had told me to divorce him, claiming he was no good. And yet, his mother was a big part of Tom's problem. His family life was miserable. I will not bore you with all the painful details, but Tom did have a horrible temper. He was immature and irresponsible. Boys sometimes have trouble growing up. He hit me and punched a hole in the wall of a rented apartment. He kicked in the furniture. During our short marriage he was thrown out of college, because he was playing basketball with the boys instead of studying. There I was working to pay the rent and feed us. Altogether, Tom lost six jobs in two years. I had to pay the bills. Tom got the car payments. I got the furniture payments. With the car repossessed in months. I should have listened to Mildred!

Several months after my divorce, an old Mormon boyfriend, Bruce LeMarr from Monrovia, showed up at my door one Sunday afternoon. We had dated at age 16, and I had once said that I could understand practicing polygamy in the early Church. I sympathized with the life style.

Guess what?

Bruce was a member of a Mormon polygamist group. He already had two wives: one 27, a few years older, the other 18, five years younger. At that time we were both 23. Bruce wondered if I might maybe like to be his third wife. He was very handsome but perhaps not nearly as intelligent as I had once thought he was.

That day I was smoking a cigarette and sipping coffee. That had to put him off. The Church is against these disgusting habits. But the thought of sleeping with three women, together or separately, seemed fully agreeable to him. Imagine that?

I wonder how many wives Bruce ended up with.

Third? Give me a break!

While working at Foster & Kleiser Outdoor Advertising, I was secretary to a group of energetic salesmen. More than few of the men had taken a shine to me. But I only dated Gary, the man in charge. A year earlier, Gary had caught a co-worker, supposedly his best friend, in bed with his wife. Gary had been hurting ever since. His wife and the guy never stayed together. I only went out with him a few times. Once, at midweek, Gary asked me to play hooky with him to celebrate the finalization of his California divorce at the Hollywood Park Race Track.

I had never been to the horse races before. Mormons frown on gambling. But on that day I picked all the horses without realizing that I was psychic. I preferred long shots, since there was a greater chance of making real money. I never bet myself. But Gary placed small bets on every horse I picked. He ended up making around $800, which was a lot of money then. He never gave me a cent. He just bought me a nice dinner and took me home early, so I could get up and go to work the next day.

Another time, Gary and I were out having dinner and one boss from the office saw us together. The next day, Gary was called on the carpet. Fraternizing was frowned upon. A couple months later I went on vacation with my Leo friend Nikki McMillan to Laguna Beach and left Tomi with Tom's family. When I returned for my daughter, she was running around in the yard in only her underpants and burning up with a fever. Although Tom's mother was a nurse, she summarily dismissed my child's temperature. I was furious. I needed to go to work the next day.

At the time I had no car. Another employee picked me up for work. Tomi was in day care while I worked. They refused to take a sick child, so I had to stay home with her until she was well enough to go back into day care. My mother was dead. My father lived far away. There were no relatives near to help out. I had no telephone. I had to walk to a pay phone to even call my office.

When I finally returned to work—I was fired! No one believed my story of a sick child and having to stay home to care for her. It was the truth. But they thought I was trying to extend my vacation. That was how I met my second husband, Bill Jacobs. Karma can be interesting, but usually only much later after the fact!

An employment agency sent me out on an interview with Mr. William Oliver Jacobs (Cancer Sun, Virgo Moon: June 29, 1922) for a secretarial job in his one-man office in downtown Los Angeles. Bill had premature white hair that went nicely with his blue eyes. He looked much older than 38. I was 23. He gave me the impression of a married man with at least four children. I had no desire to work in downtown Los Angeles. I had no car. No telephone. I had run up a large long distance bill with an old Aries boyfriend named George who never gave me a cent. Handsome George, who looked like a cross between

Paul Newman and Elvis Presley (not bad with his green eyes) had asked me to marry him, but since high school, George had become an embalmer. Even though I'm a Scorpio, which rules death and taxes, I was unable to see myself married to an undertaker. No offense intended. It happens to be a necessary and highly profitable business, but not my cup of tea, shall we say?

In fact, perhaps my strangest date ever was when George asked me to go with him to Las Vegas to pick up a body. The man had apparently keeled over at the crap tables from a massive heart attack! It may have been the worst day of his life, if he was winning! Or maybe a huge loss was what did him in?

We had to drive all night to get there and pick up the "body" at a funeral home. The next morning, with the deceased in a coffin on a gurney in the back of the "van/hearse" George drove him back to Los Angeles for his funeral. En route, somewhere around Riverside, the gurney cut loose and rolled free. That actually freaked me out on that day.

"You'd better make sure he's dead!" I said to George, "He seems to be trying to break free." And George was not amused with my remark. Nevertheless, I never married him. He was why I lost my telephone in Glendale, because of tall, dark and handsome George!

In my Glendale duplex, my neighbor let me use her telephone for job referrals. My decision was to take the job with a geophysical company in West Hollywood as secretary to the attorney instead of working in the one-man office of Mr. Jacobs. The geophysical job earned me another $20 a month, which was a lot in those days.

Two weeks later, my neighbor in the duplex said I had a call. Bill Jacobs wanted to know why I had never called him back. I told him about taking the other job for more money. He said he would have paid me more.

"Except, I'm not calling to hire you," he said with a smile in his voice. "I just wondered if you'd have dinner with me on Wednesday evening?"

On the next Wednesday, I put on my little black dress (the only decent dress I owned), and Bill picked me up in his new black Ford Thunderbird. He took me to Don the Beachcombers in Hollywood for dinner. No cheap Chinese food or pizza. It was tropical fish, ukuleles, and a dugout canoe. Hawaiian music serenaded us, along with the sound of the surf. I drank my first Mai Tai and kept the little paper umbrellas for Tomi. For me, it was an elegant dinner, my first in a really fine restaurant. Much later, Bill said that if he had hired me, he might have had to exchange the typewriter for a couch! Cute!

On that very evening, however, there was a telegram from the furniture company tucked into my screen door that informed me of the immediate repossession of my furniture: $70 overdue (the last two payments). Bill Jacobs saved my furniture, cheap Scandinavian, and gave me enough money to get my own telephone. He wanted to call me instead of my neighbor. After that, every Wednesday for several weeks Bill took me out to dinner in a different fine Hollywood or Beverly Hills restaurant. He never asked for Saturday. He said he never liked the weekend rush. That made me suspicious. When I called his apartment a Spanish woman answered. Could he be married?

Still no car.

One night, my boss, the lawyer at the geophysical company, asked me to work late and said he would see me home. After leaving the office, he wanted to stop for a drink and dinner. Rather soon, the thoroughly ugly corporate attorney was trying to kiss me and insisting that I go home with him. After rejecting the impudent ogre, when I arrived at the office the next morning—I was fired! Nowadays, his ass would be sued and glued to the wall, but not then. Women were still lesser citizens in the workplace and expected to look the other way after sexual harassment from slobbering, orc-like attorneys.

I was outraged.

Bill Jacobs dashed to the rescue of this damsel in distress.

I have no plan to bore you with all the details, since there are countless stories of courtship, engagement, marriage and divorce—good, bad, horrible—and nowhere. Where my first husband was physically violent and had trouble keeping a job, my second was a wealthy, highly critical and verbally abusive alcoholic. Bill had a master's degree in chemical engineering and responsible position bidding on chemical plants and oil refineries. He had also inherited a considerable sum from his maternal grandmother. Cinderella was rescued—but the prince turned into a toad.

During our marriage, Bill sent me to his psychologist, Dr. Rose, so I could be a better wife to him. This was perhaps not a wise move on his part. Bill had convinced me that I was stupid. For that reason, Dr. Rose gave me an IQ test. He said I may have been ignorant or uneducated to some degree, lacking in knowledge in terms of higher education, but my intelligence was in the upper five percentile bracket of the general population (135-140). "You are hardly stupid," he emphatically stated.

Those results made me think back to my early days in high school when my class adviser, Mr. Kemp (who belonged to the Alhambra Ward) had said, "From the results of your tests you should be getting straight A's in high school and should definitely plan to go to college." The problem was that no one at home cared about my grades, even though I usually got A's and B's. I was the only one among my other four cousins to graduate from high school, and the only one to take classes in college. When I told Bill I wanted to go to college, one night after too many martinis, he said, "But I don't want you to outgrow me." I think you call that a "control freak."

According to Dr. Rose, one problem between Bill and me was the difference of our basic outlook on life. When I said, "Red, purple, yellow, orange," Bill said, "41, 98, 73, 114!" The doctor said we were missing each other entirely. I was a colors girl. Bill was a numbers guy. Right brain, left brain—these are issues that frequently arise between a woman and a man.

Before I stopped my weekly sessions with Dr. Rose, he said that I reminded him of "a wise old woman in the body of a girl (I was 25). And you're very much like a bumblebee."

To wit: "The bumblebee is not aeronautically designed to fly. But the bumblebee doesn't happen to know that, so the bumblebee flies anyway." I have never forgotten that definition of my particular personality.

It was during those sessions, which Bill paid for, that I decided to divorce him—and buzz on with my life in my precarious bumblebee flight! Friends of my husband tried to persuade me not to divorce the millionaire. They said my life would be easier if I stayed married to him. After all, he was the only man I had known with any tangible assets able to pay the bills. And yet, to my way of thinking, money and material things were no compensation for my unhappiness. Bill had found fault with just about everything about me, which, in fact, made me educate myself in many areas in the years that followed. Perhaps if he had approached me more like a Professor Higgins, he might have transformed me into his conception of what he wanted me to be. But that was not "in the cards." My wonderful son Mark was the result of our union—with no regrets in terms of that karma!

To explain how karma sometimes works: Bill promised me the three-bedroom house in Glendale when we separated. To quote, "I give you my solemn promise that you will never want for anything and you can stay home with our children as a full-time mother."

I'm not sure why he changed his mind. But he never should have made a promise he did not intend to keep. The Universe is always listening. No one punishes us except our own Higher Self, the Voice of Conscience. I had to legally battle Bill Jacobs for everything I got, which was pitifully little in a State where women were supposed to do well in divorce in the California of those days.

Nevertheless, I had to move out of our lovely home on a cul-de-sac that was safe for my children in an excellent school district, with Tomi just starting school. As for the two- bedroom apartment that became our home in Burbank—the entire place could have fit into our former living room. The landlady agreed to reduce the rent by $10 a month if I watered the lawn and kept an eye on things. That meant $135 a month for a two-bedroom apartment with my children sharing a room. But compared to life with Tom—and my former life with my mother and stepdad—I had definitely moved up more than a few steps on the ladder of life.

Perhaps it was not truly a coincidence that the landlady of our apartment house had recently been to see an astrologer and a psychic. Circumstances were about to change in strange and miraculous ways, which enabled me to really buzz on with my life!

Marriage is a business contract not always easy to honor. During one reading from a psychic-astrologer after my two divorces, he looked at Tom's chart and said, "You should have had a daughter from that marriage."

"I did."

"You should have had a son with him," he said of Bill's chart.

According to the Cosmos, my life was on track. After all, astrologer Franka Moore had said I have a horrible chart for marriage. My first psychic, George Darius, said, "You'd be better off if you never got married again."

And to date I'm still single!

The closest I ever came to remarrying was in 1975-76 when I was briefly engaged to a Capricorn who had not yet filed for divorce from his first wife. I met Bo at a party in the home of Gwen Davis, and in two months, he and his older son, Chris, moved in with us in Encino. Chris got the maid's room, which had been my writing room. And yet, right before we met, during my second reading from George, he described three men in my future. With the first he said, "Check his bank account. He doesn't likely have a penny in his pocket."

Perhaps not surprisingly, two weeks after Bo moved in, he confessed he had recently filed for bankruptcy. During the six months that Bo and Chris shared our home and swimming pool, Bo gave me about $100 a week to cover expenses, sometimes less or nothing. When a new car was purchased through my children's trust, Bo wanted the old car, which he paid for with a quilt made by his mother. He said the quilt was worth the Blue Book list price: $500. (I never would have paid $500 for that quilt.) In weeks, his errant younger son, only recently released from juvenile detention, totaled the car by crashing into a tree while either drunk or drugged. Sometime later, it was discovered the boy had stolen Mark's accordion, worth $750. Perhaps the accordion was sold for drug money. Needless to say, I was glad to be finished with that karma!

During my time with Bo, I told him about Gary winning money at the races. One afternoon Bo wanted to take me to Hollywood Park. Unfortunately, every time I picked a horse, it was only after the bets were closed that I actually picked the winner—race after race. The first horse usually placed or showed. By the end of the day, Bo was disgusted. I had warned him that it was unethical for me to use my psychic powers to gamble. With Gary, it had been innocent, perhaps coincidental. By the time I met Bo, I had become fully aware of my psychic powers. Plus, the Higher Self is excellent at reading character! Touché, I say.

A few of my clients have fallen in love, married, fooled around, divorced, married again, fooled around some more, divorced again, and sometimes married again. Such is the karma of evolving mortals in search of the perfect partner. It is said a soul mate marriage can be among the most difficult. Soul mates expect the best of each other. Most humans have not yet reached personality perfection. Imagine that! I guess you never noticed, huh?

My spiritual teacher, Ann, said an individual has to earn the right to a soul mate. By the way, a soul mate is not necessarily our "perfect other half" or complement yearning to find us— our Twin Flame—a romantic, idealistic concept at best. A soul mate is the soul best suited to your spiritual progress and development during a given lifetime. Therefore, should you be looking for perfection, then work on yourself and keep looking! And be prepared to work really long and hard during that particular union.

Everyone fortunate enough to fall in love initially is possessed of the same heady sensation of love at first bloom that lifts the heart and mind into realms sublime. However, not every human being is evolved enough or capable of loving, which is the higher aspect of the fourth heart chakra (spiritual center). If you love someone who does not love him or herself, your love may repulse the object of your affections, because of a lack of self-love.

Neptune, the higher octave of Venus, rules illusion, delusion and intoxication, in addition to platonic, idealist love. Neptune is the planet of the illusive, often Invisible Feminine Principle of the Godhead, the Holy Spirit or Holy Ghost. Under the intoxicating influence of Neptune, the planet of mediumship, or even of the planet Venus, one does not always see a person as he or she really is, but perceives the higher aspects of perfection. I have always thought that sexual chemistry is simply another clever cosmic conspiracy—one that keeps the planet populated with souls in need of a vehicle to continue evolving toward ultimate Enlightenment. The Love of God is the true expression of Love, which one day every soul shall express—unconditionally.

Some couples are fortunate to stay together for the long haul. After a romance ended, Pisces actress Joanna Miles arrived for a reading. I could see that she would be involved with a man she had already met while working. He was a director, perhaps married when they first met. Being the loyal type, he never would have made a move on her at the time. But now, he was divorced and things were going to be different. She would marry the man and have a son. Not long after that—Joanna ran into Michael again.

In 1980, Joanna (Miles) and Michael Brandman attended our Christmas party in Woodland Hills during her advanced pregnancy. Joanna insisted on climbing the hill to look through Mark's telescope at the stars and the planets, with some of us holding our breath that night. Was there going to be the birth of another son during the sacred season? Thankfully, Miles waited until his appointed date with Destiny: January 8, 1981. Miles is also now happily married and following in his parent's footsteps in the entertainment industry. His first film: *Sex and Breakfast*! Kudos, Miles Brandman!

Throughout the many years of my psychic work, a future husband or wife for a client at times took up to 10 years to show up, but not always. A widowed chiropractor was told he would not remarry for five years. Years later, he said he thought I was nuts that day. Five years later, he brought his new wife to our Halloween party—and she seemed perfect for him.

One unhappily married client was told that she would be widowed. She had had more than one affair during her long, unhappy marriage. Her husband was unwell, and yet, the man who died was her lover. She was devastated and angry with me: "You said it would be my husband!" The man who had died was more of a husband, perhaps. Years later she finally was widowed.

One attractive married client in her early 40s had three lovers besides her husband! Her only concern: that none find out about the others. She was an Aries with an overactive libido. With another married client, the love affair in her cards was with another woman rather than her male neighbor. Several clients were bisexual. One black female client said, "Bisexuals are just greedy!" And I thought she might have a point.

One California client, married for more than 30 years, had several affairs during her marriage. When I pointed out that her husband was having an affair, she haughtily replied, "We have three children and six grandchildren! I can't worry about where he puts his little weenie!" Perhaps such an attitude could save more marriages.

A frequently married Gemini blonde bombshell had designs on a wealthy man she did not love. "I'll just marry him and divorce him. Then I'll have a nice chunk of change to help me raise my two sons (from her two former marriages)."

"You'll have to sign an ironclad pre-nup and never get a cent. You're going to be miserable married to a man you don't love. Please don't do it."

She never listened. Besides being in a miserable marriage, she had an equally miserable divorce. Her Higher Self had taught her a lesson. After that, she listened. She was attracted to blue collar types, but was high maintenance. For years I could see a man named George (pseudonym) with whom she was going to fall in love. He was a tall, dark and handsome Leo who lived on the water and had all the money she could ever spend! I described his business. She met him seven years later. Divine timing is not always my timing!

With a real estate broker in Maryland, I kept seeing another woman in her husband's life. She swore he was too conventional and conservative to have an affair. Several months later she came back for another reading.

Her husband was supposed to travel extensively on business. For that reason, it was normal for her to occasionally open his mail. A letter arrived from the Department of Motor Vehicles that involved a late charge on the registration of a car in her husband's name at an address in Ocean City. To her knowledge, they owned no property in Ocean City. However, because of my constant reference to "another woman" she drove from Bethesda to the Ocean City address—almost three hours away.

The two-story house was lovely, grander than their home in Bethesda. The automobile with the license plate number was parked in the driveway where a boy of about 14 was getting off a bike. In a moment of impulse, she got out of her car and walked over to the boy to ask him if a man by her husband's name lived there.

"My dad is gone on business. He travels a lot," the boy said.

You can perhaps imagine her surprise?

To cut to the chase, my client was a successful real estate broker. Over many years she had entrusted large sums of money to her husband for investments. At various times he had expressed his regret over the loss of large sums in the stock market or through "unwise investment decisions." The money her husband had supposedly "unwisely invested" had purchased the lovely house in Ocean City, its furnishings, automobiles, and private school for his three children with his second wife, five years younger. He and my client had four daughters and were married for more than 25 years. On holidays, such as Independence Day, Thanksgiving, and Christmas, her husband had been "forced to travel on business." All those years, he had been keeping two wives in the dark, maintaining two separate families—primarily because of the large amount of money my client had earned selling real estate.

The man was prosecuted for bigamy in Maryland. Perhaps he went to prison the same as my paternal grandfather with his four wives at once. However could a stagecoach driver afford four wives? What about the money her husband had stolen to pay for the luxury enjoyed by his second family? Messy karma! He never would have been able to pull it off without my client's business acumen for making money.

His four daughters were disappointed for the times their father had lied about holidays when they were young. My client was devastated. Evidently, the second wife had learned of the polygamous situation three years earlier. I never tuned in to the ultimate mess. The deceit and ingenuity of her "conventional and conservative husband" was amazing! I seldom read novels because I read people's cards—and life is certainly stranger and more interesting than fiction.

During one reading, the cards of a Leo Dragon lady revealed that her Scorpio Rooster husband was having an affair. She was aware of his philandering ways, since the two of them had met at the duty-free counter in Fiji with each of them married to someone else.

My client made it a point to verify the facts before she went ballistic. Then, she reacted with the remarkable fury of an atomic bomb. Everything the Rooster owned was tossed into the heated swimming pool: expensive clothing, costly jewelry, laptop computer, briefcase, business contracts, and rare artifacts collected on trips to exotic ports of call. If it belonged to the cocky Rooster—the item was tossed into the deep end of their Beverly Hills swimming pool. Few items floated, except perhaps for his pricey silk shirts and suits! Then, her car keys were turned into a weapon and she attacked his brand new Mercedes, scratching and gouging the shiny surface on every side in the mode of an avenging angel.

The following week, the Leo Dragon brought her remorseful Scorpio Rooster to my home in Woodland Hills for his first reading. After studying his cards, without any foreknowledge of her rage that had also destroyed the filtering system of the swimming pool, I had the strangest sensation as I inquired, "Did someone attack your car?"

A sheepish expression spread across his face, although he probably thought his wife had told me of her extreme retaliation for his "passing indiscretion." In all honesty, she may have been still testing the full range of my psychic powers.

Several years after my move to Virginia, I stayed in their home in Beverly Hills with that same swimming pool with its brand new filtering system. I gave readings in their den. The Scorpio Rooster, an investment banker with Capricorn rising, was impressed by the expensive cars parked in front of his house. A few foreign clients rented limos. The success of my other clients seemed to assure him of the accuracy of my readings for him.

We remained friends for many years. I attended lavish parties in their homes in Beverly Hills, each grander and larger. His Scorpio eagles adorned the electric gate of the house near the Beverly Hills Hotel. Her huge Leo lions ornamented the living room with giant palms between them. Leo cannot be outdone, with the Dragon the most fortunate sign in the Chinese Zodiac!

In my opinion, lamentably, the Scorpio Rooster often had other women in his cards. While the Dragon and Rooster lived in their last fantastic house, now owned by a world-famous singer, the Scorpio had mistresses in three different houses within jogging distance. Since his success in investment banking was in the extreme, he started to act as he pleased with little regard for anyone else. Tragic! Excessive wealth can be at the root of evil behavior. It is my opinion that those who play should not make marriage vows. The Lords of Karma are always listening and eager to pull the cosmic rug out from under you for your own ultimate good.

Eventually, the regal Leo Dragon divorced the philandering Scorpio Rooster (Scorpio is the sign with the greatest power for good or evil), and he has since left this earth at the young age of 62. His life in itself could fill several books. He was attractive, intelligent, ambitious, successful and charming with numerous homes, private jet with his own crew, and luxury yacht. Money and power can be fun, but tend to corrupt. And yet, karmic relationships do create endless opportunities for growth and development for souls living on this earth.

One woman's husband fooled around and was discovered before she divorced him. "I'm not usually attracted to attractive women," he said. His problem: kiddie-porn and bestiality. The cover seldom reveals the contents of the book. I was surprised to learn that he had been taken away in handcuffs and imprisoned. This is the reason I do not walk around open. The husband of another friend philandered. Upon being found out, he wanted the divorce. It was no longer fun for him—and that broke her heart.

Some of my beautiful friends, including a *Playboy* centerfold and Miss USA runner-up in the Miss Universe Pageant, were betrayed by husbands. Beauty, intelligence, or excessive wealth are no guarantee of lasting happiness or fidelity in marriage. Rich and famous males have been cuckolded, as a few rich male clients discarded one woman for another without a backward glance. Money and power are no guarantee of fidelity, honor or integrity.

Early 1981, at Sheila and Edward Weidenfeld's home in Georgetown, Cancer Sally Quinn had her first reading. There was an earth sign woman (Taurus) in her cards who seemed to be pregnant. The woman's husband was having an affair with another woman that was going to create a notorious public scandal. Sally's friend's marriage would end in divorce and her friendship would help to sustain the woman through difficult times. On the other hand:

"In time, the woman is going to write a book because of her ordeal and the book will be a bestseller that is eventually made into a successful motion picture. Her life is going to change dramatically for the better because of this horrible situation."

That Taurus woman turned out to be writer Nora Ephron. Her second husband, Carl Bernstein, had a notorious affair with a famous female politician whose name by now is irrelevant. Her bestselling book, *Heartburn,* became a motion picture that starred Meryl Streep and Jack Nicholson. Nora's life dramatically changed because of the flagrant infidelity of her famous husband. Nora wrote one of my favorite movies, *When Harry Met Sally.* So you never know when your present agony is going to lead to a different kind of ecstasy in the near or distant future. Take notes!

There are those rare instances in which a marriage is "happily ever after." But that is usually because of hard work, blood, sweat and tears, high anxiety, disappointment, sacrifices, promises, insomnia, talking all night, fighting and making up, with the latter the best part.

God bless the Lords of Karma and God bless marriage— whether you are fortunate enough to live happily ever after— or not!

7

THE GAME OF LOVE – OR RAGING HORMONES

When the planet Mars (or the 'dwarf planet' with major impact) Pluto, closely aspects Venus, Sun, Moon or the Ascendant between the charts of a heterosexual or homosexual couple, erotic fireworks and remarkable chemistry are sure to follow. Mars on the Moon is "tear off clothes jump in the sack time." where people can have trouble keeping their hands off each other. **Hot and heavy** comes to mind. There are past life bonds that involve extremely personal unfinished business—more to learn, in not only a carnal sense, but every sense—on the continuing journey through our evolving Universe.

It has been the karma of some clients to have such a relationship, and yet, even with the most fantastic astrological aspects and multiple past life bonds, relationships may still wane within months—or years. Some clients have fallen in love rather often, but being "in love" is different from maintaining a long-term relationship after the blush has left the rose. Edgar Cayce said there could be 25 persons anyone might marry in a given lifetime. A few of my clients married several of these in one life, while others enjoyed lusty affairs without the messy legal entanglements involved in dissolving a marriage.

The game of love is not risk free. The fifth astrological house of romance also governs gambling, games of chance, politics, recreation, and children that may result from brief or lasting engagements of the flesh. Not all romantic relationships are destined for a seventh house marriage. Neither is it unusual for some to be *childish* in affairs of the heart, especially when spurned by the object of ardor, or upon discovering some heartless scoundrel or scheming damsel was simply toying with their affections!

One scorned client put crazy glue in all the locks of her lover's brand-new Mercedes and pierced all four tires with an ice pick (having acquired the strength by working out with a personal trainer provided by her philandering lover). Another woman dressed up like a ninja and stalked the new girlfriend, besides leaving disguised, threatening messages on his answering machine—which might be more difficult these days with the advancement in electronics. Luckily, she was never arrested and did find another man to harass. "Hell hath no fury like a woman scorned" is sometimes an understatement.

In the same year, two male clients in different states put $1,000 on their Visa cards to pay some so-called Internet "psychic" to bring back the woman each man said he loved. The guy on Maui, in the middle of his midlife crisis, went all out after only one toss in the hay with the sweet, young thing 20 years his junior. For her, he rented and furnished an apartment with an ocean view and leased a new car for her after sleeping with her twice. She must have been something!

From the beginning, it seemed to me that the pretty young thing was crazy about some hot young stud two years her senior. He was the one who actually shared that king-sized bed most days and nights with plenty of action between sheets provided by my client. The younger man usually drove the new car on which my client made payments. No fool like an old fool—even at a young age of 43.

A fascinating aspect of romantic love: no person can be forced to have "that feeling," no matter how much we yearn for reciprocation. Love is a mystery the same as life, in spite of the lucrative sex trade. Love is not a commodity to buy or sell, even though some may be foolish enough to think that way.

Sex may be bought and sold. Sex is not necessarily love. Good sex almost always comes with love.

When I tried to tell Mr. Maui, who was conned out of his $1,000 for a ritual that supposedly involved seven candles six feet tall that would burn for a month, his response was: "You don't have the power to bring her back to me."

"I'll pray for you for a month twice a day for $1,000," I teased.

The pretty young girl soon abandoned the apartment with its view of the surf to reside in a lesser abode with her young stud. Mr. Maui had trouble finding the car, ungratefully trashed. He was too embarrassed to call me again. Many of us have difficult lessons to learn when it comes to the game of love—and how to manage our abundant hormones during our younger years—and sometimes even later!

The other young male fell in love with an older, recently divorced woman formerly married to a doctor. She was used to the good life. My client was a salesman. He may have lacked prestige in her eyes. She was fond of him, but not "in love." He was desperate to marry her and eager for her to love him back. My heart went out to him.

In another lifetime, I was a witch in Italy and used black magic to create amulets and potions to win or try to guarantee love. I know better than to try that again. Bad karma is the price for such actions. Several clients have paid thousands to charlatans without results. Charlatans in the psychic business make much more than genuine psychics. The reason seems to be naive superstition, especially when it comes to emotion. Energy can be manipulated by those skilled in the dark arts, but such actions require sustained energy and concentration— more on this later. The result is usually difficult karma, now or later, for those who tend to dabble!

In 1965, my first love affair with a working actor was with Libra Allen Case. Our relationship started when Allen played Frank James on the TV show, *The Legend of Jesse James*. Several months into our affair I started to feel guilty. He had a wife and young daughter. My decision to break things off with Allen was mentioned to a psychic named Nita in Tujunga. "When you tell him, he's going to say … 'Well, if I ever get divorced …'" and strangely enough, those were his exact words two weeks later.

I was crazy about Allen. I never wanted the relationship to end, but it didn't feel right to me to continue. I was learning about karma—about reaping what I may have sown.

Several years later, Allen divorced. His acting career floundered. He turned designer and designed the first fake fur coats for men. Allen also designed the uniforms for the pilots and flight attendants of Southwest Airlines. Whenever he came to town, he asked me out to dinner. Allen was upset that he was no longer a star on television. First, he had starred in *The Deputy* with legendary film star Henry Fonda before co-starring on *The Legend of Jesse James*. His acting roles had dwindled to guest stints on episodic television.

In 1984, Allen was my date for an elegant birthday party at the Wilshire Country Club for my roommate from India, Fanya Carter. Allen embarrassed me that evening by trying to pick up the young waitress serving our table of 10. Only recently had he been released from the hospital with problems with his liver. That night Allen consumed one drink after another. It pained me to see him on a downward spiral. After my move to Virginia the fall of 1984, I was still concerned about him and called him during the Christmas holidays.

"Patricia, I've developed a serious drinking problem," he said on the telephone. Allen had always called me "Patricia" and never lost his Texas twang. Allen was born in Dallas.

"I noticed," I said, remembering the party. "Maybe you should get help."

He mumbled something about conquering his demons, but I had serious doubts. At Christmastime 1985, I called Allen again and wondered if he was sober. As Christmas approached in 1986, I was on the telephone with Susan Strasberg when I said, "I need to call Allen again to see how he's doing."

"He died this year. Didn't you know? It was announced on *Entertainment Tonight.*"

I was stunned.

That night I cried myself to sleep. Six foot three, eyes of blue, a handsome Libra with dimples too—Allen Case had been discovered singing on Arthur Godfrey's *Talent Scouts.* It seemed tragic for him to die at 51. He had a beautiful singing voice. In 1967, Allen had starred on Broadway with Leslie Uggams in *Hallelujah Baby.* He was a man of many talents, although I was always aware we would never make it as a couple. My views were far too liberal for that gun-toting Texas Republican. And yet, Allen Case will remain forever in my heart.

In the summer of 1987—a strange thing happened. I went to the theater with Libra Nancy Ferguson, who had also moved to Washington from California. After the show we had a glass of wine at a sidewalk café, and for some strange reason I started to reminisce about Allen Case and our love affair that started when I was a secretary at 20th Century Fox.

"So you were the redhead at the studio!" Nancy said.

Surprise!

As it turned out, Nancy and her first husband had lived across the street from Allen and his wife. His wife had apparently heard rumors about Allen "having an affair with some redhead at the studio."

I was that redhead!

There we were on the other side of the country talking about Allen Case 20 years later, with Allen on the Other Side of life. Karma always catches up with you.

Every Scorpio has much to learn about sexuality and that includes the Moon or Scorpio rising. I fell in love with actors on the silver screen as a girl. My first husband, Tom, was an aspiring actor. Blame it on my Leo moon. Actors are only men. Water signs (Cancer, Scorpio, Pisces) are emotional and romantic. Scorpio rules sex and reproduction. Cancer rules the home and family. Pisces rules clandestine affairs. One petite, married, blonde Pisces had a hot affair with Pisces-Aries actor William Shatner while he was Captain James Kirk of the Starship Enterprise in the original *Star Trek* series. Apparently, he did send her straight into orbit. ☺ Kudos, Captain Kirk!

During the mid-1960s I dated three men at the same time who were friends. Gemini Stewart was the medium who gave me the Ouija Board. Another was named Huck. The third man was Gemini science fiction writer Harlan Ellison. Since I desperately wanted to be a writer, I was jazzed by dating a published novelist who also wrote for the original *Star Trek* series. Harlan was very eccentric. He introduced me to my first deck of tarot cards, which were much too large to shuffle. The strangest part—all three men asked me to marry them. I was only attracted to Harlan, definitely the most interesting of the three.

While working at the studio, I learned that a Capricorn I had a crush on in my teens had divorced. He had a band that played for our LDS stake dances, but nothing further ever developed between us. In 1968, I had a leap year party for singles and he was invited. That night romance finally bloomed. Then, two weeks passed without a word. In frustration, I decided to call him.

"Oh, he got married," his former roommate announced.

Shock!

"When?" I managed.

"About a month ago."

My party had been two weeks earlier. Needless to say, I was distressed by the news of his nuptials.

Two days later, the Capricorn called. "I think we need to talk."

We had lunch in the commissary. I continued to see him for several months. Sadly, his first wife had committed suicide and left him with a young son. The present wife wanted to adopt the boy. She was also a sharpshooter policewoman. I decided it was best to end the romance, but we remained friends. He booked readings and we had great conversations about metaphysics and other far-out subjects.

Pisces men were once my downfall. Their Sun falls in my house of romance. In the early 1970s, a strawberry blond Pisces singer broke my heart. Michael and I met at an A.R.E. Conference at Asilomar in Pacific Grove. He played his guitar and sang to me on top of the sand dunes near the sea. That was romantic! He had a lovely, country-style voice. Before long, I was introducing him to my friends in show business. One helped Michael get a demo made for the recording companies. He sang in lounges at the Hungry Tiger restaurants. In my enthusiasm to launch his singing career, I invited friends and clients to hear him sing. His sister also sang, but her voice was not nearly as fine as Michael's.

Since I was a professional psychic, Michael wanted a reading. Against my better judgment, I decided to give him one. Until laying out his cards I was ignorant of his involvement with a brunette Capricorn in Orange County. That was the day I learned to never again read for the men in my life. In my clairvoyant state I can *see* much more than most men might want me to know.

In Michael's cards was a redheaded Scorpio woman, divorced, five years older than he, with two children, a boy and a girl. "You're going to marry this woman after a 6-8 week whirlwind romance," I said, and the weirdest part: I could have been describing myself.

I was a redheaded Scorpio, five years older than Michael, divorced with two children, a boy and a girl, and I was crazy about him. "In all honesty, I don't know if the woman in these cards is me."

From the look on his face, it was plain to me that Michael thought I was doing a number on him. Honestly, I did not know if the woman was me—even though we had been involved for almost two months by then. When I give a reading I become a channel for that person. All my personal interests are set aside.

Immediately, Michael stopped calling. Soon after, I found out that he had hit on two of my closest girlfriends, both named Susan. We were invited to Susan Strasberg's in Malibu for dinner—and Michael showed up two hours early and hit on her. Susan never said a word until my affair with Michael ended. The other Susan had helped him with the demo and was married to a lawyer. Michael hit on her too! Luckily, my girlfriends were loyal. Neither was interested in a struggling musician, even though Michael had talent.

That Labor Day weekend, Susan Strasberg and I drove up Route 1 to the Big Sur and stayed at a charming inn. We were lucky to get a room without a reservation. That part of California is magical. Each day, Susan and I walked through the woods and sat under a different pine tree to meditate. We had dinner at Nepenthe's sipping wine and watching the sun sink into the sea in a brilliant wash of color. And yet, all weekend I was in despair over Michael who had dumped me. I cried myself to sleep that weekend over all the lost loves of my life. Poor me!

On the third day, Susan and I took a different trail up the mountain. We reached an open place where we could see the sea covered with a million twinkling lights reflecting the sun. We each sat under a different tree to meditate.

I was feeling sorry for myself again—alone and forsaken—when, all of a sudden, I had what can only be described as a brilliant illumination. In an instant, I knew that I was not alone—that I had never been alone—and would never, ever be alone again. It was as though I was surrounded by myriad hosts of beings evolving the same as me. I was Love Eternal—never to forget the LOVE at the core of all LIFE—the absolute Love of God.

Talk about getting over a guy fast!

Eleven years later, Pisces Michael called again. Instead of singing on television and collecting gold records, he was singing in a smoky, tacky bar in Riverside, California, in a rundown hotel. And, six months after he stopped seeing me, he was singing at Harrah's Club in Reno when he met a redheaded Scorpio woman, five years older than he, divorced with two children, a boy and a girl—and he married her in eight weeks! They had the son I had also seen in his cards back in my kitchen in Sherman Oaks. His free reading had been quite accurate.

Guess what?

Things had not turned so well. Michael was divorced. He even said, "I should have married you. You should have been the mother of my son." And yet, as fate would have it—we can seldom go back. Everyone changes in different ways. The spark was gone.

And thankfully, I was able to tell Michael how he had inadvertently been responsible for my having one of the most elevating, profound experiences of my life in the Big Sur. My state of consciousness had instantly soared from agony to ecstasy on a clear day on a mountain high above the sparkling sea.

Another Pisces man in the 1970s lied to me about his age. I made arrangements for Phillip to have a birthday reading with my astrologer friend Tish Leroy. When his arrived for his reading, he admitted that he was five years younger. He was 10 years younger than I was, not five. He was afraid I would never go out with him if I knew his true age. He proposed to me on my birthday after six dates and wanted me to run off with him to Las Vegas on that night.

Phil had never impressed me as father material for my children. After his proposal was rejected the relationship turned stormy. There was something about him that never felt right to me, but I was unable to discern the reason. That New Year's, Phil went camping with some guys instead of joining me on a trip to Lake Tahoe with my friends. Finally, after further traumas, the relationship ended.

One Saturday afternoon, my hairdresser Samantha (Sam) asked about him when she was doing my hair: "Are you sure it's really over?"

"Absolutely!"

"Come with me," she said and she marched me up the next aisle in Joseph Magnum's hair salon to the station of another hairdresser who was plainly gay. On his mirror, Phil smiled out at me from his picture signed, "I love you! Phil." He had given me the same picture.

"Who's that?" I inquired, nodding at the picture with narrowed eyes.

"My boyfriend. Isn't he gorgeous?" He was watching me closely. "Do you know him?"

"He used to be my boyfriend too—but you can have him! He even asked me to marry him."

And that was that—for that 10-degree black belt!

One Sunday in the spring of 1971, after a lecture at the Tarot Temple, a highly recognizable man walked up to me. "I'm Audie Murphy. I'm a national hero," he said talking in an animated manner that amused me. He looked young with his baby face and sparkling eyes.

The manner in which he was trying to impress me with his war record and acting career was adorable. After all, Audie Murphy was the most decorated war hero of World War II. In 1945, his picture on the cover of *Life* magazine attracted Hollywood producers. Audie appeared in many motion pictures and television shows. He was also a successful country music composer and had quarter horse ranches in Texas, Arizona and California.

I assured handsome Audie that I knew who he was and that I was aware of his war record. And even though I was flattered he had hit on me, I had a strange sense that he might not be around long. Gemini Audie was 46. I was 12 years younger.

Unfortunately, months later in bad weather his small private plane crashed in Virginia, his pilot unqualified to fly on instruments. Audie Murphy was dead at 46. His grave in Arlington National Cemetery is the second-most visited grave next to that of President John Fitzgerald Kennedy. It was not surprising that Audie Murphy attended the Temple of Sacred Tarot and Holy Qabalah. He was a Freemason and Shriner. He has a star on the Hollywood Walk of Fame. It was a brief moment in my life that I shall always remember.

Since my moon is Leo, Leo men have played major roles in my life. My first big crush was on Leo Floyd Brown at age 13. I was a freshman in high school when he was a sophomore. I invited him to a Backwards Dance (girls invite the boys). My stepfather drove me to pick him up and picked us up afterwards to take Floyd home. His dad was a lawyer, my stepdad a UPS driver. Plus, my family never belonged to the Church. My crush on Floyd continued through my high school years.

Only once did Floyd and I make out in front of my house after he drove me home from church. There was plenty of passion. I had trouble keeping track of his hands. At that time I planned to be a virgin on my wedding night. Floyd sometimes arranged dates for me with his cousins from out of town. There were times I wondered if he was testing me. Chastity was preached at church.

While Floyd was on his mission, I married Tom and had Tomi. After divorcing abusive Tom, I ran into Floyd at a church dance after he returned from his mission. The remark he made when I asked him to dance was hurtful: "You're used," he said, referring to my lack of virginity. He walked away. That night, my crush was crushed. What a jerk! All the girls he dated were Mormon and from wealthy families.

Many years later at a party in the home of Bobbie and Ray Wood, Floyd was there with his second wife. He had divorced and his actions were different. Later that evening, after taking his pretty young wife to the car, Floyd returned and kissed my cheek. Then he hurried out. I'm not sure how many children he had with his wives. Some old Mormon boyfriends had as many as 13 children and lived on welfare. That made me happy to no longer be Mormon. My spirit guides had protected me.

My first serious romance with a Leo was with Ray Taylor who worked for a major shoe company. In the early 1970s, Ray and I met at the wedding of my Cancer friend Carol (for whom I did my first reading) to Scorpio Tony Spinoso. The men were friends through work. That day Ray was impressed with my Juliano shoes! When I was younger I had very narrow feet and bought expensive shoes. With his Leo Sun on my Leo Moon— it was absolute kismet!

Ray's second wife had died in her 30s from kidney disease. Two years after her death, her prescriptions were still in his medicine cabinet. Since they lived in Newport Beach on the water, Ray had scattered her ashes at sea. Tragic but romantic! And, the lady still seemed to have a hold on him.

Early in our relationship, Ray invited me to Las Vegas. Leo rules gambling. Ray loved to shoot craps. I picked a table and told him to play there. He started out with $20 and ended up with several hundred. Then I pulled on his sleeve and said, "It's time to stop." All Ray did was give me a look and he kept on throwing those dice.

Before long, all the money except for the original $20 was back in the casino's coffer. He asked me to pick him another table. Guess what? The exact same thing happened all over again. He refused to stop when he had more than enough to pay for our weekend. I tried to explain that I wasn't allowed to use my gift in that manner. I refused to pick another table. He should have listened!

Months later, Ray wanted me to read his cards. He had heard I was good. I had learned my lesson from Michael. I had no desire to know about the other women in Ray's life or if he had doubts about me. There was no commitment. Ray had his cards read by a psychic in Pasadena.

"I guess you know the woman you're dating is a white witch," the psychic said.

"But that's good, isn't it?"

"Well, it all depends on how you look at it. The lady has a whole lot of power!"

I was never sure if it was because of the crap tables in Las Vegas or the Pasadena psychic calling me a "white witch," but Ray never committed to me. He gave me a nice cameo for my birthday, which Tomi borrowed and lost when she was in her teens. Years later, another friend of his in the shoe business, Milton Barad, the husband of my client-friend Valerie, took me to dinner in Malibu when Valerie left for Taiwan on business. I had been giving readings in their lovely Encino home.

"You know you scared the hell out of Ray Taylor, right? He told me about Vegas and those crap tables." Milton started to laugh.

Ray had made it clear he was not interested in taking on a woman with children. Then, after we stopped dating, I had this dream. In the dream Ray was in a black car with his boss from New York, with a young woman seated between them. To digress, one weekend in Newport Beach I had fixed up his boss with my friend Susan Strasberg and they both stayed in a hotel. Susan was not interested. Back to my dream: Ray and I were standing behind the car and I was crying.

"This is something I have to do," Ray said.

Then, he got into the car and they drove off—leaving me there alone.

A few months later I heard that Ray had married his New York boss's secretary. She was much younger with two small children. I guess it was "something he had to do." Years later he divorced again. We got back together, but it was not the same. Our time together had passed. Ray married again after that, maybe more than once. I hope he is happy.

The next Leo man in my life was a publisher. Timothy and I met in 1975 soon after I started writing my first novel, *The Recycling of Rosalie.* When the Leo Key of the Major Arcana showed up in my cards, my first thought was usually Ray. But he never returned. The nicest part about Timothy was that he read every chapter of my story as it was written. Then he sometimes read the rewrite the next day.

"You're good at editing your own work," Tim said.

It was perfect timing. His office was blocks from our Encino house. After work, I would fix him a drink and Tim would sit by the pool reading my next chapter. Sometimes he got upset if I interrupted him! That secretly pleased me.

Timothy's encouragement with my writing was very important to me. His kind words kept me writing that story, which he insisted I finish. He also attended tarot classes for clients in our home that year. The classes were recorded for posterity, although I have yet to play them again.

As it turned out, there was another woman in Tim's life. In the summer of 1975, Timothy Welch made several trips east in connection with the memoirs of former President Richard Nixon. Our relationship ended before my novel was finished. But I always thought it was divine timing that he crossed my path that year. When our affair ended, he wrote me a note saying he needed to know how my story ends! For years, I searched for him on the Internet. Do you have any idea how many men named Timothy Welch live in the United States of America?

"Speaking of ghosts," the e-mail subject line read.

The afternoon of September 29, 2009, I was interviewed on Sirius-XM Satellite Radio by my Libra friend Maggie Linton and her co-host, Kim Alexander, on *Cover to Cover* live in Washington, D.C. We talked about my two published books: *The Wheel of Destiny – The Tarot Reveals Your Master Plan,* and my novel, *The Recycling of Rosalie.* Perhaps by divine design, the right Timothy Welch was driving in his car in Washington State and just happened to turn on his car radio in time to hear our show. Tim is still publishing. He is also married to his fourth wife and is writing his memoir, in which he plans to mention me. Wonders never cease! Clever spirit guides for us both!

The last Leo in my life was a psychiatrist. On New Year's Eve 1978, I met Frederick at a party at the home of Susan Strasberg in Sherman Oaks. Susan had raved about wanting me to meet Frederick. The way she talked I thought she meant him for me. Perhaps not so strangely, Frederick had seen a psychic who told him that he was going to meet "a redheaded

Scorpio in a green dress at a party." She was divorced with two children and would change his life—would help him to grow spiritually. That night I had on a green dress.

Frederick and I had our first date within days—and our love affair ignited. However, my romance with him started on retrograde Mars. That is not good. I learned about retrograde Mars many years later. The rule: a man can turn cruel after Mars turns direct. That was exactly what happened with Frederick.

During our affair, I turned into his interior designer and selected furnishings for the house in Westwood to which he was adding a second story. Much time was spent searching for the right piece of furniture for the flamboyant Leo. There were serious misunderstandings with Susan at the time. She kept asking Frederick to take her to fancy parties, which upset me. Her interest in him was more than she had admitted. She acted jealous of our whirlwind romance. Unbeknownst to me, another psychic, once considered a friend, had trashed me behind my back by telling Susan and other close friends' of mine barefaced lies. I didn't learn of this until 2003.

On Susan's birthday, May 22, 1979, she invited Frederick to her private party but not me. When Frederick told me, I was devastated. And yet, some men have trouble understanding close bonds of friendship between women—even psychiatrists. Later, Susan and I ended up on the telephone, with both of us crying our eyes out.

To illustrate Frederick's eccentricity: He chose me over Susan because he thought her feet were ugly. He said he could never date a woman with wide feet and stubby toes. Could it have been his Pisces Moon? Pisces does rule the feet. Susan had a Pisces moon. Their moons should have created a bond between them. Plus, Susan should have been honest and told me of her feelings before I accepted my first date with Frederick. When it comes to intimate relationships, there is a big difference between Gemini and Scorpio! Susan had lots of men friends she kept at a distance. When I am interested in a man I do not keep him at a distance. But I am monogamous.

My relationship with Frederick lasted a year. The fun part was that he wanted to learn everything about the tarot and he taught me the I Ching. We spent hours throwing tarot cards and coins on his king-sized bed. We talked metaphysics for hours. One Sunday he was on the telephone with his mother and I picked up on his deceased father being with his dead aunt, whom I named. Frederick picked my brain. He was highly intelligent. I can be a sucker for intelligent men. My Mars is in Virgo. Both my husband's had high IQs and Virgo planets.

When my affair with Frederick finally ended—it was as though a spell had broken as I drove back to Woodland Hills. That is the only way to explain it. I had awakened from a long, complicated and difficult dream.

One good thing that resulted from our relationship was my friendship with his former partner, Jim, and his wife, Beverly. Frederick never thought Bev was good enough for Jim. But the two of them are still happily married and have raised two beautiful children. Now they are grandparents. When our affair ended, Jim and Bev said they could never understand how someone as nice as I was could be with Frederick! But karma is karma.

The different aspects between the planets in two charts determine the destiny of a relationship. Nearly every woman is waiting for her prince, her king or knight in shining armor to whisk her off to his castle or even a modest apartment. Fairy tales are the way it really is, right? The handsome prince awakens the princess from her dream without turning it into a hellish nightmare.

In 1977, a young client was in a highly destructive relationship. The man abused drugs and alcohol. When he was drugged or drunk, he turned violent and abused her. She was the daughter of a good client. My advice was for her to lose the loser. During our session I had accurately described him and his drunken father in whose footsteps he followed. Another man was going to show up in her life to make her happy. At the end of the session, she said she was going to play my tape for her violent boyfriend. On the first side, I had totally trashed him. On the flip side I had spoken of her job, future children, and her marriage to a nice man. The thought of her replaying her tape for a guy who pounded on women made me anxious.

Guess what?

When she arrived home, the first side of the tape was blank. Everything on the second side was still there. Clever spirit guides looking out for both of us!

In the 1960s, Susan Strasberg referred Scorpio actress Brenda Vaccaro for readings. Brenda was then romantically linked with handsome Libra actor Michael Douglas. Brenda, Michael and I attended the same New Year's Eve party at Susan's house in Malibu. That was before Michael starred on the *Streets of San Francisco*, but his acting career was on the rise.

I didn't have a date. Near midnight, we all traipsed out onto the beach with our glasses of champagne, along with a fresh bottle. We gathered around a bonfire. Someone had a transistor radio with the countdown to midnight. Before long, people were kissing each other Happy New Year. Since I was feeling no pain, as they say—and Michael Douglas was standing alone—I walked over and kissed him. And he kissed me back!

Then, I started to walk away, but instead, turned and kissed him again. About then Brenda was watching me, but she was laughing. On the other hand, as another Scorpio, she was no doubt keeping an eye on me. I have a weakness for Libra men. And I still think Michael Douglas is a fox! Lucky Catherine! Two Libras! Can anyone decide?

Unfortunately, while Brenda was still with Michael, it seemed in one of her readings that Michael was with another woman. The relationship was going to end. Not too many years later Michael married Diandra and had his first son. I have never read for Michael Douglas, but he sure can kiss!

When Anjelica Huston was involved with Jack Nicholson, the end of their affair was in her cards. Other men would enter her life. Her future success as an actress was there, along with nominations and awards. Anjelica has had quite a career since then. I enjoy her work and wish her all the best.

In the early 1970s, in one month I read for three different women romantically linked with Frank Sinatra. Busy Sagittarius! One was a flight attendant, another a script girl, and the third woman was an interior designer, all beautiful. He did well for a skinny Italian (not so much in later years). Thankfully, Frank entertained us all until his Uranus Return, which happens with many celebrities. I probably have all his albums!

When I read for Taurus model-actress Alana Stewart, she was already divorced from George Hamilton and from singer Rod Stewart. I saw other men and much success in her future. In Texas, I read for the mother of supermodel Jerry Hall and could see her daughter's relationship with Leo rock star Mick Jagger of the Rolling Stones. I predicted the birth of their four children. I thought they might marry. In 1990, they married in Indonesia. Later, Mick challenged the validity of the ceremony and the marriage was annulled. Bianca Jagger had one telephone reading after life with Mick. Her life since then has been admirable.

In a reading for a young Englishman, I saw a romance with an Aries rock star: Elton John. When I said Elton's name, the young man nearly fell off his chair and his eyes widened. "But how do you know that?"

"I'm psychic. When I looked at your cards I could see Elton's face before me!" With key 4, The Emperor, Aries, in his house of romance I had flashed on Elton. My spirit guides are clever and accommodating!

A beautiful Virgo client-friend was torn between a famous composer and actor-singer Dean Martin, both much older than she. Dean had paid the rent for her fancy Beverly Hills house and he gave her a new Cadillac the very same week that the composer gave her a new Ford Tornado. What a dilemma! A mutual friend and I thought her mad not to marry Dean Martin, who had proposed. The composer is still married. The sexy Virgo always had men falling at her feet.

In the late 1960s, during our chummy days she invited me to dinner on Easter Sunday at her sister's house in the Valley. Bill had the children that weekend. Her sister was complaining because my friend was on the sofa instead of helping out in the kitchen.

"Get the lead out of your ass and get up and help me!" her sister demanded.

"That's not lead, sister dear—that happens to be pure gold!"

Everyone laughed, but she did obey her elder sister. That Virgo had her pick of men. She was a dazzling blonde bombshell and alley cat in one nice package! When she stayed out late with other men, our Aquarius friend stayed at her house in case Dean or the composer called. Then the other beautiful blonde pretended to be her absent friend in a breathy-sexy voice. Many nights talking to the composer, he never realized who was on the other end of the telephone as the conversation ended with, "I love you." Some men enjoy being fooled.

Dean finally dumped her. She had to move out of the Beverly Hills house with a pool after she was photographed by a detective in Acapulco with "the dentist to the stars." Karma is karma, but some karma is more interesting. She may never have seen it coming. The Virgo later married a doctor and had children. Since then, I hear she has been married a few times and is now living in Palm Springs. She should write her memoirs.

Over the years, intimate relationships have been predicted for thousands and thousands of clients: male, female, straight, gay, transgender, and ambidextrous. Some were love affairs, others involved marriage, and still others involved painful divorces. Some couples lived together, which did not always work. Relationships are never easy. There must be friendship and compassion for true passion to endure.

Matters of the heart tend to awaken our deepest insecurities, vulnerabilities and even our forgotten fears. When we are not very careful, that which we fear can descend upon us—the same as it did for Job in the Old Testament. Maintaining a positive attitude about everything all the time is nearly impossible in this dimension. Do you suppose that it gets any easier in the next?

THE RICH AND THE FAMOUS

8

STARS IN THE WHITE HOUSE

On January 3, 1967, when former actor Ronald Reagan was sworn in as Governor of California, I had been doing readings for only a few months. It was after watching Johnny Carson's monologue, since I always enjoyed ending my day with humor, when I decided to stay up for the swearing-in ceremony of our newly elected governor.

Lo and behold, I got chills from head to toe and could see the White House, Capitol Building, and the Seal of the President directly behind Governor Reagan. To me, that meant he would one day be President of the United States. What I didn't realize then was the prominent role the two terms of our 40th President would play in my life—or that 20 years would pass before the public learned that an astrologer had picked the time of the swearing-in of California's new governor.

Along with the majority, I had cast my vote for Ronald Reagan. He was the hot topic on the Fox lot. In spring 1967, I was secretary to a screenwriter of a WW II drama that was never made. I had learned that writers have a rough road to success in Hollywood.

I have never been really political. Still, when Ronald Reagan was governor I had a dream one night. In my first studio assignment on *The Legend of Jesse James,* the saloon set was where parties were held after a segment wrapped. In my dream, I was standing at the bar on the saloon set when Governor Reagan walked up in his blue jeans, western shirt, cowboy boots, and cowboy hat and placed his foot on the railing. Maybe he had done that in some old Western movie. He looked young and handsome for his age.

In my dream, I turned to the governor and said, "You want to know something?"

Governor Reagan smiled and nodded.

"One day you're going to be President of the United States."

"You know something—I think I'd like that," he said, smiling.

That's all I can remember. But it was a dream I will never forget. It was further confirmation of my vision from when Ronald Reagan was sworn in as governor.

The years passed.

Reagan was getting older and I was starting to doubt my vision and my dream. How was he going to be elected president if he was really old?

Then, in the spring of 1976, Gwen Davis gave her friend Sheila Weidenfeld the gift of a reading from me. Sheila was Betty Ford's press secretary and very short on spare time on the campaign trail in the attempt to get Gerald Ford elected to the presidency. I drove to the Beverly Wilshire Hotel to see Sheila in her room amid ringing telephones and interruptions that made it difficult to concentrate.

Sheila Weidenfeld is highly mercurial: a cute, pert, petite brunette with bright blue eyes and keen intelligence. With her Sun and two other planets in Virgo and her rising and three other planets in Gemini, she has the perfect chart for a press secretary or writer. She was under pressure and apologized repeatedly. Virgos are always in my life (husband, daughter, stepmother, friends and granddaughter). Sheila's Sun falls in the house of my friends, while my Sun falls in her house of employees or coworkers. That seemed logical.

Perhaps another divine coincidence was when I described a woman in her reading as a water sign with red or blonde hair, divorced with two children, who had an earth sign man in her life who was giving her trouble. He was going to break her heart.

"Are you a water sign?" Sheila brightly inquired. "I don't have any friends of that description, so it must be you. Are you divorced? Do you have two children?"

Talk about confusion!

Sheila's moon in Sagittarius makes her forthright. My Venus, Jupiter and North Node are on her moon. I was unsure of how to respond. We had just met. On the other hand, there was an earth sign man in my redheaded Scorpio life: Capricorn. He and his teenage son lived with me in Encino. Bo had asked me to marry him. He had yet to file for divorce from the wife he had left two weeks before we met at a party in the home of none other than Gwen Davis. The Capricorn had responsibility issues. His younger son was in juvenile detention. The relationship felt karmic, to say the least. But how could I be in Sheila's cards? I liked her although I doubted Ford would be elected. President Ford had inherited the Nixon presidency after his resignation because of Watergate.

In the summer of 1976, we moved into a smaller rented house on Aura Avenue. That summer Sheila drove to my house for another reading. It was not easy for me to tell her that Gerald Ford was going to lose to Jimmy Carter. I waffled in my effort to make her happy. And, even though Sheila had been married for five years, she had no children. Children were in her cards. By then the Capricorn man was history. The broken-hearted Scorpio was me. There are times I learn more about me in the readings of other people. I was already dating someone else.

After Ford lost in November, Sheila invited me to Washington to see the White House before the Fords moved out and the Carters moved in. She wanted me to read for her friends. I made preparations for my first trip to the nation's capital. Tomi was away at Whitworth College and Mark stayed with friends. That trip east included New York City, where I stayed with my astrologer friend, Jeanne Avery, another Scorpio, and read for her clients and friends. In Washington, I was in the Georgetown home of Sheila and Edward Weidenfeld. My extensive travel as a psychic began with that trip.

Before that time I had not realized that Sheila Rabb Weidenfeld had grown up in politics. In 1952, her father, Maxwell M. Rabb, was a member of Eisenhower's campaign and Secretary to the Cabinet during that administration. As a child, Sheila had played on the White House lawn. Her father had served under Democratic President Lyndon B. Johnson and as adviser to Republican President Gerald Ford, besides being appointed Ambassador to Italy. Maxwell Rabb held many responsible political posts until his death at age 91 in 2002.

During the U.S. Bicentennial of 1976, Sheila treated me to a private tour of the White House. Walking through those hallowed historical halls I experienced déjà vu and felt that I had been there at an earlier time in history. We had lunch in the White House Mess, the restaurant within the presidential residence, on two separate occasions. One day Barbara Walters was there, as well as senators, congressmen and women, cabinet members, and members of the press. I felt honored to be having lunch there.

In the Weidenfeld home I did readings for Sheila's friends and members of her staff, which included the boss's son, Jack Ford. Then Edward had a reading. I flashed on his having been involved in a serious automobile accident at age 16.

"Many boys that age are involved in serious automobile accidents," Ed dismissively remarked. Ed Weidenfeld is a lawyer—a natural-born skeptic.

I could think of no boy, age 16, who had been involved in a serious auto accident. I went on with the reading and spoke of matters involving his career and personal life. Children showed up in his cards. Then, after picking up the cards, Ed said he wanted to ask me one more question.

I shuffled the cards and used a spread known as the Celtic Cross to answer his question.

"The answer to your question is *yes*," I said.

"Could you elaborate, please?"

The various meanings of the cards in the spread were explained. The first card, the Queen of Cups, usually a water sign woman, commonly Libra-Scorpio: This card "covered" the question. I knew the Queen of Cups was *my queen*. The King of Cups opposed the question. Edward is a Cancer man, a water sign. All Cups are water. Suspicion started to creep in.

I no longer remember every card in the spread, but the answer: the Three of Wands of the Tarot Minor Arcana. Besides the element of fire, the number three represents the planet Mercury and relates to communications. Fire represents ideals. The answer to his question involved "honor, integrity and honesty."

Edward was amused.

Curious, I asked him the nature of his question.

"I wanted to know if I could believe the things you just told me in your reading, if you were telling me the truth."

Needless to say, I was surprised and relieved. The honesty of the Queen of Cups had been established. My cards had exonerated me. The King of Cups was Edward: opposition. Clever spirit guides all around!

In their dining room one evening, Edward inquired, "So who do you think is going to be president in another four years?"

"Ronald Reagan," I said.

They looked at each other in amusement.

"You don't believe me?"

"No, on the contrary," Edward said. "You may have something there."

The following January, Jimmy Carter was sworn in as our 39th President as the Republicans moved out of the White House and the Democrats moved in. My friendship with Sheila Weidenfeld was established—an interesting part of my life.

Back in 1973, I got psychically burned out by the time we moved from Sherman Oaks to Encino. I had been seeing too many people, usually six days a week. I selected an unlisted telephone number. For a few years, only a few people knew how to find me. By 1977, after my daughter Tomi and I purchased a house together in Woodland Hills, my telephone number was back in the directory and former clients were calling. Not long after that September move, Tomi returned to Whitworth College in Spokane, Washington.

Our new home in the foothills south of Ventura Boulevard was on three-quarters of an acre of mainly sloping hillside, more like a mountain. There had been a drought for several years, so watering was restricted. But that winter the rains came. Driving over the San Diego Freeway toward West Los Angeles the foothills looked more like the lush green of Hawaii with waterfalls everywhere, not like the deserts of Southern California.

In the summer of 1978, Sheila drove to Woodland Hills for another reading. I gave her the Cook's tour of my hillside garden in its early stages. Again, children were in her cards. Nicholas Weidenfeld, their eldest son, was born in September 1979. That year Sheila's memoir of her time as Betty Ford's press secretary was published: *First Lady's Lady: With the Fords at the White House,* by Sheila Rabb Weidenfeld. An account from one reading was in the chapter, "A Death in the Workhouse." I was flattered and pleased to be in her book. Another of George's predictions had manifested.

On a return trip to Washington, one evening at dinner in the Weidenfeld home, Edward once again inquired, "So who do you think is going to be our next president?"

"Ronald Reagan."

Sheila and Edward seemed delighted. As it turned out, Sheila's father, Maxwell Rabb, was going to assist Ronald Reagan in his bid for the presidency.

I'm not sure of the month I predicted: "It will be Ronald Reagan and George Bush by a landslide." But it was long before the Republican National Convention in Detroit in July 1980. My further prediction: "Two terms for Ronald Reagan, with one term for George H.W. Bush as president." For me, those predictions were a direct revelation of Absolute Destiny!

That summer, after the Republican Convention but before the November election, journalist Judy Bachrach invited me to The Palm restaurant in Beverly Hills for dinner and an interview. Sheila had told her about my predictions at the convention. That evening I related my earlier vision of Reagan as president at the time of his swearing-in as California's governor back in 1967 and my dream about telling Governor Reagan he would become president of the United States one day. My story, which originally appeared in the *Washington Star* under the title, "In California, What a Psychic Says Is Serious," was misquoted in some newspapers and had me telling Ronald Reagan in person he would one day be president, perhaps good for my reputation but untrue. *The Washington Star* accurately published Judy Bachrach's article.

Sheila and Edward both worked on Reagan's campaign. Sheila worked on the Reagan-Bush transition team and put my name on her list of helpers. Several months later, two impressive certificates arrived in the mail which thanked me for my part in the Reagan-Bush Transition. My work was definitely behind the scenes, but perhaps equally important. I like to think my prediction that Ronald Reagan would be president made them work that much harder.

In 1980, soon after the election, I returned to Washington to stay with Sheila and Edward again. That was when journalist Sally Quinn, wife of Ben Bradlee, editor of the *Washington Post,* had her first reading. My prediction about her friend, Nora Ephron, is in another chapter. There were other things in Sally's cards, including a much-wanted child for her and Ben. His name is Quinn.

The day after Sally's reading, Henry Irving of *The Washington Post* invited me for lunch and an interview at The Palm in Washington, D.C. Tarot cards were spread out on the table as a photographer snapped pictures of me and my cards in front of sketches of their famous patrons.

On November 24, 1980, as I was about to leave for California, Henry Irving's article headlined the *Style* section of *The Washington Post:* "THE TAROT PSYCHIC – The Once and Future Cards of Patricia McLaine," by Henry Allen. The article announced my presence at the Weidenfelds' home in Georgetown. Almost instantly, the telephone started to ring and ring.

Westinghouse Broadcasting wanted me to tour their TV stations: *People Are Talking,* WJZ- TV in Baltimore, *Pittsburgh Today"* on KDKA-TV, and *People Are Talking,* WZB-TV in Boston. Westinghouse would cover my expenses. My agreement was to tour the first of the year when I returned for the inauguration of President Ronald Reagan. Many Washingtonians called that morning. I gave out my California telephone number. Some wanted a reading in person when I returned in January.

The sudden turn of events in my life was mind-boggling. My 15 minutes of fame as a psychic had arrived. Back in 1972, when Jess Stearn had wanted me to do radio and television with him to promote his book, I was not prepared to deal with the limelight. Things had changed. I had accepted my "gift" and felt more confident with the public. The incredible predictions that George Darius had made for me in 1964 and in 1975 were actually coming true!

Through Sheila's connections, I was able to purchase tickets for the presidential gala and the California inaugural ball. My daughter, a Democrat, was appalled that her mother (then a registered Republican) and brother were going to Washington to celebrate the inauguration of the Reagan-Bush years. Mark voted for Reagan and Bush for their second term in his first presidential election in 1984. Through the years I have always voted for the man rather than the party, voting for both Democrats and Republicans depending on the person.

In January 1981, Mark joined me at the Tabard Inn in downtown D.C. My son was my handsome date in his rented tux for both the gala and the inaugural ball at the Kennedy Center. We danced as Tony Bennett sang. We strolled through the Kennedy Center star-struck as Ronald and Nancy Reagan and George H.W. and Barbara Bush appeared to the thundering applause of their California supporters. Actors are as impressed with politicians as politicians are with actors. On that night, former actor and governor, Aquarius Ronald Reagan, had been overwhelmingly cast in his finest and grandest role. A number of American presidents have been Aquarius.

That week I gave a reading to Svetlana Godillo, the astrologer who had a column in *The Washington Post*. I found her fascinating and hoped to have her interpret my chart one day. In 1984, after moving to Virginia, I learned Svetlana had passed away.

January of 1981 marked my first appearance on the *Panorama* show in Washington with Ross Crystal. It was the beginning of my friendship with Libra associate producer Maggie Linton. A limo picked up Mark and me for my first appearance in Baltimore on *People Are Talking* with co-hosts Richard Sher and Oprah Winfrey. That was years before Ms. Winfrey simply became "Oprah." During my last Baltimore appearance, with Oprah as co-host, I predicted a bright future for her, tremendous success—which seems to have been an understatement!

While at the Tabard Inn in 1981, I was watching President Reagan's parade on television that cold January when horror suddenly gripped me. There was another woman in the room, a journalist from a New York City newspaper. I turned to her and said, "Someone's going to shoot him. Someone's going to try to kill the president."

"Doesn't someone always try to kill the president?" she responded before turning back to the TV. She was the only one to hear my prediction of an assassination attempt on President Reagan that day. Sometime later, Sheila and others were told of my vision. It was a scene I had trouble ignoring.

In late January, I appeared on *Pittsburgh Today*. Later there was an appearance on *People Are Talking* in Boston with Nancy Merrill. An answering service was hired to take calls. The telephone number flashed on the screen and there were more than 200 calls. I stayed on for another week to give readings at the Hilton Hotel.

Perhaps it was no coincidence that I was on the telephone with Sheila from Woodland Hills on March 30, 1981, when John Hinckley, Jr., shot President Reagan, one policeman, and press secretary James Brady. Sheila had the television on in her kitchen.

"Oh my God, the president's been shot!" Sheila exclaimed in horror.

Our conversation ended.

In mild shock, I went to my den and turned on the TV. Moments later, I turned the TV off and started deep rhythmic breathing to meditate. In a short time I was tracking the timeline. It seemed the president would be fine, along with the policeman, but I was unsure about James Brady. He seemed to be severely wounded with a bullet in his brain. I was amazed when he lived. But James Brady had a mission to fight for stricter gun control, an important aspect of his destiny.

In August 1981, my daughter gave birth to my first grandchild, her first son, Oliver James (August 19, 1981). He was adorable, as grandchildren always are. That October, Sheila and Edward Weidenfeld welcomed Daniel, their second son. Both boys were healthy and whole.

In the spring of 1984, while I was working in Houston, our house in Woodland Hills sold after being on the market for four years. Soon after the call from my realtor, I had a client from Washington. "You should move to Washington!" she said. "You're very popular there. That's how I heard about you and told my friends here in Houston."

"I think I will," I said—and the decision was made.

On October, 31, 1984, driving into the Washington area on a holiday that my son still celebrates with tremendous imagination and enthusiasm, I remembered Aries actor Don Adams arriving for his reading on Halloween in 1972. He came up the walk just as my 11-year-old son was hanging a witch from the tree in our front yard. I think our California neighbors thought I was a witch, even though I never practiced witchcraft—in this life.

At the start, I stayed with my Mormon friends, Jean and Gary Arbuckle, in their lovely colonial home in McLean, Virginia. Gary was a practicing dentist in Arlington. Jean's father, Dr. Berry, had delivered my daughter, Tomi, and allowed me to pay over time.

In weeks, I had rented a townhouse in Vienna. In 1985, my house in Arlington was purchased: a two-story, red brick Federal colonial near Lee Highway. It amazed me to think that General Lee had once marched the Army of the Confederacy that way during the Civil War. All the early American history enthralled me. I enjoyed dinner at the Red Fox Tavern, built in 1728, in historic Middleburg. The Smithsonian museums are fascinating, the Air and Space museum Mark's favorite. Tomi's second son, Jonah (June 8, 1983), once told his elementary class in Slippery Rock, Pennsylvania, "I visited my grandmother's zoo." The National Zoo! His classmates must have been impressed.

In my Arlington neighborhood were Christians, Jews, Buddhists, Hindus and Muslims, those of every color and race, such as those scattered through the Washington metropolitan area. My move took place during President Ronald Reagan's second term—so far so good on that presidential prediction. Many new clients called, although some who had always made a point to see "the California psychic who appeared on television" seemed disenchanted with my being local. The Hollywood crowd still called, and I took yearly trips to Los Angeles.

While I was still in the rented townhouse in Vienna, journalist Barbara McConagha interviewed me. Her article, "Looking in the Crystal Ball," was published in November 1985 in *Washingtonian* magazine and featured eight local psychics, including me. Barbara had photographed me in front of my Wall of Fame with the autographed 8 x 10 glossies of Sharon Gless, Anjelica Huston, Joanna Miles, Ted Lange and Nancy Collins. Two cropped pictures disclosed only the lower part of the faces of Susan Strasberg and Goldie Hawn. Soon after the article was published I was asked to appear on the *Carol Randolph Show* in Washington, and *People Are Talking* once again in Baltimore. The new host in Baltimore was Linda Harris. Hundreds of new clients called to make appointments.

During President Reagan's second term I was once again concerned with assassination. That was the Iran-Contra Affair and character assassination. The ex-lover of a California client had sold arms to Nicaragua—more on her in another chapter.

In late 1984, Mark graduated from the University of Arizona with a B.S. in astrophysics and a minor in atmospheric science. In January of 1985, my son joined the U.S. Air Force and entered officer's training in San Antonio, Texas. His pilot training was in Vance, Oklahoma, where he eventually learned how to fly a KC 135 refueling tanker. Eventually, Mark made captain and commander of a KC 135. The thought of my son flying around in a huge gas tank refueling fighters and bombers, which looked like giant mating insects, made me nervous. But I respected his choice. After all, his Scorpio Sun is conjunct Mars, which indicates military service at some point in time.

In the mid-1970s, Sheila recommended me to a good friend who had a reading in his Beverly Hills hotel room. He was a young congressman. He wanted to know whether to run for the senate or governor of his state. My advice was to run for the senate, since he was likely to win by a landslide. That happened. He was reelected to the Senate several times and has since held significant positions with each major political party.

After my Arlington move, congressmen and women, senators and cabinet members had readings. While working in Houston in the early 1990s, I read for Governor Ann Richards, referred by Gwen Davis. My news was not good for her in 1994. That year, George W. Bush was elected governor of Texas. Ann Richards was a very impressive lady.

In view of the framed pictures of Ronald and Nancy Reagan on my wall in my Arlington home, my media clients seemed convinced that I was the astrologer to the president and first lady, especially after Nancy Reagan admitted to using an astrologer. A reporter from *People* magazine interviewed me in front of my Wall of Fame and I spoke in general terms about Sharon Gless, Goldie Hawn, and Susan Strasberg, whose pictures were behind me, only revealing that they all had had readings. Nonetheless, when Sharon and Goldie were called for confirmation, both of them said, "I don't know her." What?

But then, I knew some of their deepest, darkest secrets— things I would never disclose to the press or anyone else. I had given several readings to each woman. I had even read for Sharon's brother and friends, plus family members of Goldie's. I had attended parties at Sharon's home. Sharon had attended one Christmas party in our home and mingled with my other client-guests!

In September of 1986, Tomi was ready to give birth in Slippery Rock, so right after the interview I got in my car and headed north. That was the weekend that Joan Quigley revealed herself as astrologer to Nancy Reagan. Her picture was on the cover of *People,* with my famous client's denial of me in two small paragraphs in the article. Fortunately, I made it to the hospital on time for Shaina Patricia to arrive on the stage of life—my daughter's youngest daughter and child.

In 1987, Laura Foreman of Time-Life Books interviewed me for a new series, *Mysteries of the Unknown* and featured me in the volume: *Psychic Powers.* Those books increased my popularity and generated more clients, more articles and public appearances. George's prediction of my name appearing in books, newspapers and magazines had come to pass.

By the time that George H.W. Bush was sworn in as our 41st president, some of my clients were upset. I had only predicted one term for Bush. I had read for his social secretary. Not long after his election, she booked another reading.

"But why is he only going to be president for one term?" she sounded distraught.

"He'll be blamed for the state of our economy. A Democrat will be elected next."

After casting one last scornful glance my way, she left my house in a huff.

I have no control over the destiny of presidents or anyone. At times I am able to tune into a destiny pattern, but I have no power to create the pattern. Destiny is determined by a higher power. Patterns exist within the Akashic Record, also known as the Book of Life. It was during the only term of George H.W. Bush when I met George W. and Laura Bush at a party at Sheila and Edward's. The day I said to young George, "You have a bright future in politics," without fully understanding what I meant.

Late in 1991, I was alarmed by impressions received in meditation. It seemed someone was going to try to assassinate Mikhail Gorbachev in the United States. Some nation planned to embarrass our government. Friends and clients, including generals at the Pentagon, were informed of my impressions, as well as senators and congressmen. Security needed to be tight.

Much later, a friend who knew someone in the CIA said that a spy who was a known assassin had been picked up at one Middle Eastern embassy. The man was smuggled into the embassy under the backseat of a limousine. I have no idea if my warning helped, but I felt the need to say something even if I sounded like a fool. I wish those under President John F. Kennedy had listened to the warnings of psychic Jean Dixon in 1963. She told him not to go to Dallas.

During the election campaign in 1992, I was unable to psychically see Bill Clinton and Al Gore holding up their arms in victory until the month of August. I had done a reading for a television producer, and since the birthdays of President Bill

Clinton and Mary Matlin fell on the same day, August 19, in 1993 I was invited to appear on Mary Matlin's TV show on their birthday (which also happened to be the birthday of the wife of Clinton's vice president, Tipper Gore, as well as my grandson Oliver). Matlin had not yet married James Carville, who then worked for Clinton. Republican Matlin worked for Bush and Cheney, and then George W. Bush. I found Mary bright and engaging. It was a fun show and their horoscopes were discussed.

With President Bill Clinton, I had also sensed the possibility of assassination. That turned out to be character assassination with the Monica Lewinsky affair. Clinton never should have lied. On the other hand, I had done readings for numerous girlfriends and mistresses of married men on Capitol Hill, many of them senators and congressmen. I was appalled by Clinton's impeachment proceedings, mainly because of all the hypocrisy. Some had been clients of a certain Washington dominatrix. If walls could talk, the gossip in the nation's capital would be endlessly titillating. Even male pages have been sexually harassed—hear tell!

During Clinton's first term, I moved to Camden, Maine, and Sally Quinn gave my telephone number to columnist Maureen Dowd. Early 1995, Maureen interviewed me on the telephone. Whatever was gleaned from that conversation ended up in an article in the *New York Times* magazine called "First Horoscope." I had talked about patterns in the horoscopes of Bill and Hillary Clinton and matters in his administration. I happen to be a fan of the Clintons. I voted for Bill in both elections.

It seemed that Ronald and Nancy Reagan had a wonderful love story. Sadly, among the predictions on my website (posted December 12, 2003) for the Year 2004: *A long black hearse on PENNSYLVANIA AVENUE, a sad parade with honors as thousands file through the Rotunda of the Nation's Capitol to view the GREAT ONE!*

This prediction marked the passing of Ronald Wilson Reagan, 40th President, on June 5, 2004. The black hearse slowly advanced down Pennsylvania Avenue as it had for other presidents—this time to honor the Great Communicator. Thousands filed by Reagan's casket in the Capitol Rotunda. Reagan's funeral was in the National Cathedral as leaders from around the world, including Margaret Thatcher and Mikhail Gorbachev, attended his final farewell.

The American flag was lowered to half-staff as our nation mourned the passing of one of its leaders, his body no longer the prison of a once-brilliant mind and sparkling wit. President George W. Bush was known to have said, "Ronald Reagan belongs to the ages now. But we preferred it when he belonged to us."

I predicted the election of Al Gore as 43rd president. It seemed to me the American people had decided exactly that by a majority popular vote. I pray the decision of another presidential election never ends up in the Supreme Court.

In 2004, I predicted Howard Dean, and then, Senator John F. Kerry. I was wrong on both counts. My bias had gotten in the way of my objectivity. I disagreed with the policies of George W. Bush, especially regarding the Iraq War. I sensed another "Vietnam-type" no-win situation. The people of Iraq still seem to have a great deal to be resolved.

From 2007–2008, I wanted Hillary Clinton to be the first woman president of the United States. After all, she is a Scorpio and highly capable. Many other women of my acquaintance, both Democrats and Republicans, also wanted Hillary Clinton as our first woman president. I thought the Democratic ticket would be Hillary Clinton for president with Barack Obama as vice president. My bias got in the way the same as it does with friends and family. What I may "want" for anyone does not mean it is his or her destiny. Bias and personal opinion block precognitive powers. No objectivity.

In 2004, when I heard Barack Obama give his brilliant speech at the Democratic National Convention for the nomination of Senator John Kerry for president, it was easy enough to see him as our first African-American president. I felt this deep down in my bones. I still wanted Hillary, however, thinking perhaps she would be on the ticket as vice president. Of all cabinet posts, I wanted Hillary for secretary of state. I am glad President Obama was on the same wavelength. I still expect Barack Obama to be president for two terms.

At this point, I have no clue about other future presidents. Yet, I think everyone around the world will be surprised with the eventual outcome of the administration of President Barack Obama!

9

STARS IN TINSELTOWN

Since I worked at a film studio when I started to give readings, actors, producers, directors, writers, composers, special effects technicians, cameramen, film editors, makeup artists, secretaries and file clerks were among my early clients. After meeting Susan Strasberg, I was invited to parties in her home and to parties in New York City and Los Angeles hosted by Lee and Anna Strasberg. All those champagne brunches and evening parties were attended by the talented, the rich, the famous and the almost famous.

I'm clueless as to how singer-actor Ted Neeley heard about me in the late 1960s. He was doing the role of Claude in *Hair,"* the American tribal love-rock musical that depicted the rebellion of the times. Ted was interested in another role, which I thought had his name on it: Jesus in the rock opera, *Jesus Christ Superstar* by Tim Rice and Andrew Lloyd-Webber. Ted also played Jesus in the film. He continues to perform the role on stage. Excellent insight for a $5 reading! Ted has enjoyed a fantastic career on the stage.

I am unsure how Aquarius actor Gregory Sierra heard about me. Greg had readings in Sherman Oaks during the early 1970s. I predicted his role as Dynamite in *The Thief Who Came to Dinner*, which starred Ryan O'Neal and Jacqueline Bisset. Another actor was going to get sick or have an accident, and Greg would assume the role. That happened. Other predictions included his role as Julio Fuentes on *Sanford and Son* and Detective Sergeant Chano Amenguale on the *Barney Miller* TV series. There were also parts in the *The Towering Inferno* and *Papillon*. The longer I read for Greg and the better I got to know him, the more difficult it was to be accurate. We lost contact for years. Even though Greg has retired from acting, he still has readings. I danced at his second wedding with his co-star, Cancer actor Ron Glass, who played Detective Ron Harris on *Barney Miller*. Ron Glass and his sister had many readings.

Capricorn actor Ted Lange of the *Love Boat* TV series had one reading and autographed a picture for my Wall of Fame. Gemini actress Alexis Smith attended a tarot workshop in my home with Leo actress Mary Munday, another client. Both actresses autographed pictures for my Wall of Fame. I may have been more impressed with Alexis than she was with me. She was one legendary Hollywood actress with a long, happy marriage.

Starting in the 1970s, I did many readings for Aries Jay McIntyre. She was married to a U.S. attorney and the mother of three. At first, Jay made appointments every six weeks, much too often to suit me. She had made up her mind to be an actress and had a lovely singing voice. She changed her name to Jay W. MacIntosh (numerology) and sang in a Beverly Hills club. In 1978, Jay also sang in the film, *Sgt. Pepper's Lonely Hearts Club Band*, which starred Peter Frampton and the Bee Gees: Barry, Robin and Maurice Gibb. Prior to that, Jay guest-starred on many different television shows and supplemented her income by selling real estate. Acting truly has its ups and downs. Years later, Jay attended law school and passed the bar. She is now an entertainment lawyer. Numerous predictions were made for Jay over a long period of time.

In the early 70s, a pretty young woman was warned about the older, married Pisces film director she was dating. He seemed like an "alcoholic womanizer with a penchant for violence." I could see that his mother had ruined him with her unacceptable, insane behavior. The reading was taped.

The next week I had a telephone call from a deep, sexy male voice asking for me.

"Who am I speaking to, please?"

"Sam Peckinpah."

As it turned out, Sam Peckinpah was the Pisces film director! He had listened to her entire tape, which made me nervous in remembering things said about his mother! Sam's office was on the lot at the MGM. He invited me to lunch. Sam said that I had touched upon some sensitive and amazing details about him and his life in the young woman's reading.

Years before, *The Wild Bunch* had brought a big bunch of attention to Samuel "Bloody Sam" Peckinpah. *Straw Dogs* with Dustin Hoffman and Susan George had only recently been released. None of Peckinpah's films generated a warm, fuzzy feeling in the audience. His last major release, *Bring Me the Head of Alfredo Garcia*, he both directed and wrote. Sam Peckinpah was a fascinating, talented, and highly troubled man.

My curiosity was piqued. I agreed to drive to MGM to meet Mr. Sam Peckinpah in his office, knowing that Sam was one of the original bad boys. It was noon when he offered me a drink and poured himself a double. I passed. There was only the faintest light in his shadowy corner office as he tilted back in his chair and studied me. He never finished that drink. Instead, he called for a driver to take us to a nearby popular restaurant. It seemed that Sam drank all day every day. He had learned not to drive himself or anyone else—perhaps the hard way.

As soon as we were seated in a booth, Sam ordered a double martini while I ordered lunch and iced tea. Sam picked at his deep fried zucchini and drank at least three double martinis as we engaged in a long, drawn-out, somewhat serious conversation over our leisurely lunch.

Water signs have a tendency toward addiction: drugs, alcohol, food, sugar, emotional attachments or sex. Water signs need to develop moderation and a sense of caution. Sam Peckinpah was a sensitive Pisces. His moon in Aquarius made him a natural-born rebel, as well as talented and fully magnetic. Alcohol and drugs just happened to be numbered among Sam's closest and dearest friends.

He talked to me as though he had known me forever—or as if I were his long-time therapist and aware of his deepest, darkest, most dangerous secrets. Psychics can be therapists. My guess: Sam thought I knew him as a man and a person, through and through, heart, mind, body and soul. I didn't, actually. Sam Peckinpah was a masculine, rugged, magnetic male who spoke in a soft, enticing tone. And yet, the disconcerting turbulence beneath his somewhat gentle exterior seeped through from his psyche to mine. He was a charming, fascinating gentleman who looked much older than his 45 years at the time. He was too slender, since he preferred to drink alcohol rather than eat anything of any nutritional value.

Director Sam Peckinpah had a reading in Sherman Oaks. He also sent his secretary and several friends. One day, Sam went as far as to extend an invitation to me to bring my two children to his ranch in Durango, Mexico. However, I was not about to take the bait from that persuasive, dashing renegade. Being romantically involved with one alcoholic had been sufficient for me, although Bill Jacobs was nowhere near as fascinating or tempting as Sam Peckinpah. And frankly, with Sam's lifestyle, I was amazed he lived to 59. Bill only made it to just short of 47!

In the early 1970s, it was fun to read for singer Keeley Smith. She was married to jazz singer Louis Primo. I love their rendition of "That Old Black Magic has me in its spell. That old black magic that you weave so well!" I should have asked her to autograph my album.

Around then, "Cuchi-Cuchi" Charo called. Her sister was in town from Spain. I fail to remember if Charo had a reading, but she was her sister's interpreter. Imagine that! My

Spanish involves about four words and counting to 10. It was a challenging experience! I had no way of knowing if Charo was accurately translating what I said. That was the last time an "interpreter" was allowed to sit in on a reading. I know I predicted Charo's divorce from bandleader Xavier Cugat, who was old enough to be her grandfather. I could also see that Charo's career might flourish. She was such an adorable woman.

Actress Suzanne Oliver's mother, Ruth, was among the many astrologers who interpreted my chart. (Susan Strasberg had many readings from Ruth.) She was the astrologer who said, "It doesn't matter what you do or what you write, you have the chart of a public figure." Ruth said what the public was interested in was ME! In 1984, I was delighted to see Ruth as the "library ghost" in the film *Ghost Busters*, which starred Bill Murray, Dan Aykroyd and Sigourney Weaver. It was a charming movie, and Ruth Oliver happened to be a brilliant astrologer.

During the late 1970s, Gemini actor Kale Browne started to have readings. I predicted his role on *Another World*, along with parts on other shows. His marriage to Libra actress Karen Allen was in his cards, along with the birth of their son, Nicholas. A few times I stayed at their home in the Berkshires on my way back to Camden, Maine. They had 40 acres and an impressive beaver dam on the property. Kale sings and is also talented with carpentry and building things—and he is still one of my favorites.

Our rental house in Sherman Oaks was the former home of the parents of Capricorn actress, Tippi Hedren. Her second husband, Noel Marshall, repainted and fixed things for us. The strangest part: I had a dream about Noel about three years before we met. He had on the same brown sweater, and the very same three dogs jumped on me as in my dream. I remembered the dream after seeing Noel about renting the house with its 40-foot pool and two fireplaces. I was amazed.

My love affair with Noel took place off and on for three years. I dreamed that he kissed me in front of the living room fireplace. For that reason, I tried to avoid the fireplace whenever he was there. And yet, that was where he kissed me the first time. It was a passionate relationship. My marriage house is ruled by Aries—Noel is an Aries.

Tippi Hedren had readings during those years. Strangely enough, her readings only took place during times when things had been broken off with Noel. I broke up with him about six times. Whenever I dated a single man, I would stop seeing him. Then, Noel would show up again right after the other relationship ended. It was uncanny! He once left a gift for me on the windowsill outside the front door at Christmas. Joy perfume! Noel paid for my first trip to New York City.

There were often acting jobs in Tippi's cards. One of her endeavors involved a humanitarian mission after a natural disaster, perhaps an earthquake in Central or South America. A group of actors and doctors had chartered a plane to fly clothing and medical supplies into the country. The glitch: the U.S. government stopped the plane from taking off. The situation puzzled both of us. From her cards it seemed that it was going to happen. Everything leading up to the plane taking off did happen. And yet, the government thwarted the mission.

Aries Noel Marshall was fascinating and charming, the attraction one of the strongest I have ever known. He was an agent, writer and producer of films, which got my attention. We had many long conversations about his projects in the house in Sherman Oaks. Noel had suggested that I help him write a script. Once he bragged about bedding nine women in one day—which hardly made him marriage material, to my way of thinking!

During those years (1969–1973) Tippi and Noel collected wild animals, mostly lions and tigers. There were also an elephant and a bear in the animal compound outside the city limits. Tippi's extensive efforts in animal rescue and the establishment of her wildlife preserve happened years later and long before the film *Roar* was released in 1981. Perhaps the script Noel had in mind for me to help him with.

One afternoon Noel called. He had what he referred to as "a young male lion" at the house, along with its trainer. The van had broken down. Noel wondered if he could borrow our station wagon to take the lion back to the animal compound.

"You can borrow the car if you bring the lion by so my children can see it."

The idea of what turned out to be a fully grown young male lion in the back of our station wagon on the San Diego Freeway seemed extraordinary to me. Noel agreed. He said to make sure our dog and cat were out of sight, since the lion would consider them as prey.

Our critters were locked inside. Mark hovered behind the yucca plant as my gutsy daughter Tomi, with her three planets in Leo the Lion, petted the stunning adolescent male on his noble nose with the back window rolled down. I was apprehensive, since my first past life recall was of being eaten by lions in a Roman arena. On the other hand, that male was a magnificent young king of the beasts.

Sometime later, my Scorpio friend and house guest Lisa wanted to see the animal compound. Noel invited us out. There was one large enclosure with 19 young lions and tigers of various sizes and ages, some as big as a Great Dane or Saint Bernard. After advising us to be assertive with the young beasts, Noel and the trainer entered the pen with us. The wild cats needed to know who was boss. Easy enough for them to say! My heart started beating considerably faster and I had to remind myself to breathe.

I had on brown jeans and brown leather boots when the young lion, with its mouth opened wide, lunged for the inside of my left thigh. Alarmed, I bopped the beast on the nose as my heart pounded faster. The open mouth of the lion had left a wet imprint on the inside of my jeans. I was convinced there was no way for me to prove to all those young lions and tigers that I was the boss. The numbers were definitely in their favor. You can perhaps imagine my relief when we were once again safely outside of their domain with the gate securely locked behind us.

Another time, I had ordered gold satin sheets and pillow cases from a magazine. I had only slept on the sheets once. They were too slippery to suit me. And I never slept on those sheets with Noel! They were washed and in the linen cupboard.

During those days, young Melanie Griffith, Tippi's daughter, was involved with actor Don Johnson. Tippi purchased the sheets at the original price, perhaps for Melanie and Don. The first time I saw young Melanie with her long blonde hair, she looked like Alice in Wonderland. Melanie was a year older than Tomi and has had a terrific career. I can neither confirm nor deny that Melanie Griffith and Don Johnson ever slept together on my former gold satin sheets!

When Aquarius actor George Kennedy had his reading, he had already played Joe Patroni in the first *Airport* film. George was so nervous when he tried to light my cigarette that he extinguished the match and had to strike another. He was not at all the tough guy he played in *Cool Hand Luke,* but his divorce and remarriage showed up in the cards.

In the 1970s, aspiring actress Judy Luciano had several readings. Judy was an animated, beautiful brunette who dated several successful men in show business. Often at the Playboy Mansion, she had friends on the Hollywood "A- list." One suitor was a Taurus producer with his Moon in Aries. Another man was an Aries actor with his Moon in Taurus. That made it tricky for me to differentiate. Both men had readings in

Sherman Oaks. The Aries was actor Don Adams, whom Judy finally married. They had a daughter. Don was terrific as Agent 86, Maxwell Smart! He was also a really nice man.

Judy Luciano's mother also had readings. She generously invited me and my children to their ranch in Montana. After we took a commercial flight to Spokane, Judy's father picked us up in his small plane and flew us to their huge ranch. Tomi learned how to drive on the property. The house was filled with kids, so my two had fun. The saloon in town was like a saloon in the Old Wild West. An Indian squaw could walk up and tap some guy on the shoulder and he had to go home with her—or else! What an interesting Native American practice—for women!

Their Montana neighbors were nervous when the Lucianos bought up so much acreage. In those days, Judy denied being related to Uncle Lucky, the notorious gangster and racketeer. These days she admits that he was her uncle.

In the late 1970s, my Gemini friend Susan Strasberg had a role in a TV miniseries, *The Immigrants*. Working on that show, Susie told Gemini actress Sharon Gless about my readings. Sharon was on *Switch"* which also starred Robert Wagner and Eddie Albert. Many of Sharon's acting roles showed up in readings. She stopped by our Christmas party looking gorgeous in a long, white gown, with a limo waiting outside. My other guests were impressed.

In the 1980s, when actor Pierce Brosnan appeared on *Remington Steele*, I was convinced he was going to be James Bond—007. Pierce never had a reading. Finally, in 1995, he became a brilliant James Bond! Some destiny patterns are tricky to determine in terms of time.

Initially, I met Rosemarie and Robert Stack at a party at the home of Gwen Davis. In Rosemarie's readings, scandals were often picked up that involved her rich and famous friends.

The widowing of Betsy Bloomingdale was in one reading, in addition to Alfred Bloomingdale's notorious affair with his mistress, Vicki Morgan. Morgan had filed a palimony suit, but was murdered a year after Bloomingdale's death. That affair was the plot of the book, *An Inconvenient Woman*, by Dominick Dunne.

For years, it seemed that Capricorn Robert Stack was going to have another TV series. He was constantly guest-starring in TV shows and appearing in films. In 1987, Robert became part of the cast of *Falcon Crest*, soon followed by his narrative of 29 episodes of *Unsolved Mysteries*. Robert Stack was a working actor and producer until his death at age 84 in 2003. It amazes me how many celebrities leave this earth on their Uranus Return (ages 82-84). Robert Stack never lost his good looks. He was charming and talented. All my predictions for Robert showed up in readings for his lovely wife, Rosemarie.

In 1978, 6 foot 9 inch Scorpio author Michael Crichton started to have readings. In a normal house, Michael had to stoop for lower ceilings. However, his talent was as tall as he was! Michael always called me "Patricia." For several years I told him to write something for television. He said he wasn't interested in writing for TV. He seemed to think writing for TV was beneath him. Every year he published another novel, with several made into successful motion pictures. Still, I insisted that Michael should write something for television. That show would bring him nominations, awards, and tremendous financial success.

Finally, with his M.D. from Harvard Medical School, which he never used to practice medicine, Michael Crichton wrote the pilot for *E.R.* The series first aired in 1994. As a result of Michael writing that pilot, my predictions of his enormous success in television finally came to pass. He received nominations and Emmys for *E.R.* In fact, that TV show may have earned Michael Crichton more money than all of his novels and films combined, although his *Jurassic Park* films are constantly on TV. When I saw the original *Jurassic Park* in a dark theater, I thought it was the scariest movie ever. I wrote Michael a note to tell him so. I never see horror films! On a TV screen, no film is as scary as on a big screen in a darkened theater.

Eventually, I stopped hearing from Michael Crichton. Over the years I had read for his fourth wife, Ann Marie, and several family members. Michael had referred many of his famous friends in the film business to me for readings. However, when Michael divorced Ann Marie I expressed my sympathies to her sister. Perhaps not coincidentally, I learned from an actor client that Michael had fallen in love with his young yoga instructor. Perhaps she was his fifth and final wife. I was saddened by the news of his death at age 66. Michael Crichton was a fantastic talent and lived a truly fascinating life.

In 1982, I had a long telephone conversation with legendary screen actress Gloria Swanson. The year before her autobiography, *Swanson on Swanson,* had been a bestseller. Our conversation included life after death, reincarnation, premonition, past life recall and psychic phenomena. My question was, "What was it like to be in the movies from their early beginnings?" We spoke of organic food, vitamins, and things I no longer remember. We talked for more than an hour. Gloria Swanson graduated the following year at age 84, on her Uranus Return. I hope our talk helped her to prepare for her otherworldly journey.

Many trips were made to Beverly Hills to read for Scorpio actress Brenda Vaccaro. Gemini singer, songwriter and actress Michelle Phillips, of the Mamas and the Papas, had several readings in Woodland Hills. I remember seeing a bright future for her daughter, Chynna. Singers from the Fifth Dimension had readings. Pisces actress Cristina Raines was once a regular and another friend of screenwriter, film director Joan Tewkesbury.

The threads in the tapestry of my life continued to weave a more interesting and colorful picture for us all.

WALL OF FAME

Pioneer in entertainment journalism, writer, businesswoman client: "To Patti, Thank you for all your help and wisdom, Always, Rona Barrett."

My client actor Kale Browne: "Best wishes, Kale," written on back, "This is all I've got at the moment! X Kale." I predicted Kale's roles on *Another World* and *One Life to Live*.

My late client author Michael Crichton. "For Patricia, Love, Michael Crichton." Perhaps my best advice to Michael was to write something for TV: *E.R.*.

My client-friend novelist, playwright, screenwriter, songwriter, journalist and poet Gwen Davis in the picture for her book: *How to Survive in Suburbia When Your Heart's in the Himalayas* published by Wyden Books, 1976. "To Pattie, The Seer of Seers. Love, Gwen." (Photo by Harry Langdon, Jr.)

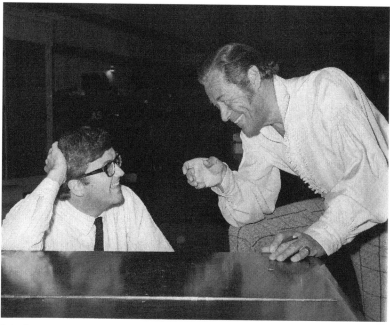

My boss: composer, lyricist, writer Leslie Bricusse rehearsing the
late actor Rex Harrison in the title role of *Doctor Dolittle,* 20th
Century Fox, 1966.

"Patti, Every time you look at this photo you will be Blessed in
"White Light." Best Wishes, Carushka, 1982."

My client actor Ron Glass: "Patty, Better late than never! Smiles and Love, Ron Glass"

My client actor Sharon Gless: "Patty: Thank you for the many years of friendship and helping me to see that we do create it all. Love and Happiness, Sharon"

My client-friend actor Myrna Hansen, Miss USA 1954. Insert: Myrna as a showgirl for the 1958 MGM film *Party Girl* which starred Cyd Charisse and Robert Taylor.

ANJELICA HUSTON

My client actor Anjelica Huston: "To Patty, with much love and thanks for your help and guidance, Anjelica."

My friend and client Diane
Ladd: "Patti, My special friend –
whose energy and talent is a
Consummate Channel. God Love
You, I Do, Diane Ladd."

My client actor Ted Lange: "To Patty,
Thanks for being a friend. Love, Ted
Lange"

My client entertainer and composer Gloria Loring: "Pattie, Thank you for the insight, Gloria"

My client Gilda Marx, designer and owner of Body Design by Gilda: "Dear Patricia, Sock it to the world! Fondly, Gilda (11/ 23/1981)"

My client actor Joanna Miles: "For
Patty, I think you're terrific, Joanna."

My client actor Cristina Raines:
"You are absolutely the best!
Thank you, Thank you, Thank
you, Love, Cristina"

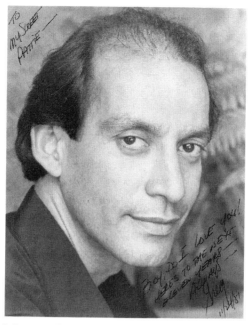

My good client friend actor Gregory
Sierra: "To My Sweet Pattie: Boy, Do I
Love You! Here's to the next eleven years!
Always, Greg, 11/24/81" In addition to
other roles, I predicted Greg's parts on
Sanford & Sons and *Barney Miller*.

My dear friend Susan Kelly, May 1961 Centerfold, *Playboy*,
and actor. Her former roommate Sheryl Stagg did some
acting. 1966

My client-friend dancer, actor, screenwriter, director Joan Tewkesbury: "To Pattie, With love since grammar school. Joan Tewkesbury." I predicted her success as a writer and director of film.

My client, dancer, actor, director Gus Trikonis: "To Pat, A friend since 1968 and still going strong. We live forever, Gus Trikonis." I predicted his success directing film and television.

My late client actor Peter Sellers with actor Shirley MacLaine
from *Being There* produced by United Artists, 1979. This photo
was a gift from a woman who worked on the picture that Shirley
recommended to me for a reading.

My client-friend actor Brenda Vaccaro: "Pattie, With Love,
Brenda Vaccaro"

My client-friend, actor Goldie Hawn: "For Patti, I wish
you everything good. Love, love, Goldie Hawn."

10

22-KARAT GOLDIE

It was summer of 1970 when Scorpio Gus Trikonis and Capricorn Don Mitchell showed up in Sherman Oaks for their first readings—months before their famous wives arrived. My friend Susan Strasberg had touted my psychic abilities at parties. Producer Don Mitchell was married to talented Taurus novelist, lyricist, screenwriter Gwen Davis, who had a bestseller the year before with her spicy novel, *The Pretenders*. Broadway-Hollywood dancer, actor, director Gus Trikonis was then married to a talented Scorpio blonde bombshell of Rowan and Martin's *Laugh In* fame who had received an Oscar for Best Supporting Actress the prior year for her portrayal in *Cactus Flower*. Gus's superstar ex-wife is still known as Goldie Hawn.

Since most of my clients are female, it is always a pleasure to read for a talented, good-looking man. Reading for women all day drains my chakras (which correlate with the endocrine system), whereas men "polarize" me: yin-yang, moon-sun—you get the picture! I end up feeling charged after reading for a man. Besides, I was impressed that dark, curly-haired and handsome Gus Trikonis had played Indio in the film *West Side Story*.

In addition to being friendly and outgoing, Gus was another Scorpio on the cusp of Sagittarius born the same day as Goldie, although she was eight years younger: November 21. Gus also recommended me to his Capricorn sister—actress, dancer, costume designer Gina Trikonis. Gina was another animated, charming actor-dancer in *West Side Story*: Graziella, Riff's girl.

It was not long before Don's wife, Gwen, turned into a regular. Sometimes Gwen brought along one of her famous friends such as singer Jaye P. Morgan. Many people had readings from me because of Gwen. She also invited me to her parties, which were attended by many celebrities as well as by somewhat ordinary folk like me.

Early 1971, Goldie Hawn had her first reading. That morning my life was like a scene out of a comedy motion picture. As the sun rose higher in the sky, our beautiful, highly intelligent tomcat, Smokey Joe, brought a live baby squirrel into my bedroom through a window left open for the "purrfect" nocturnal hunter. The squirrel got loose and jumped and ran all around my room. The terrified creature dashed under my bed, over my bed, and across the dresser, with our trusty tomcat in hot pursuit. The squirrel chattered in a frenetic, upsetting, disconcerting manner.

By then, I was hysterical myself. I closed my bedroom door to prevent the escape of either Smokey Joe or the terrified squirrel into the rest of our house with all of its nooks and crannies. Then, I ran out the front door to stop my neighbor's husband (Al Schultz, the makeup artist who left Shari Zack to marry actress Vicki Lawrence) from getting into his car, since he was ready to leave for work at the studio.

Gratefully, Al caught the baby squirrel in a wastebasket covered with a dustpan and returned the frightened creature to the tree with its nest in the backyard. All the while, Al chastised me about the cruel hunting habits of my terrible though proficient tomcat. (I never chastised Al for breaking Shari's heart, which perhaps I should have done.)

During the squirrel pandemonium, this hysterical flight attendant called and threatened to kill herself over some married airline captain who dumped her! I had warned her of his less than honorable character, told her he was only interested in a playmate. But this client had a knack for getting involved with less than promising romantic partners, something that continued throughout her numerous readings. Her horoscope was difficult for relationships. I talked her out of taking her life on that particular morning, something she tried without success later, after destroying all the tapes from her countless readings, which she lived to regret.

That was how my day started out the first time I gave a reading to Goldie. I found the pretty blonde actress bright, adorable and charming, not at all the bimbo portrayed on screens, small and large. I am unsure what was covered in her first reading, but future roles were there. I must have been accurate, since that was the beginning of a long and interesting relationship. More than a few astonishing and magical things happened during our extended journey as psychic and client-friend.

In another reading for Gus, it seemed that their marriage was coming apart at the seams. In Goldie's readings there were always other attractive men interested in her. Each of them had other interests, which seemed sure to come to light. Over the years, it has always been extremely difficult to read for a husband and a wife, especially when trouble is brewing. In my opinion, whether a marriage goes on or ends should never be decided by a psychic, psychiatrist or marriage counselor, except in a case of severe abuse.

In the 1970s, Goldie's sister, Patty, had readings and attended our parties in Encino. In California, in the 1970s and 1980s, I hosted many parties: Halloween costume parties, champagne brunches, Fourth of July bashes, Christmas parties, and Labor Day barbecues that included clients and friends. In the 1970s, Goldie was making one film after another. She invited me to lunch at her lovely home with a swimming pool designed like a natural pond with rocks, plants, flowers, and a waterfall. You could walk right in, as if into a lake. The antiques in her guest rooms were exquisite.

Soon after the completion of *The Girl from Petrovka,* Goldie and Swedish Aries actor Bruno Wintzell (also in the film), double-dated with me and Capricorn Don Russell who I was dating at the time. Don had some healing ability. He worked on Goldie for a few minutes before the four of us went to El Torito's for margaritas and a Mexican dinner. It was a fun evening.

Soon Goldie was in *Shampoo* with Aries Warren Beatty, an actor who was romantically linked with several of my clients and friends. Warren was rumored to have a highly active libido. In those days, Goldie was offered one role after another as her salary increased. In those years, I picked up on a handsome, younger, dark-haired Libra man coming into her life. Soon to enter: singer-songwriter Bill Hudson, less than two years her junior. It seemed that Goldie might marry him and have a family. Her first child would be a boy, with a girl later. Not too many years later, Oliver and Kate Hudson arrived.

However, when Goldie was in Colorado filming *The Duchess and the Dirtwater Fox* and eager to marry Bill, she called me one day. It wasn't a reading, just girl talk. Before that time I had been to her house in Malibu for lunch. Her friendship was important to me. I no longer considered myself as just her psychic.

During that conversation, Goldie was her usual effervescent self and so "in love." Suddenly, she invited me to join her on the set in Colorado. I was thrilled. I planned to book a flight the next week. I had never seen a Western being made and my former studio, 20th Century Fox, was making the film. I was really excited about going.

"This is it, isn't it, Pattie?" Goldie asked me in this dreamy tone in reference to Bill Hudson—her "happily ever after." After all, I had predicted him. I had said that she might marry the handsome Libra and have his children.

All at once, I had this strong catch in my solar plexus and a strange sensation swept through me. I had learned to trust my body whenever anyone asked a question. My body is often a receiving station for the Cosmos. At times but not always, I absolutely *know* how something is going to turn out without any doubts at all. In my work, I have to tell the truth—it's my sacred task—to tell the whole truth and nothing but the truth. This is not always easy—especially when it comes to people I care about.

"Do you really want to know?" I cautiously replied, with not the slightest desire to burst Goldie's lovely pink bubble.

"Of course!" she said with a definite smile in her voice.

"You'll be together for several years. You'll have children together, but you won't grow old together," I said, and a horrible sense of dread instantly filled me.

There was silence on the other end of the telephone that delivered a tangible blow to my solar plexus. I could feel her disappointment, along with my own, because I had told Goldie the truth. I love happy endings. At that moment, I wanted to disappear.

Needless to say, our conversation came to an end.

After hanging up, I remembered her invitation to Colorado to watch her make the movie with George Segal. I tried calling Goldie back. I left my name and my number. But Goldie never returned my call.

The next day I tried calling her again. And yet, in my heart I knew that Goldie was not going to talk to me. The messenger of ill tidings was sort of being "killed" in her mind. Perhaps that would cancel out my dire prediction about her forthcoming marriage. One Scorpio seemed determined to prove another Scorpio wrong!

I had been true to my gift in giving Goldie an answer to her question on life with Bill Hudson, even though it truly upset me to do it. Telling the truth had cost me her friendship and that nearly broke my heart. And yet, somehow deep down inside, I *knew* that one day Goldie Hawn would be back in my life. I was unsure of how or when or why—but I *knew* I was going to hear from her again—someday.

The years passed.

No more referrals that included family, friends, business associates, employees and co-workers because of Goldie. In magazines or tabloids I learned of the birth of a child or about a film she was making. All the while, in the back of my mind, my spirit guides were whispering, "It's not time yet. Be patient. She'll be back! Goldie will return!"

In 1975, after finishing my funny love story about life after death and reincarnation, psychic researcher Jess Stearn suggested his agent friend, Reece Halsey, to represent me. Reece found my story "charming, enchanting, and delightful." During the next year he tried to get my story published, but only gave it a year. Then actress Diane Ladd had trouble getting a studio to go for a metaphysical story. It was the same year that Goldie gave birth to Oliver Hudson.

Although I knew better, I sent Goldie my screenplay version, which she promptly rejected. I guessed she was still angry with me for the cloud I had placed over her marriage.

In the summer of 1977, I gave the screenplay to successful director, Gus Trikonis, Goldie's ex-husband. Gus came in person to our house on Aura Avenue to return the screenplay.

"Have you given this to Goldie? She'd be perfect in the role," Gus commented.

Without giving him the dreadful details, I said, "She rejected it." It seemed unfair to let her ex-husband know of the possible short duration of her second marriage—or that she no longer even spoke to me. Gus had happily remarried.

"They only let me direct action films with car chase craziness. They'd never let me direct something sensitive like this, although it's something I'd like to do sometime," Gus said.

That year his *Moonshine County Express* was released. Gus had also directed a horror flick: *The Evil*. He was doing episodic television as well, so my predictions of his success as a director in film and television had come true.

That afternoon, Gus said he had had a dream about me in which I wore a silk blouse and gold jewelry and charged $150 for readings. He also dreamed I was on television. In 1977, I charged $75, but two years earlier another psychic had said the same thing. In fact, she said, "Someday you'll charge $300 for readings—or more!"

Scorpios tend to be psychic and have precognitive dreams. My television appearances in silk blouses and gold (costume) jewelry started three years later when readings were $125. Gus's son Nicholas paid $150 for a half-hour reading in 2008. Nicholas is a lovely young man and was about the same age as Gus when he had his first reading. I wonder if Gus ever dreamed that I would read for his son one day!

In 1980, not long after the release of *Private Benjamin*—the film that Goldie Hawn produced and also starred in, and for which she was nominated by the Academy for Best Actress and for a Golden Globe—the tabloids started running these tawdry rumors about the end of her marriage to Bill Hudson. There was gossip about some affair with a French actor.

Upon first noticing those tacky headlines in the supermarket checkout line—with Goldie's picture on the cover of those harbingers of ruination and sensationalism—it seemed to me that it would only be a matter of time before I heard from Goldie again. The marriage had ended sooner than I had expected. But Goldie had Oliver and Kate. Sweet! I was sure everything in her life was as divinely intended. And, my spirit guides had provided accurate information on that dark day in 1975.

Then, a really bizarre thing happened—stranger than anything that has happened in my entire clairvoyant experience.

Psychics can also be surprised. Trust me! Life is a mystery, even for those of us who work with different vibrations, the Akashic Record, invisible entities on the inner planes: discarnate souls, astral workers, spirit guides, nature spirits, elemental beings, angels and archangels. We all dwell in a wondrous, multidimensional, Divine Universe, which awaits discovery by those willing to explore its many realms through any number of reliable methods. No individual or religion has cornered that market—you can also trust me on that score!

What happened with Goldie?

Well, a flight attendant with United Airlines had a reading. I think it was the only reading she ever had. And did I ever surprise US! At the time about 50 flight attendants were clients from that one airline, not to mention pilots, mechanics and other airline personnel. She was a senior flight attendant who worked first class between Los Angeles and Honolulu.

The woman was ready to leave the room when I had this extremely clear and strong impression. You can even call it a *revelation*.

"You're going to have Goldie Hawn on a flight in first class," I said with certainty.

Precognition is similar to remote-viewing the future.

She looked amused, but she watched and she waited.

"When you see Goldie, I want you to give her my telephone number. I've moved since I last saw her—and she's going to want to see me now."

It was plain that the woman thought I might well be completely insane.

"She'll be on your flight." I *knew* this without a doubt.

"When you approach her and tell her about me, Goldie is going to react something like she does in the movies, maybe scream in her giggly, girlish manner. But she'll be happy to have my telephone number."

To wit: Two weeks later the flight attendant called. The Hudson Brothers, as they were known, were on her flight in first class to Honolulu, along with some famous actress as Bill's companion. She never spoke to Bill, but to one of his brothers.

The brother replied, "Yeah. I imagine she'd like to talk to *that psychic*. She's the one who said the marriage wasn't going to work."

"It's not the Hudson Brothers or Bill," I said. "Goldie will be on your flight. She may have the children with her." It was something I ABSOLUTELY KNEW.

I am uncertain as to how much time passed. However, Goldie did one day show up on her flight in first class between Los Angeles and Honolulu—and Goldie did shriek, as predicted. After the flight attendant told me—I waited for the telephone to ring. That time I even found myself rather amazing! Wow!

One Sunday morning about a month later, I was drinking a cup of coffee and reading the newspaper when the telephone rang. "Hello!"

"How did you do that?" The caller whispered on the other end of the line.

Unsure of the caller's identity, I inquired, "Who is this, please?"

"It's Goldie."

"Goldie who?" I actually did have another client named Goldie.

"Goldie Hawn!"

And the conversation went something like, "I guess our spirit guides wanted us to get back together again."

I was as amazed as Goldie. Honest! On the other hand, I was happy to hear from her and pleased to hear about Oliver and Kate Hudson, her two adorable children.

Since my neighbors across the street heard that Goldie Hawn was coming to my house for a reading, they loaded their new camcorder with film and shot a home movie of Goldie getting out of her car and walking up my driveway. I never knew about it until years later when Valerie and Philip D'Addona confessed. It was their "secret celebrity home movie"!

That day Goldie heard all about how much I had enjoyed *Private Benjamin* and the other pictures she had made over the years, including *The Duchess and the Dirtwater Fox.* She kind of apologized—perhaps just by showing up.

Goldie admitted that she was devastated when I said her marriage would not be "happily ever after." However, in 1980, Goldie was "in love" with a French actor that a French psychic had told Goldie was her soul mate. But somehow, that didn't feel right to me.

Goldie looked cautious as she inquired, "Well, what do you think?" and she sat there watching me ever so closely.

I had been in that particular position before—and this time the reading was official. "Do you really want to know?" I inquired with the same marked hesitation.

Goldie scowled, sort of nodded, and appeared to brace herself.

"You know the movie, *Private Benjamin?*" Life can imitate art.

Her smile faded but light filled her pretty blue eyes.

"You know how in the movie, the guy has another woman who has been in his life forever and he can't get her out of his system—and finally—the girl realizes the truth and walks away?"

After all, she had played that girl to the point of being nominated for an Oscar.

Goldie did not appear the least bit pleased with my response.

After glancing at her cards again, I said, "There's a Pisces-Aries man about to enter your life. He's younger, another actor, one you may even know, but the time wasn't right. Presently, he's beneath you on the ladder of success. But his career is going to take off and he may catch up with you. You'll do films together. This man is your destiny and you'll never be able to get rid of him."

In 1983, actor Kurt Russell, born on the Pisces-Aries cusp, five and a half years younger, starred with Goldie in *Swing Shift*. They had actually appeared together in 1968 in Disney's film, *The One and Only, Genuine, Original Family Band*. Goldie was married to Gus at the time. Kurt was only 16. A relationship had not been an option.

In 1986, the son I predicted for Goldie and Kurt was named Wyatt. He had one reading. When Kate Hudson was under two-years old, I told Goldie that Kate would follow in her footsteps and become a successful film actress. Another delightful blonde bombshell now entertains us on screens large and small, the same as her mother. Kate was nominated for an Oscar in her first major role in *Almost Famous*. In 2001, Kate Hudson won the Golden Globe for Best Supporting Actress. Sometimes it is fun to be "psychically gifted" and right!

By 1981, Goldie was again sending her friends and associates to me for readings. Actor Richard Romanus was married to her business partner. In 1984, the first movie I saw after moving to Virginia was *Protocol*. Goldie was the girl who took a bullet in her butt for the handsome sheik, played by Richard Romanus. No one can do comedy better than Goldie Hawn.

When my son Mark was a captain in the Air Force, Goldie autographed a picture for him. Mark had her picture prominently displayed in his den so his military buddies could see that Captain Mark Jacobs knew Goldie Hawn. Goldie was also friends with the parents of one of Mark's high school friends. She had been in our various homes several times. Her autographed picture is on my Wall of Fame. Most pictures were signed in the '80s and '90s, so everyone is younger. That is how we prefer to be remembered, naturally.

Over the years, Goldie had many telephone readings from various cities. Her permission was not granted for this chapter. In my opinion, such information, which is in no way harmful, should be in print. Then, perhaps those open to discovering that consciousness exists well beyond our three-dimensional awareness—and that life is eternal—will have some confirmation.

My client-friend, dancer, entertainer, actor, author Shirley MacLaine performing in her One Woman Show: "For Pattie McLaine, Best Always, Shirley MacLaine, 1979."

11

STILL OUT ON A LIMB SHIRLEY

In 1978, the initial reason that Taurus actress Shirley MacLaine had a reading was because my daughter Tomi resembles her. A journalist friend of Shirley's had a reading in a room that had a favorite picture of my daughter, age 16, on the wall above the table (a different picture than Tomi's graduation picture from Birmingham High featured here). I used Tomi's room to do reading while she was away at college. Since my last name is McLaine, the journalist asked, "Are you related to Shirley MacLaine?" To our knowledge, we are not related. But if you go back far enough—everyone in the family of humanity is related.

Tomi, 1976.

MacLean is the maiden name of Shirley's Scot-Irish mother. My maiden name, McLain, is the surname of my Scot-Irish paternal grandfather. From the time my daughter was young, people have told her, "You look like Shirley MacLaine." When Tomi was five, a neighbor wanted to take her on an audition to play Shirley's child in a film. Bill Jacobs, who had adopted my daughter, refused his permission. Tomi was an adorable five-year-old and surely could have passed for Shirley's daughter. The journalist said, "Your daughter looks more like Shirley than her daughter, Sachi, does."

Since I had always been a fan and seen most of Shirley's films, I told the journalist to tell Shirley about me. If she was into readings, perhaps she should call for an appointment.

Days later the telephone rang.

"Who is this, please?" Tomi inquired, home from college for the summer.

"Shirley MacLaine."

Wide-eyed, my daughter handed me the telephone and said, "It's Shirley MacLaine."

Shirley made an appointment for a reading. And Tomi realized she was finally going to come face to face with the famous actress-dancer-performer she had been told she resembled so many times during her life. That day, Shirley arrived in Woodland Hills in her sweats and tennis shoes with little makeup.

Tomi answered the door.

After entering the house, Shirley looked from Tomi to me and said, "I can see the resemblance."

That was the beginning of my metaphysical association with a woman who is fearless when it comes to placing herself really far out on a limb: Shirley MacLaine—movie star, actor, dancer, singer, entertainer, author, pretty, bright, talented, clever, curious, far out, worldly and otherworldly explorer of the known and unknown.

After that, Shirley called for many readings. She scheduled my Master Spread, which is delineated in my book: *The Wheel of Destiny: The Tarot Reveals Your Master Plan.* The Master Spread takes hours and is usually taped. Several of Shirley's past lives were picked up during that extended reading, besides patterns in relationships and friendships, her work and recognition received for film, television and stage. Soon Shirley was sending her friends to me as well.

Shirley invited me to her place in Malibu on the ocean. She owned the building and had converted several apartments on the top floor into a comfortable home complete with dance studio for working out and rehearsing. Shirley was still doing her one-woman show so she stayed in shape. We discussed our borderline hypoglycemia in terms of our polarity: Taurus-Scorpio. Orange juice was her quick fix. Shirley MacLaine is highly intelligent, well informed, and candid, besides being open and receptive. I enjoyed her company.

Shirley is Taurus with Mars and Uranus in Taurus, a conjunction of planets that bestows enormous energy, some tendency toward irritability and eccentricity. Shirley has a tendency to push herself. She has portrayed some pretty kooky characters on screen. Her rising is Virgo (29 critical degrees) on the cusp of Libra. She may not have always had the greatest confidence in herself, but her chart indicates an ability to rise above almost anything. Her horoscope bestows keen analytical abilities and makes her overly sensitive. Her Virgo Moon conjunct Neptune makes her naturally psychic and somewhat mediumistic, perhaps with some skepticism. These aspects make Shirley intuitive, artistic, creative and romantic. The Moon-Neptune is perfect for acting and entertaining.

One day in Malibu, Shirley and I took a walk on the beach and talked about different metaphysical subjects: books either or both of us had read: the Qabalah, Madam Blavatsky and the Ascended Masters. Sitting on the sand not far from the surf, we spoke of things of interest to us both on a bright, sunny day.

At one point, a man called out, "Shirley!" She turned, but he was a stranger who had simply recognized her.

"I never know if it's going to be someone I know. I guess they all think that they know me from my films."

Such is a price of fame for actors. Strangers think they know a person when it is only the character portrayed on the screen or a song and dance number performed on stage. Only a close circle of friends really know an actor or entertainer, which is probably true of any public figure.

By the time I entered Shirley's life, she was heavily into mediums such as Kevin Ryerson. She had a brief association

with J.Z. Knight who "channels" Ramtha. All trance mediums
channel some entity, usually one long departed, with wisdom.
Shirley was also into UFOs, Unidentified Flying Objects, which
I had not yet explored. She spoke of ancient astronauts who had
genetically altered the species on our planet to produce our
race: the mysterious missing link.

Years later, I read the books of Zecharia Sitchin: *The Twelfth
Planet* and *The Earth Chronicles,* which I found fascinating,
whether historical or fanciful! It was the 1990s when these
subjects captured my attention—more on that in another
chapter.

For many years (1954–1982), Shirley MacLaine and Steve
Parker maintained an "open marriage." While Shirley pursued
her acting career and became a star, Steve brought up Sachi in
Japan. In one reading for Shirley I could see another woman
in Steve's life and that he was using her money for his own
purposes. Initially, Shirley was reluctant to believe me. She
trusted him. She said they had a "special relationship." She had
married him when she was young. I saw a divorce in her future,
which surprised her. Shirley did divorce Steve Parker in 1982.

At that time we met, Shirley had already published three
books. However, in one reading I could see her writing books
on spiritual subjects that might help people be more open
to their true potential. The first, *Out on a Limb,* was released
in hardcover in 1983. While Shirley was writing the book, a
mutual friend called me, my old friend from grammar school
and high school, film director Joan Tewkesbury. Joan said she
had read Shirley's manuscript and I was in the book. Right
after that, I called Shirley and repeated what Joan had said.

"You were in the book," Shirley said, "but I edited you out. I
took several psychics and put them together into one fictitious
character. Otherwise, the book would have been too long."

I was disappointed to be "edited out" of Shirley's first metaphysical book, a book I had predicted. Joan had said that while reading Shirley's manuscript, she just knew it was me from the philosophy and manner in which the material was explained. Joan had several readings. Then again, others surely had said the same things to Shirley. Years later, I was disappointed to have been left out of all Shirley MacLaine's books.

Medium Kevin Ryerson has become world famous because of Shirley MacLaine. And yet, the better part of me, on a higher level, was never disappointed. Michael Crichton left me out of his memoir after telling me I was the "best psychic in the world." In all honesty, I have done my psychic work kicking and screaming most of the way. I resisted publicity for 15 years. There was never a time I had given up on just being a writer. Much of the time it has not been easy to live on the freaky fringe of society and be treated with a lack of kindness by those stuck in the left brain with a limited sense of awareness. God bless them all.

After *Out on a Limb* was released, some of my other notable client-friends were outraged that Shirley had left me out of her book and not given me any credit. They said the book was "superficial" and that Shirley didn't know what she was talking about. Were they trying to heal my bruised ego? The lower ego is our primary challenge in this dimension. Without a huge ego, no actor would ever act, of course. The ego drives entertainers and anyone else—as something to eventually rise above and place in perspective. The personality is actually an instrument of the Higher Self.

Once, when Shirley was having a reading and we were in my kitchen fixing tea, Shirley said, "I want to do what you do."

Talk about a surprise!

I had once yearned to do what she did—be a superstar on the silver screen. That seemed like more fun to me than reading people's cards, looking into the distant past and predicting the future, helping others get through deep disappointment and suffering. I had taken dance lessons. I had sung in the church choir, except, when asked to sing solo I was so terrified that I lost my voice. I love musicals. Shirley was fantastic in her one-woman show. I have always been too shy to perform and too sensitive to accept the criticism necessary to perfect talent. After all, few criticize my readings, although some wish I had never added astrology into the mix.

Shirley has used a psychic in New Mexico for past life regressions. I never read all her books. Nonetheless, anyone in the serious business of metaphysics has as much knowledge as I about our different bodies, the various planes of existence, karma, the law of cause and effect. I have learned most of what I know and understand by reading hundreds of books, attending numerous lectures, completing classes and initiations in a highly respected mystery school, and by deep meditation, in addition to paying very close attention.

There was a time when I could not get enough information written over the past 100 years or more. I have been privileged to study with highly enlightened teachers and spiritual masters from various disciplines. Every metaphysician has his or her own personality and unique way of describing Universal Truths.

In California in the early 1980s, Shirley invited me to her one-woman show in Las Vegas. My son Mark went with me on the long drive through the desert. We stayed at the hotel in Las Vegas with the show. Shirley not only paid for her fabulous show that night, where we visited her backstage, but she paid for another show by comedian Rich Little at another hotel. I only paid tips. And there was no charge for the room! I found her to be very generous.

One year in Woodland Hills Shirley attended our Christmas party and brought along about a half a dozen of her friends. We usually had 150 or more at our annual Christmas party in our 1,800 square feet house. Many contributed food to the buffet, brought along wine or hard liquor. A turkey was baked, along with my famous huge pot of chili. My Taurus friend, Les Szarvas, always provided the hot mulled wine kept warm in the electric coffee pot. The homemade eggnog was so thick it had to be eaten with a spoon, as well as being potently laced with brandy and bourbon.

At those parties, Mark always set up his 14-inch telescope on the hill (he had poured the cement for the pad for the telescope himself). Weather permitting, our guests observed the craters in the moon or the Rings of Saturn. My son always knew which part of the sky held a heavenly wonder. His telescope was a highlight of our Christmas party, as a fire blazed in a ring where children roasted marshmallows. Shirley seemed to enjoy looking through his telescope. Mark had ground the lens himself, at age 14, in our kitchen on Aura Avenue.

Interesting incidents occurred at that party. Shirley had given me some gifts: a felt ring and perfume. The ring fits on a light bulb and infuses the room with scent. The other gift was a gold stickpin of her as a dancer.

There was an odd-looking gentleman standing in the middle of our living room with people all around him, talking and gawking, especially at the actors. I had no idea who he was, so I walked up to him and said, "Hello, who are you?"

"What do you care?" he gruffly replied, perhaps thinking I was hitting on him. He was hardly my type!

"I'm Pattie McLaine and this is my house and my party—who are you?" That time my tone equaled his rudeness.

His response was a name no longer remembered and he said, "I'm a friend of Shirley MacLaine's," as though that was an excuse for his offensive behavior.

A list of names was never required. Many clients or friends brought someone, but they usually introduced me to their guests. Shirley never introduced me to her friends that night. That one man had a Damon Runyon look straight out of Vegas. He may have been a character actor. I directed him toward the self-help bar, since we never hired a bartender. Very casual, our California parties.

Another incident was when a writer-client approached Shirley with: "So you're one of the tapes!" Shirley found her remark odd. But then, my readings *are taped*.

My regulars were impressed that Shirley MacLaine was there. Shirley arrived early and stayed late. She was the same as any other person, eating and drinking, chatting and gazing through the telescope. It was almost impossible to introduce 200 people to each other. Plus, I always enjoyed my own parties! One Christmas, someone who had worked with Albert Einstein was there—and my client introduced me to that physicist. I was impressed with him.

In 1985, after my move to Arlington, Virginia, one July Fourth holiday I was out in the front yard pulling weeds and who should drive up but Shirley MacLaine! Bella Abzug was with her. That was a pleasant surprise. There I was in my dirty gardening clothes with no makeup. Shirley's mother also lived in Arlington. I was surprised that Shirley had not bothered to call.

Shirley and Bella each wanted a reading. Since I had no plans for that Independence Day, I cleaned up and gave two short readings to two famous ladies. Then, we went about our business. It was fun to meet Bella, the famous feminist, political activist, and U.S. congresswoman! She was not wearing one of her notorious hats that day.

In days, Shirley's stately, elegant mother, Kathlyn MacLean Beatty, arrived for her reading. She held herself erect and walked with a cane. Tall and slender, she was a touch indomitable, in my opinion.

"How long am I going to live?" Kathlyn asked, staring into my eyes.

No one had ever asked me that before, except George Darius.

It was easy to see where Shirley and Warren (Beatty, her brother) had acquired their uncommon candor. Shirley's mother was 84—and I was on the hot seat.

"You'll probably make it into your 90s," I cautiously replied.

Shirley's mother was some lady. She passed away in 1994, so I seem to have been right.

When Shirley did her one-woman show in Washington, she had a ticket waiting for me at the box office. I loved the show. However, I was at a loss afterwards. It was midweek and I had a client first thing in the morning, so I went home.

The next day Shirley called, wondering why I never came backstage. I was sorry for not spending time with her. Being on the road can be lonely. I had traveled extensively for my psychic work for years. I have to hand it to actors, musicians, singers and comedians. Long days on the set are no fun either. But then, everything has its downside.

After the 1990s, Shirley no longer called for readings. Sometime she called to chat or to ask questions about politics. Shirley has always been extremely politically active, while politics still rarely captures my attention. She always seems to be writing another book or appearing in another film. All her films have entertained me.

Shirley MacLaine is someone I am happy to know, a person I hope to keep in touch with—maybe even in other dimensions—or on some other planet!

12

STARS OF A DIFFERENT VARIETY

Josephine Abercrombie was my first billionaire client. I no longer remember if she had five or seven houses in different states or countries (New York City penthouse, Beverly Hills mansion, London and Paris flats, Texas mansion, Swiss chateau). Josephine had a complete wardrobe at each house as well as an automobile and servants. Her private jet flew her wherever her little ole heart desired! There were the thoroughbred race horses and championship boxer (the kind that KOs a guy in the ring). In my opinion, that represents—as they say in Kansas—living high off the hog.

In 1981, Josephine drove herself to my Scorpio friend Kathy Barbour's (later Barnett) apartment in Dallas for a reading. Her transportation: White classic '55 Ford Thunderbird. My tip: $20 for a $75 taped reading. Hairdressers tend to tip. Ladies of the night pay up front, something perhaps necessary in their profession.

In the Lone Star State many clients are millionaires, a few either the current or ex of a gazillionaire. Joanie Schnitzer's ex-husband built the Houston Astrodome. In 1983, on a summer trip to her fair though muggy city, Joanie invited me to her lavish home where the swimming pool could transform into a huge fountain with colored lights for parties. In her massive living room were museum-size modern paintings by artists Jackson Pollack and Pablo Picasso. Her huge dining room with its magnificent crystal chandelier had several round tables that seated 10 to create greater intimacy for dinner parties. The cozy dining room downstairs in the red brick and wrought iron wine cellar was a cool place to dine in more than ways than one—especially during those long, hot, Houston summers.

In her massive study with its elegant bar, Joanie only had to push a button for a large screen to descend from the ceiling to view newly released motion pictures. Her bedroom closet was an amazing walkaround room in itself, with her clothing organized. The right shoes, handbags and accessories were in drawers or cupboards beneath the gowns, suits, dresses or casual wear. Everything made dressing for any occasion a simple task for a socially active lady with invitations to spare.

In 1981, when Joanie had her first reading in my Houston hotel room, I was impressed by the diamonds in her gold and silver belt buckle around the waist of her designer jeans. Her jewelry was high-karat gold, her diamonds many karats. Her long blonde hair nicely framed her vivacious face. However, she was upset after that reading. I had predicted the passing of her parents and her remaining grandmother, as well as trouble with her ex over money.

A year later, Joan Schnitzer was on her way to California and asked me to come to the Beverly Hills Hotel to give her another reading. The number of suitcases in the room was astonishing. One large case held only shoes and handbags. Her room was spacious with a sitting area. Joanie insisted she see me *immediately*: Have tarot cards—will travel!

"I threw away your last tape as soon as I got home," Joan announced. "I was so upset over the deaths and the horrible news. You were right, of course. Both my parents died and so did my grandmother. There were difficulties over money. Later, I was sorry I didn't keep the tape, especially when the good stuff started to happen. Tell me what's going to happen next?"

I did my best on that day!

In Texas, one Houston socialite had the Dalai Lama as a house guest. Another had shipped in potted, blooming, cherry trees for her daughter's lavish wedding. However did those trees keep their blossoms? Texans seldom seem to think of those things. They just buy, ship and enjoy! That can happen in states other than Texas, I suppose. A beautiful blonde from Fort Worth had a new 35,000-square-foot house with Florida palm trees growing in her indoor patio. It must have been a fantastic place for kids to pay hide and seek. It sounded like a palace.

The stock market crash of 1987, which became known as "Black Monday," upset many clients and not just in Texas. That year the market went up, up, up, and FELL DOWN (2,600–1,600). One Houston client called, distraught. My insight: the market would level out around 1,800 and rise again at a slower rate. That happened. The stock market continues to go up and down and all around. Buying stocks is a gamble!

Pisces Carushka was a lovely, talented client who designed sexy bodywear for women. Carushka was the first designer of workout clothes and dancewear who used color and patterns, besides designing the first thong for women. Carushka invited me to her lavish wedding at the Bel Air Hotel. That evening the entertainment included a young Janet Jackson who sang for the disco dancing. Carushka knew how to throw a party. Her success was always in the cards!

Fashion designer Libra Mark Eisen still fills the runways with beautiful clothing for women. Mark once gave me with a lovely white outfit he had designed. Diane Von Furstenberg had one reading in her New York City office. I have always been fond of her wraparound dresses for travel. Veronica De Laurentis, daughter of the famous Dino De Laurentis, acted and also designed sexy lingerie and elegant body blouses for women. Veronica sent me one in lacy black and another in lacy white. Her marriage was in her cards, along with her honeymoon to Bora Bora.

Another client in the world of fashion was beautiful Gemini supermodel, Karen Mulder, who recommended me to her jet-set friends all over the world. After one appearance on "Panorama" in Washington, Esther Lauder of Estee Lauder Cosmetics had a reading. For years, we exchanged Christmas cards.

In 1982, on my first trip to India and England, I read for a princess in Bombay (more on India later) and after India, I rented a flat in the Chelsea section of London for three weeks. My son met me in London for spring break from the University of Arizona. Among other things, Mark and I visited Stonehenge and the Tower of London. In London, some clients were members of royalty and not only from England, but Italy, the Philippines, France, Spain, and Saudi Arabia.

Lady Rutherford had her first reading in California. In London, I arrived at her home early one evening and discovered Patricia still in bed. She had her reading on her bed in her nightgown. In the society columns, her nickname was Bubbles. That evening she invited me to a fashion show, followed by dinner with a different course at three different restaurants, not the way I like to eat dinner. Her daughter had accused her of trying to steal her rock star boyfriend. The young man was younger than the daughter. Bubbles was a touch eccentric.

In 1984, on another European work trip that included London, Sarah, the daughter of Lady Rutherford, offered me her guestroom where I slept off and on for a month. Sarah was often up late, drinking and playing cards with her royal friends, one of whom was Prince Andrew. Koo Stark was a soft porn actress romantically linked with Prince Andrew. She booked a reading and canceled. That was before Prince Andrew became the Duke of York. Years later, I read for Sarah Ferguson, the ex-wife of Prince Andrew. The Duke and Duchess still shared a home for the sake of the children.

On my 1984 trip to Europe, my California client-friend, Aquarius Valerie Barad, designer of handbags and women's accessories, planned to be in London at the same time. Valerie invited me to accompany her to Paris, Milan, Florence and Rome, cities new to me in this life. We stayed in suites at Valerie's expense. I was delighted to be invited. Valerie was born in Manchester, England, but had married an American.

That September, when I was walking through a London shop, my wallet containing my credit cards was stolen. My American Express card was replaced. I had to use it for the rest of the trip. Valerie knew the finest restaurants in London and other cities. In her generosity, she bought me a small gift in each city on our trip. The next stop was Paris. My two days in that beautiful city were gray and rainy. In the Galeries Lafayette, where money or credit cards are sent through those old pneumatic tubes, we had to wait a long time.

Finally, I heard a whizzing sound and turned to Valerie, "This one is yours."

It was.

"You really are psychic!" Valerie exclaimed.

It was late when we arrived in Milan. We had to take a bus from the airport to the train station to get a taxi. Valerie's large suitcases filled with sample handbags and fabrics were a challenge, but she needed everything for the show. She was going to purchase other fabrics in India, with the final products to be made in Taiwan.

Finally, there was a taxi to take us to the Hotel Grand Duomo on the Piazza Duomo next to the great cathedral ("duomo" means cathedral). Our suite had a sunken tub in which I soaked in absolute luxury on one evening.

Then again, in the taxi on the way to the hotel, Valerie suddenly realized she had left her other handbag with her passport, airplane tickets for her trip around the world, and a significant amount in traveler's checks under the seat of the bus from the airport. By then, the bus was gone.

I tuned in: "When we get to the hotel have the concierge call the bus station. If the bus is there, send a taxi to pick up your handbag. You'll get it back."

"You don't know Italy," Valerie replied shaking her head in distress.

"Come on, you could use a drink." We headed for the dining room.

Soon after we were seated at a table, the manager rushed up all excited. The taxi driver had returned to the hotel with Valerie's lost purse!

"Be sure and give him a nice tip!" I called after as Valerie rushed off to retrieve her purse. Then, we relaxed and enjoyed a tasty dinner, with no bad meal to be had in Italy.

Several of Valerie's competitors booked readings during our five days in Milan. Sometimes it was a wife with free time on her hands.

A year later when Valerie returned to Milan, a man tapped her on the shoulder and she turned to him and said, "How are you?"

"Divorced," he glumly replied, "It's because of your psychic friend you brought with you last year. She told my wife I was fooling around—and I was. My wife had me followed and I got caught."

I have been responsible for more than a few divorces. Clandestine affairs and extra-curricular activities often show up in the cards of not only the guilty—but the betrayed.

I fell head over heels in love with Florence, especially with Michelangelo's David. I saw an exhibit of paintings that had been done by Adolf Hitler! On the Pontevecchio, I bought a 22-karat gold bracelet that is still my favorite, and cameos for Tomi and me. In Rome, I toured the Vatican and the Sistine

Chapel with Michelangelo's famous ceiling. Before my tour, however, Valerie and I wanted to have lunch.

"Who do you know named Charles?" I asked her on the way to a hotel.

"My father-in-law?"

"No, in the near future, you're going to be surrounded by Charles."

At the table in the restaurant, Valerie picked up an ashtray: The Charles Restaurant. Valerie was indeed surrounded by Charles.

My advice on a business deal was for Valerie to ask for more money. It was agreed she would receive what she asked for when she sold her name. For that reason, in 1990 Valerie invited me to join her family and friends at the Club Med in Tahiti. On the island of Moorea, gratis readings were given to her friends and daughters as my thank-you. It was my second trip to Tahiti. Those islands are among the most beautiful in the world.

In the early 1970s, I had a very brief romance on the island of Tahiti with a younger, tall, dark and handsome Aries Englishman. Keith was a geologist who lived on the island of New Guinea. He had fascinating tales to tell of giant insects, including a poisonous centipede whose sting had nearly killed a 200-pound man who worked for him. It happened at midnight in the dark jungle when it was impossible for anyone to fly a helicopter in to get the man out of the compound to a hospital.

On Tahiti, we enjoyed a long, lingering French lunch before visiting the Paul Gauguin museum. We fed hungry, mewing kittens under our table leftover fish from our plates as we sipped wine and watched the surf roll in over the wide coral reef beyond the sand. In truth, on that trip I was running away from Noel Marshall, born April 18. Keith was also born on April 18, although he was 13 years younger than Noel and five years young than I.

In the 1990s in Washington, many readings were given at a luncheon hosted by the wife of the Saudi Arabian ambassador. Most the women were royalty from various Middle Eastern countries. One woman had 18 children, and several had at least a dozen offspring. My quiet place to read was in a large solarium with multiple skylights and windows, which was tastefully furnished with orchids, tropical flowers, potted palms and a bubbling fountain. The powder room bidet had gold-plated fixtures. The elegance of the house gave me some idea of the opulence of the royal palace in Riyadh.

Months later, one young princess called for another reading. Soon a man called for directions. At the appointed time, two limousines pulled up in front of my house, one a stretch. An older woman covered from head to toe walked in with the pretty teenage princess in her blue jeans, T-shirt and sandals. My Saudi female clients in the United States and London never observed the strict Muslim dress code necessary in Saudi Arabia and other Middle Eastern countries. Her chaperone was asked to wait downstairs while the princess and I went upstairs for her reading—but not before a bodyguard checked the upstairs and the basement of my humble abode. One bodyguard stayed in the living room with the chaperone, while several men in dark suits with bulging jackets positioned themselves on every side of my house—with the limos waiting at the curb.

After the reading, everyone climbed back into the two limos and sped off. The princess had her tape, which was of little concern to me.

Later, my inquisitive neighbor called. "Saudi royalty?" His suspicions confirmed, Paul said, "That's what I thought."

My neighbors had to be curious about some people who entered my house. Besides Middle Eastern royals, my clients included numerous Washington hotshots: senators, congressmen, and cabinet members. My clients are seldom boring.

A Swiss banking client in Washington on business invited me out to dinner. The restaurant selected was owned by another client. A banking associate of his from Mexico City joined us. The two men had business in Arizona or Florida involving the construction of moderately priced houses and were about to embark on another business venture with a wealthy Saudi businessman.

Both men appeared shocked when I mentioned the name of my prominent Saudi male client. He was the one. All those threads in the colorful tapestry of life seemed to be jazzing things up again. Another divine coincidence? Probably not!

In 1991, at Book Expo America in New York City, I signed my book, *The Wheel of Destiny: The Tarot Reveals Your Master Plan*. It was exciting when Llewellyn Publications finally released the book I had worked on for so many years. I was the first Llewellyn author asked to sign books at Book Expo. After New York, my private book tour took me to London, where a private publicist had been hired.

In the United Kingdom, I was interviewed on BBC Radio in London, Cornwall and finally Scotland during my Gothic Image Tour of Glastonbury, Merlin's Cave, and the islands of Mull, Orkney and Iona. Iona is where Irish St. Columba introduced Christianity to the British Isles in 560 AD. St. Patrick introduced Christianity to Ireland. First, Patrick was kidnapped by Irishmen but later escaped. Many year later, Patrick returned as a priest on his famous mission to convert the pagan Irish to Christianity.

In London, several journalists interviewed me. Unfortunately, the articles never appeared until months after I returned to the States. One article in *You* magazine of the *London Daily Mail:* "Most of us have to wait and see; not so Patricia McLaine, psychic to the stars. Lulu Appleton ponders her own fate, 'Altered States and Planet Spotting.'" Another article appeared in *Empire* magazine: "Patricia McLaine, Psychic to the Stars" by Phillipa Bloom. In *You* magazine, the journalist must have written down Susan S., which was supposed to be Susan Strasberg. However, Susan Sarandon and her picture were featured. My apologies to Miss Sarandon—for we have never met.

The London publicist secured an excellent rate for me at a charming hotel. Most interviews were done in the parlor with its exquisite antiques and huge bouquets of fresh flowers. There was no restaurant at the hotel. That first evening I walked down the street to an Italian restaurant.

Seated in the next booth were a gentleman and his son from New Zealand. They were in London on business and were having coffee when I ordered dinner. They started talking to the American newly arrived in London to promote her first published book.

To digress, months earlier my friend Susan Strasberg had appeared with me on a late night New York City TV talk show to help promote *The Wheel of Destiny*. The next guest that evening was best-selling suspense writer, Mary Higgins Clark. And Mary happened to be the favorite author of Susan's daughter, Jennifer. Mary and I ended up exchanging books. She autographed *Loves Music, Loves to Dance* and sent it to me.

In London that evening, as I was ordering dessert, I looked up and whom did I see but Mary Higgins Clark being seated alone at another table. If the two men from New Zealand were impressed with meeting me, they were about to meet a world-famous author with 11 best-selling mystery novels. What a treat!

I went over to Mary and asked her to join me in the booth. Mary ate dinner while I had dessert and sipped another glass of wine. By then, the two gentlemen from New Zealand had joined us in the booth—with Mary and me side by side. They had a cognac, and those nice gentlemen paid for our dinners and drinks. But then, they had met Mary Higgins Clark and had a great story to take home to New Zealand.

Another divine coincidence: Mary and I were guests at the same hotel. Rather late, we sat in the lovely parlor sipping cognac and talking about men, marriage and writing (my secret passion) until around three in the morning. Mary was once a flight attendant for Pan Am. Some of my clients worked for that airline then—and one writes mysteries!

Mary Higgins Clark is charming and lovely, in addition to having a gift for keeping us turning those pages. She writes a book a year, sometimes more, all best-sellers. My friends read every book. Many of her stories have been adapted for film or television.

It was fun to "accidentally" run into Mary Higgins Clark in London that night—which made for still more colorful threads in the tapestry of my life!

13

NOT SO ORDINARY PEOPLE

My clients are involved in all kinds of professions: doctor, lawyer, accountant, banker, estate planner, financial adviser, real estate broker, stock broker, taxi driver, corporate executive, agent, representative, entrepreneur, salesperson, lobbyist, secretary, maid, chef, personal assistant, bookie and gambler. They work in just about any occupation, including those that may not be considered legal.

Career information is always important to those who want a reading: new job, raise, bonus or promotion, getting along better with co-workers or leaving a lousy work environment. I have often pointed out the need to be careful of what we wish for. One girl was fired two weeks after her reading.

"But you said you hated your job and your boss! The Universe was listening and accommodated you!"

Most male clients are extremely career-oriented. Without a decent job, men feel inadequate in terms of providing for a wife and a family. European men are more concerned than their American counterparts, who often expect a wife to work. Nowadays, the average household requires two working partners to provide for more than basic necessities. Today many women are as ambitious as men. Among my successful female clients have been strong, interesting women such as Gilda Marx. She was at the forefront of exercise classes for women, in addition to creating workout videos and designing workout and dance clothes for women. Jane Fonda enrolled in Gilda's classes. Gilda Marx has a dynamite personality and tremendous determination.

Another female business executive was Jean Nidetch, founder of Weight Watchers. I could see her business flourishing for years. Little did I know in the 1980s I would one day read for her royal spokesperson, the Duchess of York! Jean was a sweet, no-nonsense type. There was no way for her business to go out of style. Many friends and clients still benefit from her weight loss program.

In the early 1970s, my Scorpio friend Pat Hawkings worked for Steve Krantz of Bakshi-Krantz Productions on the *Nine Lives of Fritz the Cat*, a popular cartoon. Pat recommended me to the boss's wife, Capricorn Judith Krantz. Judy had already written several novels under various pen names, but had yet to achieve a best-seller. In one reading, I saw the novel she was working would be a hit and adapted for film. I asked her its title.

"Scruples," she said.

The novel *Scruples* rapidly reached No. 1 on the *New York Times* best seller list. Then, Judy wrote *Princess Daisy*, another winner. Six of her novels have been turned into TV miniseries. Judith Krantz has had remarkable literary success since she sat at my kitchen table to have her cards read. Another client said she had read my name as a psychic in some Judith Krantz novel. The author failed to remember which one when I asked her about the matter. But another of George's predictions had certainly come true!

In the early 1970s, Gemini Jerry West was a major basketball player for the Los Angeles Lakers when he had a reading. Tall, charming and handsome, he had awards and recognition in his future—a basketball championship. I predicted he would coach the Lakers one day. That was 1976-79. Later, Jerry West was the Lakers' General Manager. It was plain to me that Jerry West would remain vital and important to the sport of basketball. He is numbered among the "50 Greatest Players in NBA History." Kudos, Jerry West!

In the 1970s, Gemini hairdresser Jon Peters arrived for his reading with one of my clients, beautiful Gemini brunette, Sharon Winters. Jon was married to Lesley Ann Warren at the time. However, in his future was a Taurus woman, powerful and highly magnetic. The lady would bring major changes into his life, the fulfillment of his fondest dreams. Enter Taurus Barbra Streisand, Jon's new romantic partner. In 1976, Jon Peters co-produced Barbra's film, *A Star is Born*, in which Kris Kristofferson co-starred. All of Jon's future success was in the cards.

Starting in the 1970s, Aries Susan Pompian had many readings. Her move from California to Washington showed up around the time of my move East. Susan had a Master Spread, which she found insightful. Her blurb is on my book cover:

"The many psychic readings I've had with Patricia McLaine have provided me with valuable insight and guidance in every phase of my life, but my Master Reading enabled me to develop a kinder, more accepting attitude toward life and myself, making me a happier person. I highly recommend the Master Reading to anyone interested in viewing his or her life with greater clarity and compassion."

There were often famous men in Susan's life. She lived in Japan for many years, which resulted in the publication of her successful book, *Tokyo For Free*. If you plan a trip to Tokyo, Susan's book is a must. It has excellent tips for travelers. Susan's writing career was in the cards.

In 1976, Gemini Christina Crawford came to see me. It was plain in her reading that her mother had treated her badly when she was a child. I was appalled to discover the woman who had adopted and abused her was legendary film star Joan Crawford. My sense of her mother's treatment gave me the chills. I advised her to write a book about her childhood with her famous mother. The book would be a best-seller and major motion picture.

In 1978, the controversial *Mommie Dearest* was published and made into a motion picture in 1981, which starred Faye Dunaway as her tyrannical mother, Joan Crawford. With what was previously tuned into in Christina's reading, I had no desire to read the book or to see the film. Over the years, I have seen far too much inhumanity, cruelty and insane abuse by close family members just by reading people's cards. It seems that many human beings have a very long way to go to become fully human and humane.

An interesting, handsome, rugged male client, an optometrist, had decided on a radical career change. He said his parents had worked hard to give him a college education and put him through medical school to insure a solid future for him. At the time he was abandoning optometry to become a fulltime Chippendale Dancer. He wanted to know how to break the news to his conservative Midwestern parents. What a dilemma! In addition, he invited me to a show, with several girlfriends eager to join me. He had a fantastic body and craggy good looks. Of course, he always had optometry to fall back on when he was past his prime for turning on the ladies with his bumps and grinds. These days he might be gazing into women's eyes with a slightly different motivation—and without receiving tips!

During the late 1970s, Scorpio Geri Cusenza was a good client. She recommended many friends for readings. Geri was the power and inspiration behind the creation and production of Sebastian Hair Products which were sold worldwide. Her success was in her cards.

Another California client, Capricorn doctor Mark Saginor was a close friend of Hugh Hefner's and his private physician. A line of beautiful women sashayed through Mark's life, often at the Playboy mansion. Several of his high-profile friends had readings.

In the early 1970s, during a reading for a producer with a major Hollywood studio I could see that someone at work was embezzling a lot of money. The culprit was a "little old lady from Pasadena" who was likely to "run off with the money to Argentina." That happened. The Pasadena bookkeeping employee, pushing 60, embezzled $250,000 and ran off to South America. That was a lot of money at the time. I wonder if she was caught. The producer found it amazing that I had all the facts right in advance of her clever larceny.

The producer had been involved with an Aries friend of Susan Strasberg's. In the cards of Aries Stephie I described a man in detail and insisted, "You are going to end up marrying him."

"NEVER!" she screamed. "No way!"

In spite of her adamant denial, the two of them did get together and stay together. She married him. Sadly, Stephie is no longer with us. She is probably hanging out with Susan in the meadows of the Summerland. Stephie appeared in *Rebel Without a Cause* with James Dean. She was Jennifer Jones Strasberg's godmother and one of Susan's closest friends.

Treasure hunters—those searching the vast sea for sunken ships and pieces of eight— sometimes called for a reading. I'm unsure if I ever helped find buried treasure. If so, do I deserve a finder's fee? Edgar Cayce worked with treasure hunters. But this is not the way clairvoyants are supposed to use their gift. On the other hand, I have predicted lottery winnings for several clients.

In one reading, the conservative California client was going to hit the jackpot in the next year, perhaps in Las Vegas. She was not a gambler and rarely went to Vegas. That year she accompanied her husband on a trip. Late one night, after shooting craps and playing blackjack for hours without success, she just wanted to sleep. The hotel had this huge slot machine

and every guest was allowed one pull of the handle to win
$25,000 or $100,000, I no longer remember the amount, but
it was a decent sum of money.

Everyone in the group pulled the handle without success. It
was her turn. She told her husband, "You pull the handle. I'm
too tired." And the manager said, "It has to be you, only one
pull per guest."

Resigned, she reached up and pulled down the handle.

All of sudden, bells and whistles and lights were flashing at
three o'clock in the morning—with her husband jumping up
and down shouting, "Pattie McLaine! Pattie McLaine! She told
you! She said you were going to win! Pattie McLaine!"

Evidently, her win was written up in a Las Vegas newspaper.
For months, dealers arrived from Las Vegas to see if a big win
was in their future. All the dealers looked like dealers. No big
wins. It was apparently not their karma!

Sagittarius Lynda in Boston had a boyfriend with a gambling
addiction. He often took her to Aruba to the casinos, usually
without any luck. One year it seemed that Lynda was going
to win money gambling. She ended up winning $35,000 at
a roulette table, and after that, she won a car and took the
money instead. To say her boyfriend was distressed would be
an understatement. Lynda had five children and the money
was used for them. She was amazed by the accuracy of that
prediction.

Dates to buy lottery tickets were given to some clients based
on the progressed hits of their astrology chart. A Pisces client
in Florida won money on every date, sometimes thousands,
other times $50. One year her solar return looked good in the
South Pacific. Her cruise to Tahiti was paid for with her lottery
winnings purchased on one of those dates! A client in Virginia
won $100,000, which she used as a down payment on a house.
Some people are just born lucky.

While planting our extensive California hillside garden in Woodland Hills, on the steepest part digging in the dirt, I found a gold man's signet ring. Since my son had worked so hard on that hill as a teenager, I gave Mark the ring. It fit him at the time. Later, I wondered if my spirit guides had intended the ring for me. Perhaps I should have kept it. Many magical, mystical moments were experienced in that garden.

One day not long after that, an ornate gold ring appeared on my bedroom nightstand. I kept the ring. The world is filled with wonders—a treasure had been teleported to me!

In the 1980s, one client was Capricorn scriptwriter Leah Markus. In several readings I could see that she was going to be the story editor on the TV series *Dallas* (April '78–May '91). Leah had written for soap operas and sold scripts to *Dallas*. Yet, the job of story editor eluded her. Her getting the job was something I *just knew* would happen. Leah was going to be Story Editor on *Dallas*. By the time I moved to Arlington in 1984, Leah had given up on me.

Then, early in 1985, while packing for a work trip to Los Angeles I turned on the TV just as the credits were running on *Dallas*. Lo and behold, **Leah Markus** was **Story Editor**. My spirit guides were right! Leah had a reading on that trip. "Your prediction took five years to happen!" she said, as had the man I had predicted. Divine timing is not always mine.

In 1985, my Gemini client Frankie Hewitt had restored the historic Ford Theater where John Wilkes Booth shot President Abraham Lincoln in 1865. That box at the theater is reserved as a memorial to President Lincoln. When Frankie invited me to a party in her Maryland home, I realized the famous Gemini man forever in her cards was President John F. Kennedy. Pictures of our former handsome president were in every room. Frankie had worked on Kennedy's election, and if instinct serves me right, she was romantically linked with our

35th President. Kennedy did like the ladies. Fickle Gemini is sometimes guilty of having a roving eye.

In 1991, in her generosity, Frankie gave me two tickets to the Presidential Gala for our 41st President, George H.W. Bush, at Ford's Theater. Her ex-husband, Don Hewitt of *60 Minutes* fame, had not made the big time until after their divorce. Such is the karma of some women! It was always fun to read for Frankie, who is now with the others on the Other Side.

My clients include psychologists, psychiatrists and therapists. A few encouraged me to return to school to get a PhD in philosophy or psychology to give me more credibility. In my opinion, furthering my education would not have helped others to believe in my psychic powers. Many famous mediums and psychics have been simple, uneducated folk. I have some college education. Mostly, it has been my lot to read books on psychology and philosophy.

In 1980, Susan Strasberg was going through Reichian therapy when I stayed in her New York apartment. At the time, Dr. Elsworth Baker, who had worked with Wilhelm Reich, had a reading. Dr. Baker wrote an important book, *Man in the Trap*. The psychiatrist fell in love with a patient and stopped treating her. But they ended up married.

In those days, Susan was dating Sagittarius Dr. Richard Blasband, a Reichian psychiatrist and associate of Dr. Baker's. Dick had a reading and we instantly hit it off. I have Venus on his Sagittarius Sun and my Scorpio Sun is on his moon. We have past life bonds. Even after Susan and Dick stopped dating, we remained friends.

Dick Blasband had many readings, some in Princeton. Later, readings were given in the San Francisco area to Dick and his friends. In the summer of 1981, Dick rented a house in Aspen and invited me to stop on my way to Denver to meet my new grandson, Oliver James. Readings were also given to his friends in Aspen.

That summer, Dick's primary reading was my Master Spread, a life reading that involves past life patterns and overall spiritual growth. In spite of Dr. Blasband's usual scientific approach to life, his sensitive spiritual side emerged, aspects of his nature that enable him to be a natural, remarkable healer on many different levels. More recently, Dr. Blasband is Director of Research for the Center of Functional Research and co-director for the Institute of Transformational Integration.

Some clients are members of the clergy. One Protestant minister embezzled $250,000 from his church, but was never prosecuted by his compassionate parishioners. This was actually one of my predictions to the other minister! Then a married minister had an affair with an equally married parishioner, which created a major scandal and ended his marriage. Both he and his wife had been my clients from the time they were young. Her heart was broken, along with the hearts of their children. Their marriage, their children, and his Christian ministry were among my predictions. Scientology practitioners and Buddhist monks have also had readings.

During a reading for a Catholic nun, she asked me if she was ever going to get married. I thought she was married to Jesus! It seemed to me that she had her eye on the widower who had brought her to see me. She wore street clothes, and yet, throughout the reading, I had the strongest inclination to call her "sister."

Finally, she said, "I'm a nun and Catholic High School principal." The educational cards were in her reading.

A Catholic priest inquired, "Am I ever going to make Cardinal?" It did not seem likely, but there are few dull moments with my clients.

In the reading for Leo hair stylist Susan Schwary I could see recognition for her work on the series *Star Trek: The Next Generation*. Her Klingon wig is on display in the Smithsonian Museum. Other awards predicted included a nomination in 1998 for an Emmy for Outstanding Hairstyling for a Series for *Buffy the Vampire Slayer*, and again in 2000, for the series *Providence*, and again in 2004, in the same category, for *Deadwood* on HBO. I predicted that Susan would be involved with a Western long before the series was even cast.

In 2002, I said to Susan, "You're going to the Caribbean to work on a film that will be highly successful and receive many nominations." That film was *Pirates of the Caribbean: The Curse of the Black Pearl*, which starred Johnny Depp, Keira Knightley and Orlando Bloom. Susan continued to excel in her work in film and on television until her passing in 2009.

In the 1980s, patterns in a reading prompted the client to tell me a remarkable story. In the mid-1940s, as a child in Poland, she was part of a march of more than 300 children through the snow in winter. The Nazis herded the children, their clothing sparse, some without shoes, to a concentration camp. Not all the children lived through the ordeal.

At age six, the little Jewish girl survived by repeating some words over and over in her mind, words whispered to her by her dead grandmother on the Other Side: *I'm not tired ... I'm not cold ... I'm not hungry ... Keep walking ... I'm not tired ... I'm not cold ... I'm not hungry ... Keep walking!* She repeated the words over and over again, sometimes mentally, other times in a nearly silent whisper.

Our loved ones beyond the veil do assist those of us still in this dimension, especially when we find ourselves in desperate need—at times, to the extent of keeping us alive to fulfill some purpose on Earth.

Throughout the years, I have been privileged to read for many remarkable individuals. Many intelligent, talented, sensitive and wonderful persons have placed their trust in my insights. I do my best to remain objective in response to their needs. Sometimes I may not tell them exactly what they want to hear, but I am true in terms of what I am able to discern.

"When I listened to your tape again, everything you told me happened. It's just wasn't exactly how I had thought it was going to be," I have heard many times.

"You told me about seeing someone off on a cruise ship with all these streamers and celebration," Juliet said. "I did that 20 years later. If someone waits long enough, just about everything you predict is going to come true, but sometimes it takes a very long time!"

"You kept telling me I was going to China and I had no such plans," Janene said. "Twenty years later I finally went to China. You are farsighted in more ways than one, my friend!"

My friend Barry Ross Parnell, my friend
Susan Strasberg, her daughter Jennifer
on Susan's lap, and me at one of Susan's
parties in her home, 1973.

Me, author Jess Stearn (who featured
me in two books) and my client Elaine
Lerer at an A.R.E. conference in Pacific
Grove, California, 1978.

My friend Jennifer Jones Strasberg and her late mother
Susan at home, 1980.

My good friends Edward, Daniel, Nicholas and
Sheila Weidenfeld in their Georgetown home, 1982.
I predicted the birth of their sons.

Me on my trip to India to the conference in Bombay. Northern Indian cities were toured to include Kathmandu, Nepal, 1982.

Me and my good friend Janene Sneider in Dallas, Texas, 1982.

My dear friend Susan Kelly and client Jeanne Lolmaugh at a party
in my Woodland Hills home, 1983.

My good client-friend, handbag designer Valerie Barad, and me at
Alfredo's restaurant in Rome, 1984.

I'm doing mini-readings and signing *The Wheel of Destiny,* published by Llewellyn, at Book Expo America in New York City, May 1991.

My party in Arlington, Virginia, with my good friend and guest Maggie Linton, (neighbor Roberta Stopler and client-friend Elaine Montgomery in background), 1992.

Me with a metal Don Quixote in Spain, 1993.

My teacher, author Warren Kenton (Z'ev ben Shimon Halevi) and me on the Kabbalah Tour of Spain, 1993.

Me with the staff of the Bali Spirit Hotel in Ubud, Indonesia, 1994.

My client-friends Pattye Horne and Joanna Basso in Camden, Maine, 1997.

My client-friend Lolly Sturtevant, dear friend Carol Kruger (my first reading in 1966) and me at the International UFO Congress in Laughlin, Nevada, 1998.

Dr. Brian Weiss, me and medium James Van Praagh on a Greek Island cruise, 2000.

KARMIC CHALLENGES

14

SEX, LIES, AND PSYCHIC SPIES

It is not easy to remember exactly when those operating outside the long arm of the law first started to have readings. It is not my task to judge people for what they do, as long as murder is not involved and the person behaves in an acceptable manner. Karmic judgment is up to Higher Powers. Should it be someone's karma to get caught and go to jail because of acts contrary to the law, I will let them know without turning them in. I am a high priestess of sorts. My task is to shed light. An ethical psychic **never** tells anyone what to do or how to live! It is not my intention to manipulate or control. I know of psychics who do that. Beware—and keep your distance!

I feel a need to state my position on the seamier aspects of life. Why not legalize prostitution with regular health inspections and blood tests in states other than Nevada, perhaps in all states? Outlawing these practices will not stop women or men from selling sexual favors. With prostitution legal, there might be less deception and dishonesty. Credit cards could be traced by curious mates or lovers, with sexually transmitted diseases such as syphilis, hepatitis, and HIV, along with new STDs resistant to antibiotics, kept under better control. Lives might be saved, with perhaps a qualified psychotherapist assigned to every brothel.

In my opinion, drugs should be legalized. Then there would be more room in the prisons supported by our tax dollars, with fewer cases for the courts to try. Alcohol is legal and is the occasional cause of promiscuity, infidelity, vulgarity, profanity, cruelty, rank stupidity, terminal illness, even assault and murder. People are known to behave badly "under the influence." Could legalizing drugs bankrupt the world economy? Rumor has it that governments and international banking covertly deal in massive sums of money from trafficking in illegal drugs.

End drug trafficking by legalizing addictive, lethal drugs. Use the tax dollars to establish rehabilitation centers for those smart enough to clean up their acts. No more would vicious drug lords get rich by enslaving the gullible, no more would outlawed substances produce outlaws in fact. Folks are going to do what they are going to do, legal or otherwise. Our educational system needs to teach children from kindergarten the results from smoking cigarettes, that using alcohol and opiate drugs is detrimental to mind, body, and soul of not only the user but to loved ones and even to strangers.

I'm not sure if I ever gave a reading to the D.C. Madam, the Mayflower Madam, or some other notorious peddler of the flesh and sexual astuteness of certain attractive, youngish females. I knew Heidi Fleiss (December 30, 1965) had to be an earth sign with her carnal entrepreneurial skills. Capricorn is the sign of the "madam." She has fire for feistiness (Aries Moon) and Neptune in Scorpio to help her lure others into the sex trade. Does Heidi own a brothel-spa for women in Nevada? What sort of woman in a vast number is willing to pay for sex from some young stud, knowing the guy is only performing because of his highly bankable ass-ets? Many men have no problem with paying for sex. Are ordinary men, or handsome movie stars, unable to get release other than by paying a prostitute? Some men may prefer variety without strings or may want a guarantee before buying dinner.

In my early 20s, recently divorced and between husbands, a pimp approached me the first time. I had been out drinking late one night in Hollywood with a young Mormon girlfriend. In my teens, I had gone out with her big brother once. Richard was a great dancer. I always liked the dancers. And yet, something about him made me uneasy and that puzzled me.

What I finally found out: Richard used to pay his pretty, young sister a quarter to give him a blowjob from the time that she was 7. Naturally, her price went up as she grew older and wiser. Unwittingly perhaps, the creep had lured his young sister, not only into incest but into prostitution. That information made me happy to have been an only child.

The creepiest part of my first offer to enter the world's oldest profession—the man in the business suit in his early 40s at my apartment at midnight—was in the mortuary business. My imagination went wild with that knowledge! He gave me the willies, even though he never looked like a pimp—and looks can be deceiving. His reasoning for me to enter the "lucrative trade"—if a girl is going to give it away she might as well get paid. To my young way of thinking, I might *give it* to a guy I was attracted to, but without an attraction, I could never *give it* to anyone. Sex with a stranger held no appeal, even after reading those sensational Jackie Collins novels—and even though sex, death, and taxes are ruled by the 8th house of Scorpio!

Several years later, the headline in the *Los Angeles Times* announced a raid on a prostitution ring run out of a mortuary. The pimp was busted for his infamous sex and death trade. Had my old friend from the Mormon Church also been busted? I sincerely hoped her brother was no longer an incestuous pedophile.

Many years later, one past life recall was of being born into a brothel frequented by sailors in some seaport in Malaysia. The madam was French. While a small child, my mother committed suicide over an English sailor who never rescued her as promised. She said he was my father. At 11, as a young virgin, I was auctioned off to the highest bidder and became a prostitute. I died a horrific death from syphilis at age 22.

Perhaps my subliminal memory protected me late one summer night when I was a young and pretty 23.

My other encounter with a pimp happened after my second divorce. Out late one night partying with friends in Hollywood, while Bill had the children, our group broke up early. I had no desire to go home alone yet. Therefore, at midnight I went to an all-night coffee house on a hill. Actor Dan Dailey was at a table near the wall. Seated not far from him was a seedy-looking man straight out of a Damon Runyon tale of hustlers and gangsters with his dark, beady eyes, pockmarked skin, and prominent Adam's apple.

Several attractive girls with big hair, wearing too much makeup, in short miniskirts and clingy blouses traipsed in and out. One girl would go up to the creep near the wall phone and soon leave again after another call. The coffee house seemed to be "his office."

I was taking mental notes, thinking the situation might be something to use in a play. With all the action between the girls and the telephone I started to get the picture. The guy looked like a pimp. He was downright scary.

All at once, he started watching me closely. Next, the greasy-looking guy got up, came over to my table and sat down opposite me. The creep narrowed his eyes to appraise me when out of the corner of my eye, I noticed Dan Dailey watching the guy watching me. Dan seemed to be assessing my suddenly unsavory and repugnant situation.

"What kind of work do you do?" the scumbag inquired, looking me over and maybe wondering if I was some kind of competition for his girls.

My solar plexus tightened. Most of his girls were out on call. He may have been interested in adding one more to his stable of ladies of the night.

"I'm a secretary," I said.

"Where do you work?"

"20th Century Fox."

Dan Dailey sat up straight. He seemed to know the creep, but he had also heard me. After all, Dan Dailey had worked at 20th Century Fox a time or two. His old song and dance movies were among some of my favorites.

"How would you like to make a lot more money than you do as a secretary?" the creep with the beady eyes inquired. "You could work for me and make a lot of money ... have a nice apartment ... pretty clothes."

"I like my job," I said, suddenly feeling anxious. "I'm not interested in making a change." By then, I was really nervous. It was almost one o'clock and I was in there alone.

Just as the pimp started to get really pushy, Dan Dailey called his name from the back and in a loud voice added, "Leave her alone, okay? Just leave her alone!"

I paid my bill and left, making sure that both car doors were locked. When I got home I took a hot shower to wash away the scummy feeling. Prime creep pimp was working the ladies of the night on the Sunset Strip.

The cards in the spreads of most prostitutes and call girls are much the same as those of an actress, topless dancer, or porn star. After all, they are actors! One young client in the D.C. area worked for an escort service to put herself through dental school. Her hair was over- bleached, her fingernails exceedingly long with a different decal or jewel on each nail. She was chunky and no great beauty. The brassy hair made her look cheap. But some men prefer a cheap look to help make them feel superior.

Most of her customers were married men from out of town in Washington on business. A few just wanted to hold her after an expensive meal in a fine restaurant. Had they been unable to perform? I wondered how she was going to be happy as a dentist after being a call girl. The optometrist became a Chippendale dancer, but I doubt he sold sex. Am I naïve? Nowadays, he may be working for Heidi Fleiss in Nevada!

In 2002 in Virginia, another young client had a website featuring her nude with turn-on techniques. She liked all kinds of sex: the age, race, or looks of a man were unimportant. She was getting paid to do what she enjoyed most—SEX! She was pretty. I wondered what her childhood had been like, and how many sexually transmitted diseases she had contracted. And whether some twisted psychotic might decide to snuff her out one day.

Many prostitute clients had been sexually abused by trusted men during childhood or adolescence. Sexual molestation in childhood shows up in readings for women and men more often than I like to remember. Usually, the abuse involved a trusted friend or family member. One handsome young man in his 20s was in a sexual identity crisis about whether he was straight or gay. When he was 10, his drunken father had sodomized him in the backseat of a car. Another client-friend was first sexually abused at age seven by her father in the Sunday school room. He was the minister. By the time she was 12, her father was raping her repeatedly, entering her room at night. Another client had multiple abortions because of her father.

Sordid situations detected in readings are too numerous to mention. I am grateful for the relative protection and normalcy of my childhood, in spite of each parent marrying multiple times and being forced to attend 15 grammar schools and two high schools. I have never been sexually molested, although I dodged a few perverts at various times. Maybe my guardian angels were working overtime—or it may have been that tribe of spirit Native Americans!

The D.C. Dominatrix looked just like a lobbyist in her prim navy blue suit, white silk blouse, tasteful makeup and conservative jewelry—not anything at all like Lady Heather on *CSI*. Most of her clients were in politics on Capitol Hill. The tools of her trade: black leather, whips, chains, and handcuffs, standard equipment for those with such a preference. Apparently, some Washington power brokers need to be punished for passing policies detrimental to the American people! There were questions I would have liked to ask, but I respected her privacy. She told me of her line of work. I am not all-seeing or all-knowing—not everything can be picked up through tarot cards or clairvoyance. Besides, I am not putting everything in this book!

My call girls clients are also looking for love, naturally. Like many others, they want to change their lives. I was surprised to learn that one so-called "friend" ran an escort service. I spent a night in her house, with the telephone ringing all night long. In the morning, I asked her why. She said she ran a credit bureau and businesses needed to check out credit cards. Then, she sent a young woman for a reading who kept track of me. When I was in Camden, Maine, the young woman called for another reading. During our conversation she disclosed her line of work and said she worked for my French friend. Even psychics can be surprised.

"I thought you knew she was a madam and a hooker."

The "friend" was a spiritual seeker and had been married to another friend. I wondered if he was aware of her line of business. Owning an escort service on a spiritual path seemed odd. But then, in Tantra Yoga temple prostitutes are provided to practitioners without a partner.

One dope dealer was worried about getting caught and going to prison. That never was his karma. At parties in the 1960s, with drugs free, I kept my distance. Deep down something said that drugs might short-circuit my brain and destroy my psychic abilities. I never read for anyone after drinking alcohol.

My perception would not be trustworthy. Sometimes I can be psychic "under the influence," but not all that reliable.

In the late 1960s, I had my horoscope interpreted and took meditation classes from my Virgo astrologer friend, Tish Leroy. One afternoon, John Barrymore, Jr. stopped by and Tish introduced me. They had been friends for a while. Tish tried to keep Johnny off booze and drugs, but he ignored her. Sometimes she cleaned out his aura with her hand to sober him up, which ticked Johnny off.

In her classes I learned how to rise in the planes into my higher bodies. The physical body is the smallest. According to Tish, in a past life I had been a priestess in Atlantis and in Egypt. She said I had returned to serve again. We had been friends in several lifetimes. Tish also interpreted the horoscopes of my children. She said I had been entrusted with great souls, never to be underestimated. Another reader had said my son's aura was silver-white. Tish was sure that Tomi would rise to greatness one day.

Tish Leroy also had a penchant for intrigue. Her claim: "Virgos do what Scorpios get blamed for," meaning sex and secrets. On one wall was a picture of Virgo the Virgin, winking. In those days, Tish was romantically linked with a man she said was a "double agent."

"I haven't heard from Dennis for a while," she said, "I think he's in Europe. The last letter was postmarked Paris." Then she said, "I'd like you to do me a favor, Pattie. I'd like you to rise in the planes and find Dennis. Then, I want you to tell him to get in touch with me—immediately!"

"I can do that?" I replied in amazement. I had never met Dennis.

"Of course, you can. Your chakras are more highly developed than anyone else I've ever known. Promise me you'll at least try to find him."

I promised. Tish showed me a picture of Dennis.

The next afternoon, I sat cross-legged in the middle of my king-sized bed in Sherman Oaks and went into deep meditation. I visualized myself rising up through the different planes connected with my higher bodies. Tish had suggested the Plane of Uranus, which is concerned with clear vision or clairvoyance about a foot above the head. Once there, in a state of heightened sensitivity, Tish had said to start searching for Dennis. His picture looked like a James Bond type—but not as handsome as Sean Connery. Had Dennis given the genuine 007 a run for his money?

Wherever Dennis was it seemed very dark. I could smell salt water and sense a seaport somewhere in the South of France. Then, after fortifying my will, I demanded that Dennis sit down and write Tish a letter. She needed to know how he was. After I felt the contact was complete, I lowered back down through the planes. Then I called Tish to report on my findings. I had no clue if my experience was authentic or just more of my "overactive imagination."

Within a week, Tish received a letter postmarked St. Tropez. The letter had 3 a.m. written under the date and started out: "Dear Tish, I don't understand why, but I just awoke from a sound sleep in the middle of the night and felt compelled to get up and write you this letter..." After she finished the letter, Tish called me in a state of high excitement—to reprimand me.

"But that's what you told me to do!"

"Well, I know. But I didn't expect you to wake him up in the middle of the night!"

"I told you it was dark where he was."

"You're more powerful than I even suspected."

Needless to say, I was puzzled as to why Tish was upset with me for doing what she had *commanded* me to do. At least the "double agent" had finally written to her. Dennis was fine. I had not made him do anything terrible or unlawful. And honestly, I was as amazed as Tish by the accuracy of what I had sensed and perceived—and that Dennis had even written the letter. Double wow!

Years later, during my BOTA (formally known as Builders of the Adytum) studies in the written lessons, Paul Foster Case taught us how to "rise in the planes." Nowadays, this might be considered as an aspect of remote viewing, except somehow my will had been superimposed onto the will of Dennis—without his permission. Perhaps it was because he was sleeping? Such actions are inadvisable unless the intentions are the highest and the purest. Otherwise, it is black magic—a no-no on the spiritual path.

After I moved to the Washington area, I found that many clients worked for the FBI, CIA, Secret Service, Justice Department, Defense Department, and other branches of government. Not all of them were spooks (spies). During the first Gulf War, I read for military men and could see them being sent off on secret missions.

"Where am I being sent?" the young marine inquired.

"I don't know. It's a secret!" All I could see was somewhere in the Middle East.

One pretty woman in a high executive position in the corporation of a high-profile CEO received not only an exorbitant salary, but anything else she wanted. She had been the boss's mistress for 20 years. She never wanted him to divorce his wife, but preferred her relative freedom to do as she pleased. Previously unhappily married, she was not interested in repeating her mistake.

Another woman's lover was an arms dealer in the Iran-Contra affair. Later, she told me he had been a pimp who strangled two prostitutes for withholding money: handsome but scary! She stayed in my basement. A meeting was arranged for her with editors at *The Washington Post*, but nothing came of it. The crook used her money and forced her Beverly Hills mansion into foreclosure. After that, he bought the estate at a reduced price. I wouldn't want his karma—or hers, come to think of it!

In 1984, another client-friend moved from California to Alexandria, Virginia. Pisces Ginny worked on Reagan's campaign and received a job in the Department of Housing and Urban Development (HUD). I had predicted her government job when Ginny had no plan to stop being a flight attendant. We became good friends during our move east. In one reading I had warned her of car theft and her car was stolen. In another, there was a major scandal at her place of work: heads were going to roll.

Several clients, some of whom were involved in the scandal, worked for HUD. The prediction was made years before the upset in 1989.

Early in 1994, I attended a weekend psychic workshop at the Association for Research and Enlightenment (ARE) in Virginia Beach. That was where I met Dale Graff, an attractive older man. After I told Dale my plan to attend lectures on consciousness at the Smithsonian, he suggested we meet there for the lectures. I had read books and taken a workshop with one speaker, Deepak Chopra.

After the first lecture, Dale invited me out to dinner. He wore no wedding ring, so I was unaware he was married until one evening when he mentioned "my wife." I was puzzled. Why was Sagittarius Dale attending lectures with me and taking me out to dinner? He had conducted himself as at gentleman and never made a pass. Nonetheless, I was mystified.

"Have you ever done any remote-viewing?" he casually inquired one evening.

At the time I wasn't sure. Looking back, I realized I had "remote viewed" many times.

In spring 1994, I booked a flight to Ireland to attend the International Transpersonal Conference in Killarney. That is where I met Donald Ware, a retired Air Force fighter pilot and UFO investigator. Don told me about the International UFO Congresses held each winter in Nevada.

During my first UFO conference the next winter in Mesquite, Nevada, "Project Stargate" was outed on several programs on national television. As it turned out, Dale A. Graff had been the man in charge of the U.S. government's secret, psychic, remote viewing spy program. Dale had chosen the name "Project Stargate." That was when it hit me that Dale had been "recruiting" me to be a psychic spy! He was not courting me. He had to be intuitive enough to see I would have been a lousy spy. My position is too universal with respect to my understanding of karma.

Difficult karmic issues become resolved through the raising of consciousness. When a soul reaches a higher level of awareness, there is no longer a reason to abuse the mind or body of oneself or another. How many souls with sufficient self-love would sell their body or the body of another for any purpose? How many aware individuals continue to abuse the body and the mind with excessive use of toxic substances that may even lead to death?

According to my spiritual teacher, Ann Davies, we take on the karma of the person with whom we engage in sexual intercourse, so not only sexually transmitted diseases but karma is exchanged. Consider the complex karma of a call girl: her many customers end up exchanging multiple karma—that keeps on multiplying, indefinitely!

Value yourself and value others—and now I step down from my soapbox. We all have many lessons to learn on this magnificent and wondrous planet.

15

MURDER, I SAID – MAYHEM

To my knowledge, the first murder psychically picked up by me was during the summer of 1969 in a reading for a Playboy bunny. She was tall, voluptuous, blonde and beautiful, an obvious Hugh Hefner selection. Not long after laying out her cards, I was overcome with the impression of drugs, alcohol, guns, knives, and the sadistic killing of several innocent people. I was unsure of how many might be involved in the murderous mayhem, or of where the grisly business was going to take place, but the impressions received were strong and clear.

"The woman you know is a blonde actress. She's young and beautiful, often in the spotlight, and she's married. More than one person is going to be murdered. This is going to be on the radio and television and in all the newspapers all across the country."

Among her cards were Swords: three, four, five, six, eight, nine and ten come to mind, plus the Queen of Swords, which usually indicates a Capricorn-Aquarius woman. There were Key 15, The Devil; Key 16, The Tower; Key 12, The Hanged Man; and Key 20, Judgment. Combinations of cards invoke visions and images to suggest patterns and events in the present or future. Things did not look good.

Fortunately, I had been able to give her some good news. It was not all doom and gloom on that day. I could see a man who played polo and had royal blood, perhaps Italian. The tall, dark and handsome gentleman was fully described. Years later, I learned she had married an Italian count and resided in a grand villa near Rome. During that July reading, however, I started to feel sick at my stomach in view of the impending horror.

"This is their fate," I said. "There is nothing that can be done to prevent this from happening. But I can't look at it any longer—it's making me sick."

When the reading ended, I felt shaky even after she left. After a reading it takes several minutes to return to my regular state of mind. After gathering up the cards, the events and patterns are wiped away. My work is done. For that reading I received $5.

Three days after the Tate-LaBianca murders were still being talked about on television, with all the gruesome details in every newspaper, she called again. I was about to leave my apartment to see a movie when she said in hushed tones, "Pattie, these are the murders you told me about in my reading a month ago. I've been so upset I had to wait until now to call and tell you. I was friends with Sharon Tate (born January 24, 1943). She's the blonde actress who was in my cards. Jay Sebring was my hair stylist. You described Sharon perfectly, and you told me more than one person was going to be killed."

Suddenly feeling weak in the knees, I sat down. Five people had been killed on the first bloody day, including Sharon and her unborn child. I remembered the news reports of graffiti on the walls written in the victim's blood. My close friend, Susan Kelly, and her lawyer husband lived down the street. Susan purchased a shotgun and learned how to use it. The seemingly random killings had produced panic in those canyons. No wonder I had become nauseated tuning in to the homicidal massacre.

As a further instance of irony, I gave readings to several members of the Manson family. Two of the girls invited me to the commune in Topanga Canyon. In 1970 and 1971, I got the willies double-time when the group was tried and convicted.

I had given a reading to one Manson lawyer, as well as to a lawyer for the prosecution. I have no idea if any client was directly involved. I had heard stories of drugs and group sex. One girl that slept in my den for two nights had commented, "Sex is my Zen."

There was talk of sex orgies and drugs at some yoga ashrams, but to my knowledge, no murders such as those ordered by psychotic Scorpio Charlie Manson and carried out by his sadistic, drugged-out pawns that will, I hope, remain in prison until the end. Too many criminals revert to evil. Not one Manson murderer should be released, in my opinion.

For years, it upset me that I had not received enough to warn the victims and prevent the bloodbath. What good was it to predict horrors that I was unable to prevent? Then again, my client reminded me, "You said it was their destiny to die in that manner." It was karma. I have no desire for the future karma of the men and women involved in that horror story.

Not only the Tate-LaBianca murders, but other chaotic patterns have made me consider justice meted out in terms of Universal Law. No one gets away with anything, although it may seem so at times. Most evolving souls are not prepared to recall patterns or relationships from other lives and times that set the awful Wheels of Cosmic Justice in motion. Past lives are not remembered until individual consciousness has reached a point to be able to deal with not only past triumphs that might inflate the sense of self-importance, but to review past evils, such as jealousy, envy, rage, and even murder, with objectivity. My spiritual teacher said we all have been murderers at some time. And yet, every murderer will one day be murdered, perhaps in the same manner as the crime committed. Those who kill an innocent child are destined to lose a life as an innocent child.

Compassion needs to be cultivated toward all life, which is an enormous task for individual souls. In considering the recorded history of our planet for just the past 5,000 years, rather than hundreds of thousands of years, there are not that many happy endings. Consider biblical accounts of one individual or tribe smiting another over something that might have been resolved in a more humane manner. What about the plays of Shakespeare? Is hate not often fostered in the name of religion, with an "eye for an eye" a common practice in some cultures, and revenge too often sanction for murder? Humanity seems to have many lessons to learn before harmony may finally prevail on this planet. Hopefully, one day Mass Consciousness will evolve beyond the need for any kind of barbaric act to include war.

In 1968–1969, with the Zodiac Killer on the rampage, tarot cards were sometimes left at the scene of a crime. A newspaper reporter from San Francisco called me about certain tarot cards. I agreed to discuss the cards provided he never used my name. I had no desire to be the next victim.

The article appeared in a San Francisco newspaper without my name. I wish I had been able to solve the crimes that remain a mystery. Some claim there were 37 victims, others, five. In some lifetime, the murderer, or murderers, will be the victim, or victims, perhaps for the same number of times. Genuine remorse alters the score in terms of karma, the same as in a court of law. It is easier to pay now than be reborn into miserable, dismal conditions and ignorantly suffer from dire infirmities and seemingly unfair disadvantages. Universal Law is just in spite of appearances to the contrary. Your conscience is your Higher Self guiding you. Pay attention—or pay the price!

When Jill St. John had her reading, she remarked, "However did you ever find a house on Aura Avenue?" I absolutely thought my spirit guides were having fun with me in Reseda.

In Jill's cards was a tall, handsome Aquarian widower with three children. Several years later that man turned out to be Robert Wagner. In 1977, Wagner was married to actress

Natalie Wood. He was not destined to be widowed for another four years.

While living on Aura Avenue, my son Mark, age 14, took over the kitchen counter to grind a 14-inch lens for his telescope. It was the same size as the telescope at the Griffith Park Observatory. Mark was also on the Board of Astronomy at Griffith Park and assisted with the newsletter. Unfortunately, he over-ground the glass and had to regrind it. I thought I would never get rid of fine glass silt in my kitchen. But I asked myself: had the mothers of Copernicus or Galileo whined about glass silt?

That summer, Cancer actor Ron Glass, who portrayed Detective Ron Harris on *Barney Miller,* called and said in a strained voice, "Do you remember telling me that someone I knew was going to be murdered?"

"Vaguely," I said.

"My mother has been murdered in New Orleans."

"Oh, no!" I sank into a chair. "I'm so sorry."

"Is there anything you can tell me that might help us find out who did this?"

My solar plexus tightened and a scene flashed before me. "Was she found nude?"

"Yes."

"Was she strangled with a telephone cord?"

"Yes."

"Was she sexually assaulted?"

"Yes."

My heart went out to him. His ex-brother-in-law was in prison. I remembered thinking he could have been murdered by an inmate. I needed to meditate and asked Ron to call me back in 20 minutes.

"I see a tall, slender, young black man about 25. He has an Afro and he's on drugs. Your mother knew him. He needs to be stopped or he might kill someone else."

He thanked me. The conversation ended.

The years passed.

Ron Glass attended a Christmas party in Woodland Hills. The subject of his mother's murder was very difficult for him to talk about.

More years passed. Had his mother's killer ever been caught?

In the early 1990s, Ron called for another reading. Finally, I broached the sensitive issue. "Whatever happened with your mother's killer? Did they ever find him?"

"Oh, yes. You described him that day on the phone. He's serving life without parole."

Finally, I knew I had been helpful! I could never charge for that kind of insight. I was happy justice had been served. When someone you love is murdered it is beyond horrible.

Late in 1980, Mark left for the University of Arizona in Tucson to pursue a degree in astrophysics. That year my travel as a psychic kicked into high gear. Some California clients had relocated in other states or countries. Some invited me to visit to read for friends and co-workers. Those cities: Seattle, Washington, D.C., New York City, Boston, Virginia Beach, and Dallas, where I stayed with different clients. The first time I worked in Houston I stayed in a hotel.

In the 1980s in Houston, I appeared on television in the *Harold Gunn Show* and the *Warner Roberts Show*. My name was also in the *Houston Chronicle* gossip column, usually after Gwen Davis had completed another sexy novel and a book party was held in her honor at some posh restaurant. At the lavish bar mitzvah for Gwen's son, Robert, I was seated with Rosemarie and Robert Stack. It was Rosemarie who had recommended me to the society ladies of Houston.

In the autumn of 1981, after working in Dallas, I contacted Rosemarie's friends to set up appointments before I boarded the plane for Houston. On that first trip, at least two society ladies who had readings had murders in their cards.

One crime was going to involve a woman who would lose it at the breakfast table and shoot her husband in front of the children. I was unaware of the reason for her unbridled rage. The other victim was a well-known young woman involved in a torrid affair with an older, high- profile, absurdly wealthy and long-time married Texas oilman. The gentleman was ardently and gleefully showering the young woman, many years younger than his wife, with outrageously expensive trinkets. He was also willing to pay for anything her little ole passionate heart desired.

"The wife of this man is going to put a contract on the woman and have her killed. The woman has no intention of allowing her husband to divorce her and ruin her comfortable life after giving him the best 30 years of her life and several children.

"When the body is discovered, probably in some dark alley, the mistress will still have on her expensive Rolex watch and diamonds, along with plenty of cash in her expensive wallet in her even more expensive handbag, which will prove that the murder was not a robbery. The killer is sending out a very strong message!"

Since I was a California psychic who read for movie stars and had my predictions in the supermarket tabloid, *The Star,* one woman said in a condescending tone, "That sort of thing may happen in Hollywood, but it certainly doesn't happen in Houston!"

In February 1982, my first trip out of the country was planned. After Washington, my next stop was Bombay, India, to attend a conference for a week and two more weeks touring northern India and Nepal. After that, it was London for the first time to read for royals from everywhere, along with regular Londoners.

In late March, while working in New York City before going to Boston to appear again on *People Are Talking* with host Nancy Merrill, I called Robb Butts. My son's good friend from high school was house sitting and feeding our cats.

"These two hysterical ladies have been calling you from Houston," Robb said. "I told them you wouldn't be home anytime soon, that you were traveling, but evidently you predicted some murders that happened in Houston. They couldn't believe how accurate you were!"

Despite Laurie's snotty retort, it suddenly seemed that murders *did happen* in Houston. Both murders occurred as predicted. I have no idea if anyone was caught or convicted. The lady who shot her husband had to be at least "temporarily insane." It seemed the contract killing would never come to light. Universal Law solves crimes in Divine Time! Imagine the karma of contract killers having countless contracts placed on them when they least expect it.

In the early 1980s, a California client had a reading where it seemed that someone she knew was going to be murdered. Weeks later, she called. A friend attending nursing school was missing. The woman had a small child and her husband was frantic. After meditating, my immediate impression was foul play. But I was unsure. I referred her to another psychic named Lorraine who said, "The woman has run off with another man to Colorado." That never felt right to me.

Several months later, two students confessed to the woman's murder and led police to her remains in the foothills. The Higher Self had gotten the best of them and brought closure to the family. It is better to pay now. That situation taught me to always trust my instincts.

Around then, in a reading for Rosemarie Stack, I could see a murder that turned out to be that of Vicki Morgan—the notorious mistress of Alfred S. Bloomingdale. In an earlier reading, I had tuned into the highly publicized scandal involving her friend Betsy Bloomingdale and her husband's affair. Scandals involving public figures often surfaced in Rosemarie's readings.

In the early 1970s, a man booked a reading. I was unaware of his profession. However, his cards were filled with pimps and prostitutes, drug dealers and junkies, and criminals, even murderers. Who was at my kitchen table? I got nervous.

"I can explain all that. It isn't me. I'm a vice squad officer for the Police Department in downtown L.A," he said in exasperation.

I froze. My heart started to race. Months before, another psychic had been arrested by a vice squad officer and taken off in handcuffs. She spent a night in jail before her lawyer posted bail. Even Edgar Cayce had trouble with the law. I had no license. I had on a bathing suit and cover-up with bare feet. I had been outside swimming with my kids.

I won't charge him, I thought. If he asks, I'll say, *No charge.* My fee was then $10.

The man desperately wanted out of police work. Instead, he wanted to build boats with his brother. He had tired of the seamier side of life, the intrigue and danger. The previous year a fellow officer had been killed in the line of duty. His wife was a wreck. He wanted to spend more time with his wife and children. His dream of building boats seemed assured.

When he stood, he smiled and tossed $10 on the table. He never put me in handcuffs or carted me off to the station to book me. What a relief! I hope he was successful building boats.

In the 1990s in Arlington, another client was a vice squad officer. By then, my fee was $100. Plus, the psychic detectives on television were helping to solve horrific crimes. Policemen and women were turning to psychics for help. The attractive young woman wanted me to work with her to help solve crimes against women—rapes and murders.

I could not do it. I knew I might pick up the fear and horror of the victim and had no desire for the experience. The psychic detectives who work with the criminal mind and terror of the victim are terrific, in my opinion. Their destiny is not mine— more power to them.

In the 1990s, a young massage therapist in New York City was romantically linked with an Asian customer. The man was a black belt in many martial arts. I had predicted him into her life. He was also married to a successful attorney and only wanted a playmate. I had tried to get her to break things off with him, which was none of my business. I just had this *feeling*. His wife had not conceived. My foolish client wanted to get pregnant to snag him. I sensed danger.

Then, she stopped calling.

The next year, on a Sunday afternoon there was a telephone call from a man who said he was her brother. She had been found dead in the bathtub. The coroner said it was a toxic overdose of herbs. Her brother had found my tapes and played them all before he called.

My reaction: the Asian lover had used a fatal martial arts pressure point to kill her. A special medical examiner would be needed to find the truth. Sadly, she had been cremated. No evidence. I was convinced she was murdered. Some things have to be left to the Lords of Karma. There are no doubt many such patterns recorded in the Book of Life.

In 2002, I was featured in an article in *The Washington Post*: "The Killer's Calling Card, For Tarot Readers, Divining

Meanings," by Hank Stuever and Hamil R. Harris. The article discussed tarot cards left at the scene of the sniper murders in Washington, D.C. Ten innocent people were killed. After the article, I was interviewed on XM Satellite Radio by Bernie McCain. Next I was taped for the *Early Show* on CBS-TV.

My Scorpio friend Elaine and I had given our impressions to the McLean Police Department, but our impressions were not fully accurate. My sense was a "military man" and "camouflage clothing," but not a teenager. We both thought the killer was military. Fortunately for the families, the two killers were apprehended and convicted.

In the late 1960s, I attended several meetings at the Peoples Temple. I no longer remember how I first heard of Jim Jones. So many events have become something of a psychic blur. It was 1970 when I had the rude awakening. By 1974, the Peoples Temple had moved to Guyana to establish Jonestown. One letter from Tish had made me sad and fearful. Nothing good was going to come of Jim Jones. Tish had loved a double agent. Intrigue and conspiracy appealed to that Virgo.

At first I thought Jim Jones was a New Age prophet preaching racial equality and social justice. Supposedly, his father was a member of the KKK and had shamed him. For that reason, Jim took his preaching to the black community. I had grown up in a black neighborhood and favored the civil rights movement. But on that Easter Sunday, I knew in my heart and soul that Jim Jones was NOT the reincarnated Jesus. Since that time many other cult leaders have made the same claim.

Once, at the Peoples Temple, Jim Jones traipsed down the aisle with his entourage in robes when he stopped and turned to smile in the manner of a man interested in a woman. Minutes later, a young woman came back to me and said, "Jim wants you to know that he loves you." At that moment I started to have serious doubts about the Reverend Jim Jones, a supposedly happily married father of many adopted children of various races.

Since the Jonestown horror, I have heard and read of his indiscretions with women and men. Jim Jones had a harem. He was once arrested for lewd conduct by an undercover policeman in a men's restroom after approaching the man. The article online: *Sex at Peoples Temple.*

The last Easter Sunday my children went with me to services, the Reverend Jones cried out, "I am he who walked beside the Sea of Galilee," and he lost me. My children had heard his lies. His followers were selling his laminated picture. He blessed tissues to be carried on their bodies. Suddenly, it was too much. I never returned.

Tragically, in 1978, nine friends and acquaintances were murdered in Jonestown when 914 men, women and children were poisoned with Kool-Aid laced with cyanide. Perhaps they were forced at gunpoint? Jim Jones was shot in the head. I doubt he killed himself. I did not predict this tragedy. It was just that the last time my children accompanied me to the Peoples Temple in Los Angeles to hear Jim Jones preach, I had finally come to my senses and realized that Jim Jones was delusional at best and might be dangerous.

My friend, astrologer Tish Leroy, died that day in Jonestown. Tish was my daughter Tomi's godmother. After that, Susan Strasberg assumed the role for both my children. Numbered among the mass suicides on that terrible day were Tish's two daughters, Evelyn and Erin. Tomi had been close to Erin. Evelyn had babysat with my children when they were young. Evelyn was close to Janet, the daughter of my friend Carol Sutton. The strangest part: Tish had accused me of searching for a guru, trying to find someone to tell me what to do. That had never been my intention.

When Tish and I met, I was actively attending lectures by Manly P. Hall at the Philosophical Research Society. I was also a member of an Edgar Cayce Search for God study group, and later joined Builders of the Adytum, a Qabalistic mystery school. I was assuredly on a quest to gain as much knowledge of metaphysical subjects and practices that I could. On the other hand, I never would have sold my house and given the money to the Reverend Jones. I never would have killed myself and my children for someone claiming to be the messiah. No messiah requires such acts. My suspicion: Tish had fallen in love with the charismatic voice and dark good looks of the oversexed Jim Jones.

Two children of other friends, Claire and Richard Janero, also perished that day. Richard had been out on a boat picking up supplies. Claire was flying to Guyana at the time. I had briefly dated Claire's brother, Chuck. Later, she called me hysterical. She wanted to know if her children had suffered, were they safe on the Other Side? Everyone is safe on the Other Side. As Ram Dass once said, "Death is perfectly safe." It is in this dimension that doors need to be locked and caution needs to be taken to be safe from the crazies.

Five other victims in Jonestown had been clients. Talk about having a guilty conscience! I had told them about the charismatic Jim Jones and suggested attending lectures at People's Temple. At least two were black: one a tall, slender man, also named Jim, was said to be one of Jones's bodyguards. Had his gun forced the innocent to drink poison and die?

Sadly, Jim Jones lost his way in his lust for sex, power, and control over his 1,000 cult members. Well-meaning, innocent people had followed him into the jungles to escape from supposed political persecution by the United States government. He prophesied nuclear war.

On that fateful Sunday, I was meditating to classical music in Frederick's living room when the news that more than 900 had perished in the jungles of Guyana was announced. I was in shock.

That night Tomi called me hysterical from Spokane to talk about Erin and Evelyn: "To think I wanted us to go there," my daughter was crying. "But you wouldn't listen. I wanted to be part of their community! Why do we have to know people involved in this horrible situation?"

My daughter thanked me for not putting our family in danger. The sad memory, however, remains, perhaps as a warning against ranting religious fanaticism.

In a dream I was attending a cocktail party when Tish walked up. We were talking when I suddenly remembered Jonestown. "Why are you here? You died with Jim Jones in Jonestown."

Her expression saddened and she walked away. Tish was never in my dreams again. For a time, she had been very important to me. Tish and her children had attended our parties. Together, we took our children on outings. I shall never forget her senseless, tragic end.

My spiritual teacher, Ann Davies, said, "The victim seeks the murderer the same as the murderer seeks the victim. It's the working out of Universal Law."

The vanquished becomes the conqueror to be conquered again as a soul persists in its folly. White plantation masters in the Old South who abused African slaves have returned as white or black civil rights leaders to right the wrongs of slavery. Edgar Cayce said we reincarnate to experience firsthand whatever we seriously judged or condemned, whether the prejudice involves race, nationality, gender, religion, politics, sexual preference, or any other character flaw in need of transformation.

Forgiveness and tolerance are among the most important and difficult lessons to learn on the never-ending journey of the soul in a physical body.

16

DOOM AND GLOOM – DISASTERS

When tuning into future world events, it is much easier to pick up negative patterns than the positive ones, because of the intense emotion generated within the Mass Mind. This is true for any psychic, regardless of the level of awareness or education. We are all part of one organic whole, regardless of color, race, gender, economic standard, educational attainment, political preference or religious persuasion. Everyone on this planet is a member of the human race, emotionally connected to the vital soul of the planet—perhaps existence in the Universe or Multiverse, as it is now called.

In January 1977, journalist and client Hal Jacques asked me to make "world predictions" to be published in the supermarket tabloid, *The Star.* I would not be paid, of course. I have no idea if Hal made any money on us psychics. He probably did.

WORLD PREDICTIONS? Wow!

At first, I was unsure if I could tune into patterns other than those for a particular person and others in his or her life. Most of the startling events picked up were in readings where a person's life was dramatically touched by the event.

Regardless, after my son Mark left for school one morning, I sat in my living room on Aura Avenue and meditated with world events foremost in mind. Before long, I was tracking what I prefer to call the *Akashic Record of Future Newspaper Headlines* while fully aware that timing is tricky with respect to the unfolding of any future event. However, purposeful *intention* combined with focused *attention* can produce results worthy of print.

Multiple images flowed through my mind. Two events were particularly clear: (1) The wife of King Hussein of Jordan was going to die in a plane crash; (2) Two jumbo jets were going to collide at an airport with disastrous results and tremendous loss of life. In my vision, the huge jets were in a dense fog. I made notes on a legal tablet about these things and others. Then, I went about my day.

A little over two weeks later, on February 9, 1977, H.M. Queen Alia al-Hussein, the third wife of King Hussein of Jordan, died in a helicopter crash in Amman. On March 27, 1977, in a dense fog at Tenerife in the Canary Islands, a landing Pan Am flight 747 collided with a KLM flight 747 taking off. The collision of the two jumbo jets tragically resulted in the loss of 583 lives. Both events had manifested in a relatively short time. Therefore, it seemed to me that I could tune into world events without tarot cards or an individual. The Universe had surprised me again.

Neither event was published. It is against my ethics to publicize the death of a person before their time. I would never use tragedy in the life of a public figure to my glorification. Most of the time, it is better to use general terms with predictions for publication. As psychic-astrologer Jeane Dixon discovered, when trying to warn President John F. Kennedy not to go to Dallas in 1963, I have learned there are few willing to listen to unsolicited advice. The visions or prophecies of a psychic are rarely taken seriously by those who exist in purely three-dimensional awareness. Belief systems vary. Times have changed since ancient Greece, Egypt and other mystic cultures. Most souls are not prepared, or developed enough, to open the mind to dwelling in multiple dimensions.

In 1988, my Gemini friend Janene Sneider in New York called. She was hysterical about the state of her personal life.

My immediate response: "Have you seen the television news or read the newspaper this morning?"

More than 25,000 people had perished in a terrible earthquake in Armenia. It seemed to me that she was tuning into the hysteria on the other side of the planet. Maybe her life was not truly wonderful, but that morning I thought she was overreacting because of the state of Mass Mind. Perhaps the information helped her to change her perspective on that morning.

Be aware! When great turmoil or destruction occurs on the planet, sensitive souls pick up on the frequency and unconsciously translate the disaster into personal terms. Please check the morning news before you decide to have a really terrible day.

The first major earthquake I predicted struck the San Fernando Valley at 6 a.m. on February 9, 1971, with a magnitude of 6.6. We were living in Sherman Oaks at the time. The wooden shutters on my bedroom windows over the garage rattled violently. Our dog, Irving, had been asleep on the far corner of my king-sized bed when he jumped up and started barking at the house. Soon, my children were in my room. Mark had been frightened when the water in our 40-foot swimming pool sounded like a tidal wave hitting his bedroom wall. Later, the brick patio was covered with water while the chlorinated water in the pool was down four feet. The only crash was a glass that shattered in the kitchen sink.

Later, several clients called to say that I had predicted the quake. Only the day before, my cards showed havoc in the home within a day. School was canceled. No one knew when the next aftershock would strike. Several lesser quakes rumbled and rattled for days. It was unnerving. One neighbor leaving his house had seen the street ripple. The landlord arrived to check for cracks. The worst occurred in the Sylmar area: two hospitals were destroyed and a freeway interchange collapsed. There was considerable damage to a dam. The final death count: 57. That quake inspired the 1974 film *Earthquake*—a scary movie that increased the sale of earthquake insurance up and down California.

Around then, another psychic said that when earth changes happened, as predicted by Edgar Cayce and other soothsayers of doom and gloom, a spaceship would pick me up and fly me to safety. Then I would be returned to the earth when everything calmed down. During that particular quake, California did not break up into islands—and I saw no spaceship anywhere near Sherman Oaks at that time.

The weekend of May 10-11, 1980, I was teaching a tarot workshop in my Woodland Hills home. For several weeks, volcanologists and seismologists had been paying close attention to the rumblings and shaking of Mt. Saint Helens in Washington State. The mountain had attracted media attention from all around the world.

"That mountain is going to blow within the next two weeks—and it's going to be major," I said to my class on Sunday.

A week later, on May 18, 1980, the massive eruption of Mt. St. Helens occurred. My daughter was attending church in Spokane as the huge volcanic cloud from the eruption deposited ash in the 11 surrounding states. Day turned into night. As Tomi left church, she said, "I thought it was the Second Coming!"

However, it was only Mother Nature blowing her top in a frightening manner to illustrate to all of us poor mortals how little control any of us truly have on this planet. Life exists on Earth only because of the constant fire that burns in its heart. We live on a passionate planet, referred to as Gaia in the tradition of the ancient Goddess. Earth and water are feminine, air and fire are masculine. Mixing elements together in an out-of-control manner produces major challenges for those of us trying to maintain life on the surface—and not only for us mortals!

In meditation in 1981, I could see the assassination of President Anwar al-Sadat of Egypt dressed in a military uniform and standing on a podium. It saddened me that the great man was being cut down. His efforts to establish peace between Egypt and Israel had earned my respect. And yet, it seems peace between the Arabs and the Jews will only be established by Divine Intervention or when civilization ends. My vision was passed on to friends, but never published. I respected the man and his mission.

The first hurricane picked up in a reading for those in the Southern States was Hurricane Alicia, which formed in the Gulf of Mexico in August 1983. The center of the storm passed over Houston with 115-mph winds. That first hurricane of the season caused $2.6 billion in damages in eastern Texas and Louisiana.

In a reading for a Houston client, I inquired, "Do you live in a house filled with light?"

"More so in the winter. Our acre is covered with huge trees that shade every side of the house most of the year."

The next time I saw her, she said, "Now our house is filled with light!" to confirm my accuracy. Alicia had knocked down every tree. It was frightening for her to ride out the storm as trees crashed down on every side of her house.

In January 1986, I was working in California at the Oakwood Apartments in Sherman Oaks. Winter was the perfect time to leave the East to accommodate my 2,000 clients in Los Angeles. Many wanted readings in person. When I stopped traveling, I lost interesting clients in most cities.

On January 28, 1986, I had an uneasy feeling fixing breakfast. My first client was due at 10 that morning, and yet dread filled my body at the thought of the space shuttle Challenger continuing with its launch. On television, there had been talk of ice forming on the shuttle. Things were not right in my estimation. My thought: *Don't launch, please don't launch!* My last thought as the Challenger headed skyward—*I wonder how their families and the nation are going to handle this tragedy?*

Seventy-three seconds later, the space shuttle Challenger started to fall apart and plummet to earth. The rest is history. True destiny is inescapable, of course.

By summer 1989, I had warned several Charleston, South Carolina, clients of a major hurricane heading their way. Over the years, news of my readings spread in that charming southern town. I had many clients in Charleston. With my client Gladys, I had said September as the month of the storm. The eye of category 4 Hurricane Hugo passed just northeast of Charleston on September 21. Gladys said the storm was frightening but exciting. That client with the Scorpio-Sagittarius cusp rode out Mother Nature's fury when I would have been halfway to Kansas by the time it hit.

Hurricane Hugo killed 82 and caused more than $7 billion in damages, the highest amount to date in U.S. history, with the highest storm surge—over 20 feet, north of Charleston. The home of another client on a barrier island washed away. She never wanted another reading, because she feared more bad news. However, she had been warned and had spent September with her sister in New England. Had my reading saved her life? Mother Nature can be horrific when the elements are unleashed. Perhaps it is not unusual that storms and volcanoes have human names—and dispositions.

In October 1989, during a telephone reading for Gwen Davis, I said, "You're going to have a major shakeup this week."

The shakeup turned out to be literal rather than emotional or psychological as her high-rise apartment on Nob Hill violently swayed to and fro in the 7.1 magnitude quake on October 17, 1989. Gwen was out on Clay Street walking her Yorkshire terrier Happy, and had to hold on to a car as bricks started to fall all around her.

"I hope there aren't any more shakeups this week. That was enough!" Gwen later said.

Damage to San Francisco and the surrounding area was severe—property losses near $6 billion. Not long after the quake I visited Gwen in her apartment, which felt as though it was suspended in the air. That building made me nervous even with no quake in the offing. But the view of the San Francisco Bay was inspirational.

One client in Virginia had two disasters in his cards. First, I saw that a tree might fall on his house. That happened. Next, I saw that his house might burn down. The house burned to the ground. Talk about the bad house karma! I felt badly for him.

Some become disturbed, or have strange ringing in their ears, before an earthquake, tornado, or other natural disaster. Others dream of an event beforehand. Edgar Cayce made dramatic predictions of earth changes to occur in the United States between 1958 and 1998, most of which, fortunately, never happened.

Frequently, natural disasters show up in a reading of one destined to be present for the event. I warned a Georgia client of an earthquake. Aries Jenny was a motivational speaker and often lectured in Los Angeles. After the reading, she said she was something of a wreck. During her next lecture in California, she had her husband stationed near an exit, so she would know where to run if the shaking started. In Seattle, however, an earthquake woke her up and knocked a friend of hers out of bed. The when and where of events are not easy to determine.

In 1992, the destructive nature of Hurricane Andrew, the first storm of the season in August, was predicted to Florida and Louisiana clients. Andrew was the second-worst hurricane in U.S. history in the century: property damages exceeded $26 billion, mostly near Miami. Scorpio Dr. Brian Weiss of past-life regression fame lost his office and valuable records to Hurricane Andrew. Brian never had a reading until 2000, so he was never warned about the hurricane.

Late 1993, I started to feel uneasy about my forthcoming work trip to California. The sensation might be best described as outright fear. No arrangements were made to travel.

On January 6, 1994, Gemini actor Kale Browne, then married to Libra actress Karen Allen, had a telephone reading from the Berkshire Mountains of Massachusetts. Karen was starring in a TV series in Los Angeles. They were getting ready to return to California.

"You're going to be in a major California earthquake," I told Kale.

"But I hate earthquakes!"

"It's going to be a really bad one … this January or next. Everybody will be fine, but it'll scare the hell out of you. Call me after the quake and let me know you're okay," were my last words to Kale.

Two days later, Kale and Karen took a flight to Los Angeles.

On January 17, 1994, around 7:30 a.m., I was preparing breakfast at my home in Arlington when I turned on the TV. *CNN Headline News* announced the 6.7 magnitude earthquake in Northridge. I called Kale, forgetting it was before 5:00 a.m. in California. Kale thought I was calling to say, "I told you so!" My interest was to make sure that he and Karen were fine. That prediction had happened immediately.

The Oakwood Apartment buildings, which was where I normally rented in Sherman Oaks, collapsed in the quake. The ground acceleration was the strongest recorded in urban North America. My spirit guides had saved me from a trip that would have been a disaster for me for sure. Pay attention to your instincts that speak in *feelings and sensations*. That San Fernando Valley earthquake was the most costly in U.S. history to date, with 72 killed.

Many California clients had been warned about that quake, including Aquarius Michelle Waterloo. In 1993, Michelle purchased renter's insurance the first time. That winter she flew to Singapore to visit her sister. Five days after she returned, the earthquake hit. Michelle was glad she had renter's insurance, which covered all her losses.

Earthquakes and volcanic eruptions are constant on our earth. Such is the nature of our passionate planet. In accordance with current knowledge, there are more human beings on the earth now than at any other time in recorded history. In addition, there are more industries that pollute the atmosphere and waterways, including our oceans. There is increasing concern for the health of the planet and its vastly diverse life forms.

Predictions for 2004 posted on December 12, 2003 on www.patriciamclaine.com included: "Earthquakes and volcanic rumblings could well fill the headlines." This prediction included the horrific quake in Iran with more than 41,000 people dead and untold property damage.

Another prediction: "Tsunamis, tidal waves inundate Pacific Islands. Many lost beneath the sea."

On December 26, 2004, a 9.4 mega-quake in the Andaman Sea generated tsunamis that fanned out in all directions. Nearly 500,000 were lost, dead, or missing, as entire villages were wiped out, with waves washing across islands and into the cities: property damage was astronomical. Such devastation numbs the human mind and heart, as in August 2005 when

Hurricane Katrina devastated New Orleans and other Gulf Coast states, with reconstruction and recovery still incomplete after five years.

Not long after the tragic events of September 11, 2001, I warned a Swiss Scorpio client not to travel on certain dates based upon on his progressed planets. However, the man needed to be in Buenos Aires, Argentina, on a certain day, so he booked a flight on a date he was told was bad for travel. On his flight a man tried to break into the cockpit. The flight attendants and passengers subdued the alleged terrorist, but for a while my Swiss client was saying his prayers with all the others.

"In the future, I shall never fly on one of those days again!" he declared.

The plane landed safely and the lunatic was taken into police custody.

In 1984, Aquarius actor Gregory Sierra blamed himself for my move East. In 1979, Greg had given me Jeffrey Goodman's book, *We Are the Earthquake Generation: Where and When the Catastrophes Will Strike.* With the New Millennium then approaching, everyone in metaphysics was talking about earth changes, especially those predicted by Edgar Cayce in the 1940s, in addition to the Book of Revelation of the Bible. Christians were eagerly awaiting the Second Coming of Jesus Christ in the year 2000.

It seems that in every new century, especially when a new millennium is reached, there are prophecies of earthshaking events from nearly every religious persuasion. The Buddhists anticipate the reappearance of the Bodhisattva Maitreya, world teacher and master of wisdom. The Hindus anticipate the reincarnation of Vishnu or Krishna, "the Master of and beyond the past, present and future, the Creator and Destroyer of existences who supports, sustains and governs the Universe, and originates and develops all elements therein." Wow! Everyone is waiting for a savior to deliver the earth and its inhabitants from the very appearance of darkness and evil.

In the 1970s and 1980s, a number of new soothsayers—New Age prophets—jumped on the earth changes bandwagon. Disconcerting and alarming new maps of the United States and other countries indicated the boundaries of the continents to be considerably altered after the Earth rocks, rolls and shimmies before flipping entirely over on its axis: Scary, to say the least. And yet, even some scientists have predicted dramatic changes in the earth's magnetic fields that could precipitate numerous catastrophes.

Aron Abrahamsen, David Michael Scallion, Len and Lori Toyes, and Delores Cannon are only a few who have foreseen catastrophic doom and gloom for Mother Earth that would destroy its frail creatures and sentient beings attempting to forge an existence on the surface. There is no need to be psychic to be nervous about prospects couched in biblical jargon. The prophecies of the Hopi Indians include earth changes capable of producing chronic nightmares and high blood pressure in most normal folk.

On the other hand, Divine Timing is not necessarily mortal timing.

The prospect of earthquakes and dramatic earth changes was not my main reason for leaving Southern California. Nor had Goodman's declaration of imminent disasters, including California's becoming islands as prophesied by Edgar Cayce, have a direct bearing on my move. It was the smog that burned my eyes and lungs, too many human beings in one geographical location, terrible traffic, and the simple fact that I no longer enjoyed eternal summer—my least favorite season and a long one in Southern California.

My former neighbors in Woodland Hills, Valerie and Philip D'Addona, say they continue to enjoy fall color because of trees planted on our former canyon hillside across the street. Fall color is hard to come by in California. However, in Alexandria, Virginia, and Camden, Maine, where I have resided since 1984, fall color is spectacular. Mother Nature wears a variety of wardrobes in parts of the country other than California.

By 1984, I yearned to live with a change of seasons. Many California clients and friends had already moved away. If a natural disaster is my destiny, there is little I can do to escape. However, it is always wise to pay attention to the Still Small Voice Within regarding everything and anything—and then we all should be just fine.

17

THE ANGEL OF DEATH

When it comes to predicting death, I tend to be accurate. Should anyone ask me not to say anything about death, the request is honored. Sally Quinn never wants to know about death or serious accidents, things she cannot prevent. After attending my weekend tarot workshop, Sally seemed to prefer telephone readings. That way, if Key 13, Death, comes up in a reading, Sally is unable to see it. At times, the month, week, or day of a passing is predicted, but not always. Timing is never easy.

In reading for myself, I tend to learn more about my children and friends than about me. And yet, as early as 1967 I began to see inheritance cards, trauma and the death of a father figure in my spreads. The patterns seemed to relate to my children.

My mother died in 1958, but by 1967 my father still enjoyed good health. He had always looked young for his age. But time and again, the cards indicated sudden death and inheritance. On several occasions I had expressed concern to my friend, Pat Hawkings (Warner), about the possibility that my ex-husband Bill might pass away suddenly. Even though Bill had treated me badly since the divorce, I never wanted my children to grow up without their father. I had never had the love and care of a father throughout my childhood.

In April 1969, Bill's father died in Escanaba, Michigan. He was my children's grandfather. I figured he had to be the "father figure" that would leave an inheritance. My children were sure to benefit. The Jacobs family had means, the mother more than the father. Bill's mother had already died. Moreover, Bill had done very well financially himself.

Again, I ran my cards. The same swords were in the house of death next to the King of Cups (a water sign man), along with inheritance: the four of pentacles in the house of my children. I was puzzled and concerned.

That Memorial Day weekend, some friends and I drove to Asilomar in Pacific Grove to attend an A.R.E. conference. For some reason, I started talking about Bill nonstop, especially on the drive up and down California. I spoke of the mistakes I had made during our marriage, how glad I was to have Mark, how lucky I was that Bill had always treated Tomi as his own even before the adoption. My children were with Bill and Peggy, his new wife of three months, for the long weekend. My good friend Aquarius Diane Johnson wanted to drive. She was our neighbor in Glendale during my marriage to Bill: more on Diane later.

Late on Sunday, Bill brought the children home and acted out in his usual surly manner.

Early the next morning, Peggy called extremely upset. The night before, Bill had suddenly had a horrific headache before he lost consciousness. He was taken to St. John's Hospital in Santa Monica by ambulance. Bill was in ICU on a ventilator. He had suffered a major cerebral aneurysm, the possible result of a congenital birth defect, in an artery in his brain. It was as though his brain had been shot from the inside. The doctor doubted that he would survive. If he did, his brain damage would be extensive.

It was only six weeks after the death of his father. Clearly, Bill was the "father figure" in my cards for more than two years.

I was stunned.

I had quit smoking the previous year. However, when Diane arrived to drive me to St. John's Hospital in Santa Monica, I asked her for a cigarette. I had to see Bill to assess the situation in person. I was not up to driving. I was a nervous wreck.

When I entered Bill's private room in St. John's Hospital, he was hooked up by wires to various machines, including a respirator that made an ominous sound. In silence, I respectfully stood next to his bed for several minutes. Instantly, it was clear to me that Bill would no longer inhabit his body. In spite of his serious drinking every day of his adult life, he had been an avid tennis player and loved to ski. He was athletic. Therefore, in spite of numerous martinis, scotches, beer, wine and cognac on weekdays, Bloody Marys and screwdrivers on Sundays, and all the cigarettes he had smoked, Bill had always made it a point to eat right. That was probably what kept him on earth until just weeks short of his 47th birthday.

While we were married, Bill had said that he would surely die by age 55. He knew how he had pushed his body to its limits with his bad habits. William Oliver Jacobs left this earth on June 5, 1969. He would have been 47 on June 29. My children no longer had a father to love and care for them. That deeply pained me. And I was the one who had to give them the terrible news.

My children not only inherited a considerable sum from their father and paternal grandfather, but years later from their father's aunt. What that meant to me was money for college and other important patterns as they grew up. Mark was 7 and Tomi was 10 on the day of his death. The money made our lives easier. My children's inheritance provided me with an opportunity to build my clientele before they both left for college and my financial support from their trusts left with them.

On June 20, 1970, my Virgo stepsister, Ginger (Virginia Lee), went into labor to give birth to her fourth child. My astrologer friend, Tish Leroy, went with me to the hospital to await the blessed event. Ginger was having difficulties in her relationship. For that reason, Tish and I wanted to be supportive.

All of a sudden, with us in the waiting room, Tish said, "Ginger's in trouble and needs our help. She's trying to leave her body and this baby needs her."

I was startled.

The two of us began to meditate and send light to Ginger in the delivery room. I asked ministering angels to care for her. Our concern was not whether it might be her time to pass to the Other Side—we wanted to keep her on earth for the sake of her four children. We were doing an "intervention" with the Divine.

Sometime later, a nurse came into the waiting room to tell us that Ginger had a baby boy and was fine. We would be able to see her soon. I was puzzled.

After entering her room, Ginger immediately said, "I nearly died on the delivery table in the middle of having my baby."

Tish had been right. It seemed the ministering angels had done a fine job, for Ginger and baby Phillip were fine.

In the midst of her hard labor, Ginger had found herself surrounded by darkness, but the darkness had comforted her—it was warm and inviting. Then, she saw a bright light directly ahead of her that she seemed to be moving toward. There were people all around her that she could not see, but she somehow knew they were there. Ginger remembers thinking, *So this is the way it feels to die*—and she said it was a wonderful feeling. It was calm, peaceful, comfortable, and exceedingly dark, although she could see the light. It had been as though she was moving through a tunnel.

Next, Ginger remembered that her baby was being born. She could not die. She could not leave him. She said it seemed as though she was saying this to *someone* who told her she had to go back. That was when she heard the doctor saying numbers and he told the nurses, "She's back with us now. You can go and take care of the baby."

Afterwards, Ginger had tried to apologize to the nurses for talking of dying.

"It's all right. You're all right now," the nurse replied.

At that moment, I was happy that I had Tish with me. And yet, it was unfortunate that she never listened to her angels before joining Jim Jones in Guyana—for eight years later, along with over 900 other souls, she came face to face with the Angel of Death in the jungles of Jonestown.

Since timing is so difficult, with one California client things happened much sooner. I had predicted, "Within the next three years, I see you flying over the Rockies to your birthplace in Chicago to attend your mother's funeral. While looking down at the mountains, you'll remember my prediction." Three days later, her mother died of a massive stroke in Chicago. The next day she was flying over the Rockies and remembered my prediction.

Months later, in another reading, I could see her father-in-law needed gallbladder surgery, possibly within eight months. Because of complications, he could die on the table. That evening, she told her husband, "Get ready to say good-bye to your father." He was scheduled for gallbladder surgery in eight days. He hemorrhaged and died during surgery.

Early in the 1970s, I read for an older Pisces woman whose husband had been bedridden for years with a bad heart and Parkinson's disease. He had multiple heart attacks and strokes, but clung to life. In a later reading, she said she was tired of being his caretaker. He was getting worse and demanding more of her. Then, one spring I made a prediction: "He's going to have a massive heart attack or stroke and die the end of May or first of June."

When she returned later in the summer, she said, "My husband had a massive stroke on May 31st and died June 1st You couldn't have been more accurate." I doubted that she was going to last long after being married to him for 50 years. I never heard from her again.

Occasionally, clients committed suicide, something I had tried to discourage. A woman with a wealthy husband leapt from a San Diego Freeway overpass. After being hit and run over by several cars, it took her hours to die. Her act seemed selfish, since she could have taken others with her. She knew about her husband's mistress. She had three children. After having an affair with her neighbor's son, aged 17, and getting caught, she started to read the Bible, perhaps unwise for someone mentally unstable. I had feared suicide during her last reading. She was 40.

Another client slit her wrists in a warm bathtub. She had suffered from chronic pain for three years. Two other beautiful young women in their 30s used shotguns to end their lives. I attended one funeral. All the deaths seemed pointless. Edgar Cayce warned that suicide sets one up for a lonely existence the next time. Those left behind feel guilty for not doing enough.

In 1978, Virgo actor Peter Sellers had several readings. Peter was referred by actress Shirley MacLaine during their film *Being There*. I was a fan of Inspector Clouseau from Peter's zany *Pink Panther* films. I thought perhaps we would laugh a lot, but Peter Sellers was very serious about anything to do with the paranormal. Peter was a true believer.

First, Peter had a regular reading. Then he scheduled the Master Spread delineated in my book, *The Wheel of Destiny*. Only the 22 keys of the Tarot Major Arcana are used in my life reading that covers talents, skills, career, finances, health, love, marriage, children, and past lives. The Master Spread takes a minimum of three hours. We had a lunch break in the middle. His driver waiting in the limo brought Peter a soft drink, burger and fries for lunch, which he ate at our picnic table underneath the grape arbor near the top of our hill.

Mark had built the arbor and helped me plant our huge hillside garden. The grapes were always small but very tasty. Frequently, I had lunch up there and watched the hawks circling for prey. However, for me it was nearly impossible to go up the hill without pulling some weeds or pruning something. Gardening was my hobby. My hillside garden was my attempt to emulate the garden on Key 3, The Empress, since Venus rules my Libra rising.

Late in the autumn, before he returned to London, Peter had another reading. That time, Key 13, Death, was in the first house, which relates to the physical body. I tried to play down the meaning while Peter stared and stared at the card. The card also relates to change, rebirth and transformation, besides the inevitable. At the time, the planet Saturn was in Virgo transiting Peter's Sun, which would continue for 18 months. I warned him to be careful with his health, to eat right and take good care of himself. Admittedly, several clients have died with Saturn transiting the Sun, although death is not always indicated, rather restriction and hardship of some sort. At age 38, Peter Sellers had experienced a near-fatal heart attack. He had recently received a pacemaker. His heart had been a problem for him for years.

That year other matters of the heart were also of concern to Peter. He had recently separated from his fourth wife, but he still loved her. A London numerologist had said she was bad for him because of her numbers. I told him to think for himself. If he was still in love with her, then he should be with her, if that was what he really wanted. I sensed his remaining time on earth was short, although I never told him that. The decision was up to Peter, not to some numerologist—or to me!

In July 1980, the news of Peter Sellers' death at age 54 from a massive heart attack was not a surprise. Still, I was sad that he had died so young. I placed a memorial candle for Peter in my reading room, a small votive candle that typically burns up in a few hours. Peter Sellers' candle burned for three long days. That was amazing! Perhaps his soul needed help with his numerous fans and loved ones so distraught over his passing and holding on. I wished him well on his journey to the Light.

In the early 1980s, there was a tough year when eight children died, each child related to a client. A young man with physical disabilities drove out into the desert and shot himself. That suicide was picked up after the fact. Another client was warned of serious drug use by her teenage daughter. Sadly, her only child, 17, overdosed on drugs. A boy of only 10 hung himself on his bedroom door. His father had to break a window to enter the room. It seemed like an accident, but his mother said that her son had been despondent after another boy he considered his best friend had turned on him. Another client's two-year-old granddaughter drowned in a swimming pool. The horror stories of children went on and on that year.

Perhaps the strangest death concerned a boy of nine. In his mother's reading I had warned her to watch him around water that summer. My impression: he might fall and hit his head, perhaps on the cement of a swimming pool. I was unable to shake the ominous feeling.

Summer passed without incident. Then, in September the family went to the beach for the day. There was a large driftwood log on the sand not far from the sea. Her son and another boy began digging under the log so they could crawl into the hole as it filled with water. Then, all at once, with her son under the log, the incoming tide lifted the driftwood, and as the water receded, the huge log crushed her son's skull.

News of his untimely death saddened me. However, his mother told me a story. The year before his death, her son said that he had lived as a man many years ago. He said he had lived in Chicago. He had died as a soldier in WWII and he said that he was fairly old at the time: 30. He also told her that he might not live very long this lifetime. As she told me the story we both were covered with chills.

Years later, relating her sad story to my Leo friend Nikki, it turned out that one of her sons was the same age and had attended the same school as the boy who died. A tree had been planted in the schoolyard in the boy's memory. I had sympathized with the boy's mother and had commented on her bravery at the time. Perhaps it was because of what her son had told her about living as a man before in Chicago.

In a reading for a recently remarried client, it seemed that her new husband had a serious problem with his lungs (lung cancer). Her husband smoked and was scheduled for a physical for a new job. Lung cancer was diagnosed. His possible death also showed up in the cards of her children, her sister, and her two nieces. Her husband suffered with his illness for three years and continued to smoke. He had worked as a geophysicist in Asia. During that time he explored Buddhism and yoga. In the last year of his illness, an Asian spirit guide showed up to help him. No one else could see his spirit guide. Plus, he waited until his wife left the hospital to die. Many clients have shared amazing stories of assistance from beyond the veil and stories of loved ones dying after they have left the room.

I predicted the death of Natalie Wood to several clients, not by name but by the description of a petite, brunette, Cancer-Leo actress. I seldom pick up names to pass on to my clients. One client had given Natalie a manicure and pedicure right before the tragic weekend. In her cards I saw a famous actress, married with children, dying in a boating accident. She would be the only one to drown.

When Natalie Wood's death was announced over the car radio, I was driving Mark to LAX to return to college after the Thanksgiving holiday. Both of us were shocked.

The cards of Gemini actress Sharon Gless indicated the widowing of an Aquarius actor she had worked with, Robert Wagner, in *Switch*. In a prior reading, there was another death in her cards of an Aries actor, David Janssen from a heart attack. Sharon and David worked together in *Centennial*.

In 1981, there were ominous cards in my cards again in the house of children. Someone was going to die at a distance: 9 of Swords. I lived in California. Mark lived in Arizona. My pregnant daughter Tomi lived in Colorado. Each child lived "at a distance."

Tomi had asked me to wait to come to Denver until after the baby was born. By divine coincidence, the week my first grandson was due to arrive I had no clients booked. Clever spirit guides! Tomi called early on August 19, 1981, to tell me that I was a grandmother: Oliver James had arrived. Immediately, I packed my car and was soon driving toward Colorado. My client-friend, Dr. Richard Blasband, had rented a house near Aspen for the summer. Dick had generously invited me to use his guest room and do readings for his friends. My life seemed to be in perfect order.

In Aspen, the call from Tomi came earlier than expected. The Sunday after I arrived in Aurora, Tomi and James took young Oliver to church. For some reason, I had this strange, restless feeling, so I decided to stay home.

Soon the telephone rang.

My stepsister Ginger was calling from California. Her 18-year-old son, Brian, and his two older brothers, Joel and Dennis, had gone to a reservoir to swim and cool off. Evidently, Brian had made his way out to the center of the reservoir on his own in an inner tube, but he was a poor swimmer. All at once, Brian was out of the inner tube and in trouble. By the time his brothers realized the gravity of the situation, neither of them could swim fast enough to get to him in time. Brian disappeared under the water.

Ginger was sure that Brian had made it to the other side of the reservoir. She thought perhaps he was disoriented, but safe on the distant shore. And yet, all the time Ginger was telling me her feelings I had this sinking feeling. Brian was safe all right—on the other shore of life. He may have been disoriented to find himself out of his body.

After hanging up the telephone, I felt numb. I drove to a gas station to fill my tank. In my disorientation, I forgot the gas cap and ended up having to buy another.

The following week I drove to New Mexico to stay with my Virgo client-friend, Doreen Sheafor, in Santa Fe. From her place, I called Ginger to see what had happened. The day his father and uncle had decided to make a last-ditch effort to find him, Brian's body surfaced not far from them in the reservoir. At least the family had closure.

Tragically, the dark cards of the death of a child "at a distance" had come to pass. I was in Colorado, far from my home in California. The cards had provided me with an accurate warning, but no specifics. Many times in psychic work it is only much later when the cards or a fleeting image makes any real sense.

My prediction of the death of Lee Strasberg, Susan's father, to her stepmother Anna was only months off. It was my sense that Lee would live to 79. He passed at age 80 and four months. Months earlier, Lee had had an out-of-body experience while Anna was in Caracas, Venezuela, to see her family. Lee suddenly found himself in a room filled with people. When a glass fell and shattered, he was instantly pulled back into his body in his bed in California. Lee had seen himself lying in his bed before he suddenly woke up. His experience had been similar to mine years before. Lee had confided his experience to Susan and he admitted that he was frightened. Lee thought he had died.

After her father's death, Susan attended a film festival in Japan and took her daughter, Jennifer with her. In Japan, Susan went to see a medium and a strange thing happened. Her father used his granddaughter, Pisces Jennifer, to speak to his daughter Susan, Jenny's mother. Through Jennifer, Lee told Susan to go the house in Bel Air on a certain day to pick up a certain record album and a book while Anna would not be there. At the time, there was incredible animosity between Susan and Anna over her father's estate.

The reason that Anna was going to be out of the house on that particular day was because of an event to honor Lee Strasberg—to which Susan had not been invited. Unsuspecting, innocent Jennifer, then 16, had unwittingly become a trance medium to channel the voice of her grandfather. At this time, Jennifer does not remember anything about what transpired while her grandfather took over her body to speak with her mother, Susan. A friend of Susan, one of her astrologers, Jeffrey Geist, said Susan told him that Jenny spoke in Yiddish while she was channeling Lee. Jennifer does not happen to know Yiddish. Lee Strasberg was born in what is now the Ukraine and he was raised speaking Yiddish.

On the specified day, Susan entered the unlocked house owned by her father and Anna. Sadly, Susan had neglected to write down either the name of the composer or the record. Susan had contacted several psychics and mediums to try to determine the name of the composer or the record. No one was able to pick up on it, including me. Susan had thought perhaps there was another will in the album.

Neither Susan, nor Jennifer, nor Susan's brother John had inherited anything from the wealthy Lee Strasberg. Marilyn Monroe had left her entire estate to Lee and Paula Strasberg,

Susan and John's father and mother. The Monroe estate was sold by Anna Strasberg for an extremely large sum many years later. Marilyn's white piano, which was supposed to have ben left to Susan, was sold at auction for more than $1 million. I think Paula's portion of the Monroe estate should have been passed on to Susan, John and Jennifer. The matter ultimately rests with the conscience of Anna Strasberg—and with the Lords of Karma.

On the other hand, discarnate spirits are rarely concerned with material matters. Susan told me that both the book and the record album Lee had talked about through Jenny referred to the existence of life after death. It was a "divine inheritance" her father had left Susan, who must now be reunited with her parents and her once-famous friend known all around the world as Marilyn Monroe. Susan received Marilyn's pearls, which were a gift from the Emperor of Japan, but she had to sell them to pay off debts. Susan was going to receive the check for the pearls on the day that she died. Susan has written about Marilyn Monroe in her book, *Marilyn and Me—Sisters, Rivals, Friends.*

In 1984, after our house in California sold, I traveled for six months. My initial journey involved driving across the country and stopping in various cities to work. I spent a month at the Stoneleigh Hotel in Dallas, since the locals kept calling. That August, I had a call from a producer in California concerned about a friend missing in Hawaii. His friend and two other men had rented a catamaran out of Honolulu and gone sailing. That afternoon a huge storm came up all of a sudden. I told him I needed to meditate. He should call back in 20 minutes.

It was instantly clear to me that all three men and the boat were gone.

"But he's a really good swimmer," he protested.

"Not that good."

Neither the catamaran nor the three men, all in their 30s, were ever located.

After working in Washington for two weeks, I flew on to London. That spring Gwen Davis had another reading and in her cards I could see "the death of a father figure." Her aging father lived in Tucson. Gwen planned to be in the South of France writing a novel while I was in Europe. She invited me to visit. Other clients had already invited me to England, Switzerland, Italy, and Spain. My trip was shaping up nicely. Because of Gwen I would see Cannes, St. Tropes, and maybe Monte Carlo.

In London, I called Gwen. Her trip had been canceled. Her husband, Don Mitchell, 45, had terminal lung cancer. Don had quit smoking five years earlier, apparently not soon enough. Don was the love of her life. I was stunned. I had never considered the "father figure" might be the father of her children. Eleven weeks later—Don Mitchell was gone.

After Don's death, Gwen witnessed several mysterious events involving the appearance of white feathers. Gwen is not the only one to receive white feathers from the Other Side. Spirits manifest different items: rose petals, feathers, and even coins.

In Milan that summer, when I was traveling with client-friend, Aquarius designer Valerie Barad, and I did readings for some of her friends and competitors. One man from Canada had an aging mother. I told him that he needed to spend more time with her since his mother's time was growing short. She passed away the following year. When Valerie ran into him again, he said he was grateful to have been warned of his mother's death. My prediction had softened the blow. He had spent quality time with her before her passing. My reading had provided a Cosmic Time Table.

"To everything there is a season … a time to be born and a time to die." That covers the entire Universe—and the Multiverse!

In one reading for Valerie, I could see that her mother would pass while she was away on business. Her mother died when Valerie was in Taiwan overseeing handbag production. Many loved ones do not want us around when their time comes. Our suffering can delay their passing. At times, people keep their loved ones in sickly bodies against their will. Try to let them go.

One man in his early 40s told his wife and children that he was going to die that week. He did nothing overt to bring about his death. He spent the week in bed or on the sofa. According to his wife, he was not ill. At the end of the week, he peacefully passed away in his sleep. He was a student of spiritual studies and intuitively knew that it was his time.

In the 1970s, I warned two women of the early death of their respective husbands and advised each to purchase life insurance. One woman's husband was an alcoholic but held a responsible position with a major oil company. They had separate bedrooms. She was opposed to divorce. That Pisces purchased insurance on her husband worth $250,000, an adequate sum at the time. The other client had a good marriage. She and her husband owned gasoline stations with a major oil company. He was a mechanic and smoked heavily. Her policy was for $500,000. The heavy smoker died of lung cancer. Both men died in their early 50s and both ladies collected on the policies! I was happy to be of service.

Another client, the wife of a famous actor, said that her husband went out two weeks before his death and made special arrangements with his lawyer, accountant and business manager. He wanted things to be taken care of "in case something happened to him." His will was in order and their joint monies secure, with a large account in her name. The children were grown and self-sufficient but also provided for in his will. He had a bad heart, but the doctor thought things were under control. At 59, he had a massive heart attack but he left his affairs in perfect order.

Early in 1980, one pretty actress-client, the ex-wife of a well-known film director, fell madly in love with another famous film director. The man was separated from his famous singer-actress wife, but not divorced. His wife refused to let go. My client desperately wanted to marry the director. Her former husband had long since been married to another famous singer-actress. Her question for her reading was whether the film director would marry her.

"You'll be a widow before you're a wife," popped out of my mouth without knowing what I actually meant.

The tragedy occurred not long after that: The film director made a wrong turn getting out a helicopter and walked right into the rear rotating propeller. He died hours later, but not before his wife dramatically rushed to his side. Unfortunately, my client could not even attend his funeral. The affair was under wraps until his wife agreed to a settlement. Maybe next time? Another client told me about the loss of her best friend, 42, to breast cancer the year before. While meditating, she had heard her friend's voice and sensed her presence.

"What's it like to die?" she had asked.

"It's like being reabsorbed back into the body of God," her friend replied.

Ponder *THAT.*

Moments after the father of another client died, her bedridden mother found him sitting on her bed early in the morning. There was a nurse in the room at three o'clock when her mother sat up and exclaimed, "Look, George is here! He's come to say good-bye."

The nurse was unable to see him; only his wife of 60 years watched her beloved husband walk into the Light.

Months later my client was out walking near the Chesapeake Bay, crying her heart out. She had always been close to her father, so she was upset that her father had not come to her on the night of his passing or since, as far as she could tell. She was talking to him aloud, crying and carrying on, in accordance with her true Cancer nature, bitterly complaining in the crisp autumn air. Then, all of a sudden, a strong wind whipped up a large pile of leaves and swirled them all around her as she distinctly heard her father say, "Well, Sue (pseudonym), do you get it now?"

Her father was no doubt with her all along. She had been so wrapped up in herself that she never bother to listen. Many of us are too self-centered and wrapped up in ourselves to stop and listen to our thoughts and feelings. Spirits speak inside your head, more often in thought than in audible sounds. Pay attention. Learn to quiet your mind and you will never miss out on what a loved one is trying to tell you—especially days after he or she has crossed over!

For me, November 1988 through May 1989 was extremely difficult. Ten people died in less than six months, including my father, dear friends, good clients, and the newborn son of a client with only daughters. I had to advise her to pull the plug on her newborn, even though there were no more children in her future. The doctor had said he could not be saved: multiple heart defects and other problems. That reading was difficult for me and probably worse for her.

In November, my father woke me up after his death at age 78. He was standing beside my bed at three o'clock in the morning. I looked at him in my sleepy state and said, "I forgive you for your many mistakes." He had never financially or emotionally supported me, although I was his only child. Then I promptly went back to sleep.

I had flown to California to be with him the prior year for his cancer surgery. I never went back for his funeral. The doctor had openly lied about my father's condition. He had refused to even look at me when he talked to me. Dying people are big business in the medical profession. My father had one surgery after another as he was in and out of hospitals, which is a sad scenario for too many individuals. He died within a year. What my father's plight has taught me is to have morphine, if necessary, and forget about the rest. Some people are kept alive who would be better off crossing over to the Other Side. No heroic measures for me!

My good Taurus friend Les Szarvas died in his 50s from hepatitis C. Les was gay and had volunteered to work with AIDS patients. He had lost many friends who were HIV-positive. I have lost too many talented clients for the same reason. Les used to make the hot mulled wine with cranberry juice for our Christmas parties, and he always gave me unusual gifts. After I moved to Maine, he sent me purple socks to keep my feet warm over the winter. Les always stopped by when I lived in Woodland Hills on Christmas or Thanksgiving for another piece of pie and another cup of coffee. We met in the 1960s at the Cameo Playhouse. In the early days, we spent hours in Denny's drinking buckets of decaf coffee and talking into the wee hours about our love of the theater.

That summer, Les called to tell me that he had hepatitis. Even then, I never realized how sick he really was. He was a composer and lyricist for children's TV shows and had written the music for 15 episodes of *H. R. Pufnstuf*. His enormous collection of records and albums numbered in the millions, all catalogued and organized by year, song, singer, composer, lyricist, movie, or television show. I was happy for his success, but upset when our mutual Gemini friend, Lilavati Sharma, failed to call and tell me Les was in the hospital and not expected to live. The only thing she said the day before his death was that his family was "coming to hospital the next day to take him home."

When I called the hospital early the next morning, Les had already gone to our Home on the Other Side. I sent flowers to his funeral, upset that no one had let me know how serious things were. I would have flown to California to say good-bye in person.

Days after his death, I was sitting on my bed thinking about him when the mirror on my antique mahogany dresser started to vibrate. Something similar happened when a Mack truck drove by out on the boulevard. There was no truck, but the mirror was vibrating, vibrating and vibrating!

Finally, I got up and put my hand on the mirror to stop it.

"It's okay, Les. I know you're here. I'm sorry I didn't come to see you and say goodbye in person," I said, sitting down on my bed to cry, feeling sure that he was standing there thinking, *Fine psychic she is, she can't even see me or hear what I'm saying to her!*

Months after Bill died in 1969, after we moved into the house in Sherman Oaks rented by my children's trust's, I went to an Edgar Cayce study group meeting off Mulholland Drive one evening and decided to leave the children home alone. I asked them to go to bed by nine and lock the doors. They had school in the morning. Tomi was 11 and Mark barely 8. I was anxious about leaving them alone, but thought they might be fine for two hours.

However, when I arrived home at ten, the front door was standing wide open.

My heart started to race. There was a lamp lit in the living room as I rushed to my children's rooms. Tomi and Mark were both sound asleep. Unharmed. Praise the Lord. I ran to the back door, which was also standing wide open. Quickly, I closed and locked the door, my heart racing. Then, with my sigh of relief, I distinctly heard the cruel note of Bill Jacob's sardonic laughter. I went back to the front door and locked it—as Bill really LAUGHED.

"Okay, Bill. I GET IT!"

After that, I hired baby sitters until Tomi was 12.

The same year, after the purchase of our new Pontiac station wagon, compliments of the Jacobs' Trust, one Saturday I drove to Joseph Magnum's to have my hair cut. The car radio was tuned to semi-classical music and I made sure the window on the driver's side was closed. It looked like rain. Then, I locked the car and hurried in to see my hairdresser.

Bill had always preferred classical music or jazz. He looked down his nose on pop or semi-classical. After having my hair done, I returned to the car and found the window on the driver's side down. It was my first car with electric windows, so I distinctly remembered closing the windows. Never would I leave a new car window open as an invitation to theft. And then, when I started the car, the radio came on with classical music!

"I know, Bill, it's really your car! But I'm the one driving it!" I said aloud, chuckling all the way home.

In June 1999, a client from Dallas called early in the morning to tell me that the son of a mutual friend had been killed in a car accident late the night before. Sadly, Noah had died on his Gemini mother Janene's birthday. Immediately, I sensed the accident had been Noah's fault, that drugs or alcohol were involved. Janene and I were no longer as close as we once were, but my heart went out to her in losing her only child. It was a true tragedy.

In Camden, Maine, I went downstairs to fix breakfast.

All of a sudden, Noah flooded my mind with his powerful thoughts: *Tell her how sorry I am. Tell her I was stupid. Tell her I love her. Tell her I fucked up. Tell her how grateful I am for all the things she's done for me.* He was a strong Leo and he was getting through to me, loud and clear. Noah had instantly realized his folly the moment he found himself out of his body and unable to get back in. *Tell her I screwed up* filled my mind, *please tell her.* PLEASE!

Noah sincerely wanted his mother, Janene, to know how much he loved her and how deeply sorry he was for his responsibility for his own death. He knew he had created enormous emotional pain for his mother.

At first, it was difficult to find the number. Finally, I was able to call Janene to deliver her son's message. She had immediately flown to Dallas from New York City, where she was then living, and was just entering Noah's apartment as my call reached her. It was the most mediumistic I have ever been in my entire life.

The Angel of Death is compassionate in welcoming us when our time comes to leave this dimension. Occasionally, an old model needs to be turned in on a newer edition to get on with life's endless, wondrous and remarkable journey—more on that to come!

18

WARS AND RUMORS OF REVOLUTIONS

I never realized that one of my California client's was Iranian royalty. I only knew she had been born somewhere in the Middle East. My clients come from almost everywhere. She had divorced a highly successful Hollywood film producer, and in those days, she lived on a beautiful estate in Beverly Hills. I usually did her readings in the charming solarium with its view of the lush backyard. One reading indicated "the overthrow of government in her homeland, dramatic revolution with blood in the streets. Her family would be safe in the midst of chaos." I never realized I was predicting the overthrow of the Shah of Iran and the rise of Islamic fundamentalism until much later.

Soon after the revolution started, and His Imperial Majesty of Iran (formerly Persia) was safely in exile, Parvaneh insisted that I listen to her tape. With clients in the film industry, many of them actors, directors or producers, it can be difficult to know if I am picking up on a film being made or on a person's actual life. Years earlier, I had told an actress that she was going to be pregnant, something she was not eager to experience because of her career. Sometime later, she left me a message, "Watch me on thus and so on channel seven on Thursday at 7:30—I'm pregnant!" Sometimes the reel world infringes on the real world! With my Iranian client, it was a real revolution in her native homeland of Iran.

In 1991, near the time of the first Gulf War, many young military clients had readings that indicated something big was brewing in the Middle East. Several soldiers were going on "secret missions" to a destination in a "distant desert." That year, my son Captain Mark Lawrence Jacobs of the U.S. Air Force, was TDY (Temporary Duty) in Barcelona, flying a refueling tanker filled with supplies into Saudi Arabia. The operation was known as "Desert Shield," the precursor to "Desert Storm," the first Iraq War. The American people learned of the invasion of Iraq on the evening news that January as President George H.W. Bush made the surprise announcement.

The day after the war started, January 18, 1991, I was flying out of Dulles to LAX to work with my Los Angeles clients for two months. The airport was a zoo, with one long line for security. My flight stopped at Dallas-Fort Worth (DFW), where Mark was due to arrive at Carswell Air Force Base. Mark was still in his flight suit when he met me in the airport.

"You've no idea how grateful I am you don't fly a fighter or a bomber," I said as I hugged and kissed my handsome son.

News of the war was on all the monitors. Mark was weary but glad to be home. He was living with his fiancée, Chelle, with the wedding date set for May. My daughter-in-law is now Dr. Chelle Trunk Jacobs and the mother of three of my adorable grandchildren: Justin William (May 24, 1994), Chase Mathew (July 11, 1995) and Autumn Elizabeth (April 21, 1998).

In 1991, when I reached California, the progress of Desert Storm was being reported everywhere, rattling the nerves of the American people. Our military and our allies were fighting the army of Saddam Hussein in the deserts of Kuwait and Iraq. Why they never went all the way to Baghdad that year, I will never understand.

Early 1990, one Middle Eastern college student had several readings that continued after my move to Maine in 1994. "Your Scorpio father, a powerful military leader, will one day be restored to power in his country. The tyrannical leader he wishes to destroy will be destroyed," I predicted. The girl had been born in Lebanon. I had no clue about the country involved. Her mother in London also had readings and was also born in Lebanon. Then I received her father's birth data. He was born in Baghdad.

In 2002, my prediction came true. Her father was from a prominent Iraqi family. He had been involved with organizing military actions among the Kurds in Northern Iraq. The tyrannical leader he hoped to depose: Saddam Hussein. After the U.S. invasion in 2003, her father was restored to power—and the tyrant was hanged (destroyed).

Long before the terrorist attacks on September 11, 2001, on the World Trade Center in New York City and the Pentagon in Washington, D.C., I had several strange visions without fully realizing their meaning. These visions were accompanied by intermittent anxiety and a sense of unrest. Images for 1999, 2000, and 2001 World Predictions, posted on my website (www.patriciamclaine.com) included terrorist attacks. It always troubles me when insufficient information is received with no way to prevent terrible things from happening. The airy-fairy psychics get on my nerves with their symbols, scriptures, and poetry. Even Nostradamus is not easy to understand! But he had to be extremely wary of the nasty Inquisitors.

In the spring of 2001, I read for a young Muslim man named Mohammed. He refused to give me his address. Over the years I have read for many men named "Mohammed," in addition to others with common or unusual names from Middle Eastern cities and countries who were born in or lived in Dubai, Bahrain, Lebanon, Iran, Yemen, Amman, Saudi Arabia, London, Geneva, Rome, New York City, and Washington, D.C.

This Mohammed had been born in Kabul, Afghanistan. He was having his first Saturn Return, which is a momentous time that occurs between the age of 28 and 30—a time of Destiny. He had a new pilot's license and was proud to have learned how to fly 757s and 767s in Arizona. (This fact certainly gave me pause at a later date.) He had my 32-minute, $100 reading. Frankly, there was something about him that almost forced me to hold my breath. *Apprehension* comes to mind in terms of how he made me feel, definitely anxious.

"Your wish is going to come true," I said.

Key 17, The Star, answered his wish or question. This is the "wish card" of the Tarot Major Arcana. Key 17 is Aquarius, which rules the 11th house of hopes and wishes—the Key of "dreams come true." Aquarius is the sign of Fixed Air.

His face lit up. "That is good!" he said, looking very happy.

And yet, in the pillar with that card was another card of great conflict, Key 16, The Tower, directly above Key 17, The Star (16 precedes 17). The Tower, among other things indicates war, destruction and catastrophe, as the royal figures of the conscious and subconscious mind perilously fall from the flaming tower.

"The granting of your wish could result in great conflict or war."

"But that is good!" Mohammed said, and he laughed. "That is as it should be."

His tremendous enjoyment in that moment had started to make me feel apprehensive. I got chills and wondered how a "great war" or "great destruction" might accomplish anything good, anything positive?

He paid cash. Then, fortunately, he left. There was something almost scary about the man.

Perhaps by divine coincidence, on September 11, 2001, I had no appointments. My spirit guides were up to their old tricks. I had slept in later than usual. As I was heading for the kitchen to turn on the burner under the teakettle, the telephone rang.

"Do you have your television on?" my Capricorn friend Judy Diamond inquired in a tense voice from her office in downtown D.C.

"No."

"Well, turn it on. A large jet just crashed into the World Trade Center in New York."

My television set was on in time for me to see the second plane, United Airlines Flight 175, crash into the South Tower of the World Trade Center in New York City at 9:03 a.m. My reaction was no doubt the same as that of many other Americans—complete shock and disbelief! This was not some Hollywood blockbuster—it was real and intentional—which was obvious the moment that the second plane hit the South Tower.

All I knew at that shocking moment: the first plane that hit the North Tower had been from American Airlines. My son was a first officer (co-pilot) for America West Airlines. Feeling tremendous apprehension, I called Mark's home in Azle, Texas, fully aware that my son did not fly to New York at that time.

Thankfully, Mark answered the telephone. The previous day he had worked a trip to DFW, an overnight. Moments later, the flight he was to take out that morning, the same as countless others flights at airports across the nation, was grounded by the Federal Aviation Administration. My gratitude was great, knowing that my son was home with his family during a national emergency, a tragic time for our country.

Since my rented apartment at the Park Center in Alexandria was only a 10-minute drive from the Pentagon, I heard the explosion of American Airlines Flight 77 crashing into that building. On that day our entire nation was waiting for the other shoe to drop. Where or when was the next attack going to take place? What was going to blow up next and in what American city? What about the White House? The Capitol Building? The Department of Justice? The State Department? The Statue of Liberty?

Before there was time to even think, the South Tower of the World Trade Center collapsed, looking much like the pyroclastic flow of a volcanic eruption! It was unreal!

Soon, there was news of United Flight 93 crashing somewhere in Pennsylvania. My first thought: the military had no choice but to bring down the plane with a missile. However, the brave passengers on that airplane had courageously taken matters into their own hands and sacrificed their lives in an act of extreme bravery.

Minutes later, the North Tower of the World Trade Center collapsed. Amid the horrendous rubble from the two towers and the destruction at the Pentagon were the broken bodies of many brave and innocent men and women from many different nations. The property losses of many corporations and different countries seemed inestimable. Not only Americans had died on that day. September 11, 2001 involved an international horror that resounded around the world.

Many times after that horrific day, I was forced to wonder about the young pilot named Mohammed who had learned how to fly 767s in Arizona. I studied the photographs of the hijackers on the Internet, but his face did not seem to be among them. I had only seen him the one time. Perhaps he was among those thwarted in Chicago, Los Angeles, or other U.S. cities. Because I was unsure, I never gave his telephone number to the authorities.

For years, I have had numerous Middle Eastern clients from Saudi Arabia, Iraq, Iran, Afghanistan, Kuwait, Yemen, Syria, Jordan, and other Muslim nations. A favorite client from Tehran named Shahpassand was a joy to read for. In fact, it is a pleasure for me to read for those of all faiths, races and nationalities.

When commercial flights were allowed into the air again in the United States, on the tarmac at DFW in Texas, my son Mark was the first co-pilot in an America West 737 to taxi out for his flight to Phoenix. Mark said it was very eerie to be the only plane on the runway in such a large commercial airport where so many different flights were usually taking off and landing. It has been the good karma of the United States that no commercial flights have had to be grounded since then because of further acts of terrorism. Tight airport security has been one result of that day's events.

Traumatic events in the lives of people often show up in readings, although not always enough to do anything to prevent a tragedy. I do my best to keep my clients safe. It still bothers me that our national security system failed to prevent those horrendous attacks inside the United States. The CIA, FBI, NSA, DIA, and Homeland Security would not listen to the predictions of some psychic—in spite of Nancy and Ronald Reagan and Joan Quigley and Jeanne Dixon!

Among my predictions for 2001: "Unexpected dramatic changes could well involve the threat of war. Negotiation is necessary to avert disaster."

Surprise attacks by Islamic militant terrorists led to wars in Afghanistan and Iraq. The attacks against the United States of America on September 11, 2001 were indeed acts of war.

Death rules in the South, with fire in the sky, in and under the ground, sounded airy-fairy as the words filled my mind on January 3, 2001, about events destined to transpire in 2001. What did it mean? Volcanic eruption? Why did New York City skyscrapers fleetingly enter my mind? It did not make sense to me. Still, the words were written down and posted with no mention of New York City.

The large jet that crashed into the World Trade Center on September 11, had taken off from Boston, Massachusetts. New York City is hundreds of miles to the south of Boston.

On August 7, 2001, in a reading for Betty Sue, a school teacher in Virginia, I said, "You're going to hear from someone

who will be affected by a volcanic eruption or an earthquake."
She had no idea what I was talking about.

Later, Betty Sue said, "You must have been speaking of my
son who lived in New York City at the time of the attack on
the World Trade Center. The smoke and ash appeared like a
volcanic eruption, and the news media said the collapse of the
Twin Towers had the force of a small earthquake." Her son's
friend, who worked in one of the towers, was never found.

In reading for Ava, a student in North Carolina, on July
23, 2001, I predicted, "Someone you know will be murdered,
possibly through an act of terrorism."

As it turned out, Ava knew the captain and one flight
attendant aboard American Airlines Flight 77 that crashed
into the Pentagon. They were not close, but she had worked
with them. She never re-listened to her tape until October 8.
As stated in her testimonial on my website:

"Listening to the part about the murder, I was stunned! I
hadn't remembered that part until I heard it again."

Several clients had visions or dreams of possible terrorist
attacks. Not long after September 11, I spoke with a man at
DIA (Defense Intelligence Agency) at the Pentagon. I explained
the vagueness of my impressions and predictions on terrorism.
There was nothing specific to warrant preparedness in any
city. My chief concern was for tunnels and bridges, besides the
Statue of Liberty, which symbolizes the freedom of Americans.
Freedom coveted and denied by fanatical, extremist, religious
codes in some Muslim nations.

One male client in New York City was put in touch with
the man at the Pentagon to perhaps shed some light. The
dreams and impressions received by most are too vague to be
of use to the authorities during crucial times. Hindsight often
makes our dreams or perceptions easier to understand long
after a tragedy has occurred.

When Osama bin Laden escaped capture from vast numbers of U.S. soldiers and marines deployed to Afghanistan, I had to wonder what kind of war my country was fighting. American lives were being lost for questionable purposes in a war that might never be won. Guerrilla tactics were being employed in faraway countries lacking in modern conveniences at a time of remarkable technological advancement. The enemy was not to be found in any specific location, but seemed to be everywhere—or nowhere. Men educated in the United States had turned against what they considered to be a lack of values. No small nation could invade America and conquer its vast territory. The British discovered that during the War of 1812, when the United States did not yet reach from sea to shining sea.

Since 2002, fighting wars in the Middle East has seemed futile. Before the invasion of Iraq, I told the man at the Pentagon that Saddam Hussein did NOT possess weapons of mass destruction and had NOT been involved in the attacks of September 11th. Saddam Hussein was smarter than that. The U.S. had once assisted him in fighting the Iranians, at that time allied with Russia. In my opinion, Afghanistan has become another Vietnam. And was the Iraq War won?

It seems pointless to try to convert the world to a limited concept of culture or morality. America is a nation of immigrants that still pour into the country to pursue the American dream. Perhaps we should fix what needs fixing here before we try to fix the rest of the world. There seems to be plenty of things that need attention.

UFOS AND THE ALIEN PRESENCE

In 1965, early one Sunday morning driving home from a late-night party at the beach, I stopped at a freeway off-ramp and looked up. To my utter amazement, there was a large, circular, silver disk, like nothing I had ever seen before, silently rising up in the morning sky over the distant foothills. Astonished, I sat and stared. Someone honked a horn, so I drove on. Then I stopped on the side of the road, but the object was gone. Later, I had trouble not thinking about the silver disk rising in the morning sky. Was it my "overactive imagination"—or had it been a spaceship flying off to some other world?

In my bed I had tried to sleep, vaguely remembering an event in my childhood from the summer of 1947. That July weekend, my Uncle Paul said, "One of those flying saucers has crashed out in the desert in New Mexico," and I noticed the headline of the *Los Angeles Times*—a flying saucer had crashed near Roswell, New Mexico. I never knew of the later report about a weather balloon!

Although most of my experiences since 1964 were fairly far out, I was not a UFO enthusiast. I had never read a book on the subject. Trance mediums were something else, séances, anything to do with psychic phenomena: life after death, reincarnation, past lives, mental telepathy, astrology, numerology, premonitions about the future or seeing into the past. I had read countless books on those subjects.

In 1971, a client brought me a coffee table-type book and left it with me for a week. The book had colorful pictures, perhaps taken in Switzerland or Germany, of large circular spaceships. That was years before I learned of a UFO contactee in Switzerland named Billy Meier. Supposedly, Billy's photographs were taken 1975–1982. The other pictures had been taken earlier and were published in a limited edition in Europe. Perhaps those pictures involved some of Meier's human-looking Pleiadians. There are only drawings of them on his website, no photographs. I wish I had paid closer attention to that book.

I had looked at the pictures and briefly glanced at the text. At the time, I felt strange enough without being involved with extraterrestrials and unidentified flying objects. I had spoken to dead people and seen nature spirits. I read tarot cards to predict the future and discuss the present and past. Part of me wanted to just be normal. But by then, it seemed there was a fat chance of that! Be careful of what you wish for or pray for!

In the early 1970s, a young chiropractor client in the San Fernando Valley told me about seeing an enormous cigar-shaped mother ship during his teens. At 16, he had parked in Malibu Canyon and was making out hot and heavy with his girlfriend, and actually in the process of undressing her, when the car radio playing music suddenly stopped. They sat up and stared. Directly in front of them was a huge mother ship with a number of smaller disks flying out in all directions. They were amazed. But they decided not to tell anyone out of fear of being considered crazy. After that, all attempts to get back to romancing were anti-climatic at best!

In the early 1980s in Georgetown, I did one reading for Dr. David Jacobs. He was a psychologist and the first person to ask me if I knew anything about UFOs and alien abductions. I never considered my sighting in 1965. But several clients have told me about seeing ships since then. I believed in the existence of beings on other planets and in other dimensions, but had little to share with Dr. Jacobs at that time.

In 1987, after being featured by Laura Foreman in the Time-Life Books series, *Mysteries of the Unknown,* in the volume *Psychic Powers,* I received a strange telephone call one night.

"Have you ever been abducted by aliens and taken aboard a spaceship and experimented on?" a man inquired.

"No," I cautiously replied. "Have you?"

"Yes," he said and added, "Repeatedly." He sounded anxious. "Do you think that could be why you're so psychic?"

"There are many reasons for psychic abilities, but I don't know much about aliens or spaceships. I have studied with spiritual masters and have had psychic abilities since childhood."

"Lucky you," he said in a disheartened tone.

He never made an appointment and our conversation ended. Immediately, I was sorry I had not asked him more questions. He seemed to feel as though he had no control over being abducted and taken on spaceships. Did he need therapy? Was it true? That was a scary thought to me at the time and still is. I am glad that alien abduction has not been my personal karma.

In the early 1990s, several female clients spoke of being abducted by aliens. I found their stories intriguing and unnerving. It disturbed me that another species, even more than one, would be insensitive and selfish enough to snatch someone out of a warm bed and probe their bodily parts, especially genitalia, and implant tracking devices. What strange karma abductees have, perhaps the 'abductees' were once the 'abductors'!

One woman was picked up in a bar. Three days later, she was dumped on her front lawn naked with only vague memories of being inside a spaceship and of little men with large, dark eyes and long, thin fingers. She had been the controller of a significant company. The incident had ruined her life and nearly destroyed her sanity. I am unaware if "they" ever returned for her like with the man on the telephone. It was difficult for her to even talk about it.

Another woman from Boston said that small extraterrestrials had come through the walls to take her to their ship. She often experienced missing time. That sort of phenomenon sounded "astral plane" or "out of body" to me, such as with episodes in lucid dreaming. In the astral body we can walk through walls and soar through space, but only spiritual Masters, and apparently some extraterrestrials, are able to do so at will. Those on other planets are surely more evolved than those of us on this planet. (This is my genuine hope.) They may be able to perform acts we might consider magical, the same as the natives did when Columbus arrived in the New World.

After reading Dr. Rick Strassman's book, *The Spirit Molecule,* about his experiments with DMT (dimethyltryptamine) and the pineal gland, I had to wonder about some alien stories. Many volunteers for his experiments with DMT, which is a strong psychedelic or hallucinogen naturally produced in the body that strongly affects the pineal gland (third eye) and produces melatonin (for sleep), had experiences under its influence similar to those of alien abductees. DMT occurs in some South American plants used in shamanic practices for its psychedelic properties. I have never taken a psychedelic substance and I have no desire to experiment.

Certain chemicals, and some spiritual practices, open the higher chakras associated with higher states of awareness that enable some to experience patterns, or entities, in parallel worlds or alternate realities, including encounters with angels or demons. Normal spiritual development sometimes has the same effect, accomplished after many lifetimes, where an individual directly experiences the fourth and higher dimensions of reality. One day, higher dimensions will be within reach of perhaps the majority. The physical body is nothing but a mass of electrical and chemical components vibrating at a certain frequency when inhabited by the life force of a soul. By raising vibratory frequency, higher dimensions may be experienced.

In 1994, at the International Transpersonal Conference in Killarney, Ireland, Harvard psychiatrist Dr. John E. Mack was a keynote speaker. His lecture was based on his recently published book: *Abductions: Human Encounters with Aliens*. Dr. Mack won a Pulitzer Prize in 1977 for his biography of T. E. Lawrence (Lawrence of Arabia). The subject of alien abductions was entirely another matter for the doctor.

In his initial approach, Dr. Mack suspected the abductees of suffering from mental illness, but no pathologies were present in those he interviewed. He discovered that the reportedly abducted ended up with a heightened sense of spirituality. I was impressed with his lecture. I also heard Dr. Mack speak at UFO conferences I attended prior to his death in 2004.

In Killarney, I met Scorpio Donald Ware, LC USAF (retired), fighter pilot and UFO investigator, formerly with MUFON (Mutual UFO Network). Don is still a director for the International UFO Congress and he was a guest on my blog talk radio show, *Exploring the Paranormal with Pattie*. Back in 1994, I found Don fascinating in his enthusiasm about unidentified flying objects, alien civilizations, higher consciousness, and extraterrestrial encounters of every kind.

Don is still a silver fox with an adventurous Scorpio nature. He and his wife are also birders who travel the world in search of exotic species of our fine feather friends. Don lived near Gulf Breeze, Florida, when the major UFO sightings occurred in 1987. He told me about a UFO conference in Mesquite, Nevada, the next winter.

On the last morning of the conference, I took Stanislav Grof's Holotropic Breathing Workshop before my afternoon flight back to the states. Most of my past life memories have surfaced in meditation, with some recalls spontaneous. Forced breathing had never been used before, although I had been hypnotically regressed several times.

In my Qabalistic training, dwelling on the past was always discouraged. Memories of past lives are considered of no true value unless something is gleaned to clear up a pattern in the present which results in positive changes. The past never exactly determines the future unless a person is stuck. History can repeat, but never in the exact same manner. Still, I was curious about holotropic breathing.

In the first session, my memory was of having been a young Native American boy of about 10. I was peeking under the flap of a teepee at the older braves and chief smoking and passing around a pipe. It was childhood curiosity. I was caught and severely punished by my mother. Perhaps the intense drumming had reawakened the memory. It was not my first glimpse into my former life as a young brave of the warlike Blackfoot that roamed the plains.

The next breathing session transported me to an unfamiliar place. I was in a spaceship on an operating table with muted lights shining down and surrounded by the familiar gray extraterrestrials with their large almond eyes. There was a taller being in a long gray robe to one side that seemed to instruct the others. Suddenly, I was afraid, confused about where I was or about what might happen next—when the group was suddenly brought back. It was all over before I could determine whether it was me at an earlier time in this life, or something from another life. I was confused.

Questions circled in my head on the long flight back to Virginia. I remembered the man on the phone asking me whether I had ever been abducted by aliens to account for my psychic abilities. Could the power of suggestion have been

working in my subconscious after the lecture by Dr. Mack and
my many UFO discussions with Don Ware?

In February 1995, I attended my first week-long
International UFO Congress in Mesquite, Nevada—and
had my mind blown with the first lecture. The middle-aged
woman from a Scandinavian country held a highly respected
political position, and yet, she spoke of being abducted by
aliens repeatedly from the time she was nine. She had been
taken from her bed at night and returned every morning. She
didn't strike me as the type to make up such a story.

As a novice to Ufology, my brain did flip-flops all week,
especially after hearing Travis Walton. I never saw the film,
Fire in the Sky, until after the conference. Travis was abducted
on my birthday, November 5, but in 1975. Twenty years later
he was still shaken by his experience.

As it turned out, a UFO conference is not unlike
a metaphysical conference. Delores Cannon spoke of
Nostradamus and Edgar Cayce, besides about her earth change
prophecies and her contacts with ETs. Another speaker played
the recordings of spirit entities. Others spoke of past lives, life
after death, or life between lives. I was right at home. And yet,
with every new Congress, there was something far out that I
had never heard ever before. It was an incentive to attend again
and meet more interesting people from all over the world. The
conferences were always more fun when Carol Kruger from
California, Susan Bauwens from Idaho, or Lolly Sturtevant
from Boston attended. All of us were fascinated.

In the spring of 2000, I had an interesting call from Aries
friend Carol Mitchell in Arizona. "I thought you had to be nuts
regarding all that UFO stuff, but I don't think so anymore,"
Carol admitted.

The night before, she had been out in her patio barbequing
chicken and went into the house to get a glass of wine. After

returning to the patio, Carol glanced up at the sky, and to her great amazement, high in the sky, which had been perfectly clear only moments earlier, were a number of oval lights circling each other, with a misty cloud hovering beneath them. She watched the lights circling over the cloud in the same part of the sky for perhaps 10 minutes before she started to get nervous and remembered alien abduction stories.

Her daughters were at the movies. Carol took her dinner and wine into her bedroom, as well as her parakeet, and she locked the door. When her daughters came home, Carol told them of the circling lights over the misty cloud. Both girls were highly skeptical. They said there was a concert in the area that night. The lights were probably there to attract people to the concert. She figured her daughters might also be questioning her sanity.

Then, months later, the circling oval lights and cloud reappeared. This time her daughters were there. On another occasion, her sister was visiting when the lights and cloud appeared, with no concert in the vicinity. All of them now believe in the existence of UFOs, and fully realize our alien visitors are especially fond of the clear Arizona desert skies.

Ten years after the incredible appearance of the "Phoenix lights," former Arizona governor Fife Symington, currently a Phoenix businessman, said he had also seen the mysterious lights over Phoenix in 1997, and indeed, he thought they were visitors from another world. His report was released by the media. About time, in my opinion!

My friend Jo in Maine told me a story of "missing time" that involved her and her daughter, Jennifer. Late one summer evening, driving home from a day at the Jersey Shore through the deserted Pine Barrens, just ahead they saw bright lights shining down from above the tree level. Jo thought it was a helicopter. When she approached the lights, she pulled over to the side of the road beneath it. Then, they lowered the car windows and stuck their heads out to look up.

Jo remembered telling her daughter to lock her door and not to lean out the window, because it was so eerie. She saw what looked like metal welded rivets, but she could not see the edges of the structure for the light was too bright. The most amazing part was that it made no sound, but was absolutely silent.

Until this day, Jo and Jennifer have no memory of how they left that place that night. They don't know if they drove away, if the lights moved away, or how *long* they were even there. Jo called the town police office the next morning to inquire if anyone had reported a UFO.

"No," was the answer.

Their memory of the incident was suppressed until Jo read an article on UFOs. In Camden, we talked about the matter at length, because by then I had attended UFO conferences.

After more UFO conferences that involved Dr. Steven Greer's lecture on black programs and government cover-ups, one Sunday afternoon in the late 1990s I had a surprising call from another friend in Virginia.

During various UFO congresses, I had called her to talk about the many strange things I was learning about UFOs, alien civilizations, and "alien abductions," some of which were supposedly carried out by our military. I was amazed by everything I had heard concerning the alien presence, but on that day she had something amazing to tell me.

Her husband was a high mucky-muck with a national insurance company, who recently had confided in her about the government flying him to Nevada several different times during the past nine months. The purpose of his trips was for his company to insure a top secret facility concealed in the Nevada desert. Everything was very hush-hush! He was flown out on military transports instead of commercial airliners, so his trips could never be traced back to their government source.

"Does Area 51 sound familiar?" I felt an urgent need to inquire.

"He didn't say where in Nevada, just in the desert. He was vague about where."

Naturally, her husband was never supposed to tell her—or me—about any of it!

"They have aliens out there, Pattie, beings from another planet," she said in amazement! "And spaceships ... and something like the BLOB. He said it was creepy ... just like in that old movie. Can you believe it, Pattie? The government has aliens in the Nevada desert!"

I could believe it.

On that day it seemed to me that a great many of the bizarre, outlandish claims made by speakers at UFO conferences were absolutely true. Wow!

Soon after that, my Scorpio client-friend Elaine in Virginia called with her strange tale. She and her younger son were taking her older son to his first year of college at William and Mary in Williamsburg. They needed an SUV to fit in all his belongings, so she borrowed her brother Jack's Chevy Suburban. Her brother had been a commercial airline captain for a number of years, after his service as a Navy fighter pilot flying F-4 Phantoms and F-14 Tomcats off aircraft carriers. He resided near Dulles Airport, which is where she picked up his Suburban and left her car.

The oldest son was successfully dropped off at college, and the drive back was a long one after an emotionally draining but exciting weekend. It was late Sunday afternoon—around 4 p.m. —by the time Elaine was back on the Dulles Toll Road heading toward her brother's house. Elaine is a WWII buff and airplane fanatic, so she often scanned the skies near Dulles to see what sort of plane was taking off or landing. It was a beautiful, clear, mid-September afternoon as she pulled into her brother's new housing development and quickly glanced toward the airport and airspace near the control tower.

The moment she saw it, she pulled the car off the road, which alarmed her young son.

After getting out of the car, she stared at the western sky in disbelief, for clearly visible on a cloudless day was a huge object shaped similar to that of a child's spinning top, but longer in height and narrower in width. The object appeared stationary, but it was spinning counterclockwise at a height not far above the airport's control tower, and brilliantly reflecting sunlight off its metallic surface.

Elaine was aware of exactly what she was seeing. She had worked for the military, held a security clearance, and had considerable knowledge of all types of aircraft currently using the airways. But she had never seen anything like this one before.

In amazement, she and her son watched the huge UFO in its stationary spin for about 20 minutes. The object could easily have been seen by the air traffic controllers, in addition to any passengers in the terminal.

Then she said to her son, "Where are the fighters? They should be up there right now! Where the hell did that come from?"

As if on cue, two USAF F-16 Fighting Falcons appeared and started to circle the enormous ship in a clockwise flight pattern.

What she said to me then was, "They looked like toy planes against that huge ship."

Please note: F-16s have a 16-foot wingspan and 32-foot length. That ship had to be VERY LARGE to dwarf the size of those fighters.

At that point, Elaine jumped back into the Suburban and screeched through the quiet neighborhood to get to her brother as quickly as possible, thinking Jack had to see this! Less than five minutes had passed when she reached him. At the front door, she pulled him by the arm screaming excitedly about what she and her son had just seen. She wanted Jack to see it!

Without hesitation, they all ran as fast as possible to the end of the driveway, which was the clearest vantage point to view the airspace around the control tower. Apparently, Elaine was yelling and pointing to a point low in the horizon where the spinning ship was last seen.

Her brother looked at her and in a calm, composed manner said, "They're already gone."

The extraordinary action in the afternoon sky, the ship and the fighter jets had vanished.

Elaine quizzically looked at her brother, knowing there had to be more to his reaction than he was letting on. For years, she had wanted to ask a particular question of her experienced pilot brother, but she had always been hesitant. She was aware that fighter jocks are notorious for seeing the world in black and white.

That afternoon, for the first time she asked, "Have you ever seen a UFO?"

UFO sightings in general are rarely discussed among commercial airline pilots. The subject is strictly taboo.

"We just don't talk about it," Jack said.

Pilots can and do lose jobs speaking of UFOs. Jack had seen this happen within his own airline company. He told Elaine he had seen several unusual, unidentifiable, airborne craft more than once. He and his copilot would simply look at each other, and then, either laugh or get on the radio and contact nearby planes. Within his airline, pilots often alerted each other about bogies sighted using special code words indicating UFOs. His claim was that there were numerous airline pilots who had seen

Unidentified Flying Objects in the daytime or night skies. He said a similar code of silence exists among naval aviators.

However, Jack could "neither confirm nor deny" seeing an alien, either from another galaxy or from some foreign country, working in a secret government facility in any location whatsoever in the Nevada desert—and that's the truth!

METAPHYSICAL MAGIC

20

TEACHERS, GURUS, AND MASTERS

During my youth, I was always drawn to spiritual patterns. Looking back, there has never been a time when I was not protected by the unseen and the invisible. My mother taught me about God—how to kneel at my bed each night and pray, "Now I lay me down to sleep, pray the Lord my soul to keep, if I die before I wake, pray the Lord my soul to take," leaving no room for doubt. That happened later. Praying to God to take my soul did cause anxiety to creep into my young mind on occasion. I always wondered if one night He might show up.

At 14, I read the New Testament. I tried to read the entire Old Testament, but that was a challenge. Soon, I was flipping through, reading chapters and verses. There was church school during elementary school followed by the Mormon Church and numerous services. I attended seminary before high school five days a week, partly motivated by Floyd Brown and the other cute boys. What else would get a Scorpio teen up that early? The Mormons have a great social program for the youth of their church.

At 16, checking out books at the public library, I found myself drawn to the *Ramayana,* the Hindu epic of the life of Rama, legendary king of ancient India. Rama was the seventh avatar (incarnation of a divine savior) of Vishnu (incarnation of a Supreme Being or god), the most popular hero in Hindu mythology. Rama was the "perfect man" who married Sita, the "perfect woman." The romance appealed to my youthful idealism, the perfect other half, not easy to find in the realm of mortals. One nice aspect of Hinduism—all the male gods have female counterparts, goddesses, which seemed more balanced in some aspects.

The concept vaguely touches upon Mormon doctrine. In the Church of Jesus Christ of Latter Day Saints, if you marry for time and all eternity and are sealed in the Temple by the Holy Spirit of Promise, and you live according to the laws of God, when you cross over to the Other Side and enter the highest realm of the Celestial Kingdom, eventually, you become a god and create worlds of your own. I liked that concept.

Soon, I was a serious student of comparative religion, sensing the Prophet Joseph Smith had borrowed more than a few concepts and tenets from religions and mystical traditions of ancient origin, providing a slightly new twist in translating the Book of Mormon. Polygamy was popular in ancient times. The Jews practiced polygamy. I still wonder how Solomon got around to his 300 wives and 700 concubines in one year—or several. What a guy!

Perhaps not surprisingly, my recent ancestors had studied the ancient mystery teachings: my maternal uncles were Freemasons, great-grandfather Franklin, a 33rd degree mason! Grandpa Schaible may have been, too. Fascination with secrets, the forbidden and religion in general, is in my genes. No one is born to a lineage or parent by mistake. There is Divine Method to support any soul's madness in any incarnation on the Cosmic Journey.

Throughout my adult life, I have been privileged to meet or study with many highly evolved and knowledgeable individuals. Around 1966 I read the paperback version of Jess Stearn's *Yoga, Youth & Reincarnation.* One Hatha Yoga instructor featured in his book had a studio in Hollywood off Sunset Boulevard. I enrolled in classes with Clara, and that was a major turning point in my life. Although Clara Spring was in her 70s, her husband was 55. She stood on her head every day. No facelift for Clara. Her body was toned and slender. Impressive! Not only were yoga postures and deep breathing exercises taught in that class, but how to chant and meditate on a deeper level. Her recommended reading list educated me in the ancient teachings of Yoga (Hindu mysticism) and Tibetan Buddhism (the mystic branch of Buddhism). Starting in my late 20s, I spent most evenings reading the timeless teachings that seemed familiar and exciting at the same time. Looking back, I was simply getting up to speed.

My studies in astrology started and continued for some time with Franka Moore. My Edgar Cayce Search for God study group was important for a time, including the group meditations. The Bodhi Tree Bookstore on Melrose in Los Angeles became a regular haunt, with volume after volume purchased to add to my library on esoteric subjects. I was like a sponge trying to soak up as much of the water of life as I could as quickly as possible. While my children watched television or slept, I read mysterious, serious, fascinating books late into the night.

At first, reading astrology books was like reading Greek or Chinese with no knowledge of the language. Then, all at once, late one night something clicked in my brain and things really started to make sense. It was a miracle. My mind had pushed beyond its limits as long forgotten doors to the past opened wide. I had gone the extra mile and had been rewarded. Some teachings of the Master Jesus the Christ (avatar) suddenly made sense in a new way. That was exciting!

During those years, the lectures of Manly P. Hall at the Philosophical Research Society were extremely interesting. The man was magnetic and a remarkable scholar with a dynamic speaking voice. His books on the occult and eastern religion were added to my library, especially *The Secret Teachings of All Ages: An Encyclopedic Outline of Masonic, Hermetic,*

Qabalistic & Rosicruician Symbolical Philosophy. That book covered all the mysterious subjects suddenly so important. I wanted to learn and know as much as my brain could contain. I read the Vedas, Upanishads, and Bhagavad Gita, along with the six volumes of the *Life & Teachings of the Masters of the Far East.* Books on psychic research by William James, psychology by Carl Jung, Sigmund Freud, Alexander Lowen, and Wilhelm Reich were fascinating. I was going for my master's degree in spirituality and comparative religion.

In my Cayce study group I met some women who had attended lectures at the Builders of the Adytum in Los Angeles. In the ancient Greek mysteries, the *adytum* was the Holy of Holies in the center of the Temple—*within the center of the Temple of the Soul.* They knew I read tarot cards, so encouraged me to check out the Temple of Holy Qabalah and Sacred Tarot. At first, I resisted anything that remotely resembled a church. I had become disenchanted with organized religion. From all my studies, I realized that the Masters and Avatars (Christs) were misinterpreted and misunderstood by many disciples perhaps not nearly as enlightened.

This is how organized religion seemed to evolve. The lower ego gets out of touch with the essence of the teaching. Someone decides on an interpretation of scripture as "right," and unholy wars are sure to follow. Look at the number of denominations just within Christianity!

Finally, one Thursday evening I decided to attend the meeting at Builders of the Adytum. At the time I was reading several books and struggling with concepts in *White Magic* by Alice Bailey, the *Secret Doctrine* by H.P. Blavatsky and *In Search of the Miraculous* by P.D. Ouspensky (still favorites). Some Alice Bailey books gave me the chills or caused strange vibrations in my brain. Weirdness was becoming the norm. I was meditating with my astrologer friend Tish, and in the process, I was becoming more aware of the energy levels in my seven chakras (spiritual centers in the etheric body that correlate with the endocrine system).

That night at the temple I was seated in the third row surrounded by strangers, observing the large painted tarot cards all around the room, along with the white and black pillars on each side of the stage which were reminiscent of the pillars in Key 2, The High Priestess. Far out!

Then, all of a sudden, the Reverend Ann Davies walked out—and without any warning—my heart and solar plexus chakras sent pure energy straight up into my Crown (above my brain). It was a strong, physical sensation, exhilarating and exciting, which instantly captured my complete attention. Ann had a special magnetism, Scorpio with Sagittarius rising. She had a radiant presence and was the rightful leader of the order. Perhaps the strangest part was that her lecture just happened to cover and clear up issues and points in the books I was then reading—another divine coincidence, right?

Outside, during the break before guided meditation, as I was smoking a cigarette I took note of the red brick building. Suddenly, I remembered what my psychic friend Joe in Topanga had said months earlier: "You're going to attend a church service in a red brick building and meet a teacher who will dramatically change your life."

Bingo!

Over the next 20 years, I completed all 13 courses of BOTA by receiving lessons in the mail, the same as any other member. Some courses were reread several times, in addition to taking three initiations. The teachings were familiar. Books by Bailey or Blavatsky often made my body vibrate, which could also happen with my tarot lessons. It was a sign that I was getting in direct touch with spiritual Masters on the Inner Planes.

A number of magical experiences occurred in the presence of Ann Davies, most involving a sense of bliss or heightened illumination. When Ann left this earth in 1975, I chastised myself for not attending every single lecture during the four and a half years that she was my teacher. Several months before her transition, Ann said she would not always be with us. There are times her guidance is still sensed from finer realms. While writing the *Wheel of Destiny*, I could almost hear her as I had during one of her many inspirational lectures.

After Ann's graduation, there was the usual struggle for leadership at the Temple of Qabalah and Sacred Tarot. For a time, my Aries friend Fredda Rizzo was president, but some found Fredda unworthy. I think she did a fine job. Being on a spiritual Path does not guarantee wisdom or enlightenment, only that someone is fortunate enough to have found a way back up the ladder of awareness. Occult author Dion Fortune points out in *Esoteric Orders and Their Work* that few orders survive the leader that follows the first Initiate and Founder of the Order. Many lower personality egos are less than perfect in terms of carrying on the work of the Masters of the Wisdom of the Order of the White Brotherhood. The Master R (an Ascended Master in charge of religion, ritual and magic on the planet) told Paul Foster Case, founder of Builders of the Adytum, that it was not because he was perfect that he had been chosen, but that he was the best to be found on the physical plane at that time. The perfection of the lower nature requires countless lifetimes and hard work.

In the early 1970s, Jess Stearn introduced me to Libra Ralph Winters. Ralph invited me to be his guest in his Mind Dynamics Workshop. Ralph Winters was the head of casting at Universal Studios at the time. Mind Dynamics teaches aspects of remote viewing and higher patterns of psychic awareness, including clairvoyance and the development of healing abilities.

At a follow-up meeting in group meditation, Jesus appeared to me and said, "Feed my sheep." I thought the message was for Ralph, but he said the message was mine. I had my own interpretation of the Master's directive, since psychic work involves awakening others to their divine potential. An individual needs to separate from the herd and become a shepherd instead of remaining one of the sheep. The Master Jesus taught that the Kingdom of Heaven is within.

There is no end to learning in metaphysics. In the 1970s and 1980s, I attended many workshops taught by many fine teachers. Late in 1981, a brochure arrived in the mail from the International Transpersonal Association about a conference, "Ancient Religion and Modern Science," in Bombay, India. Notable speakers from various spiritual disciplines were going to speak and teach. India? At the time I had only been to Canada and Mexico.

I had been saving money, something basically against my nature, and I had $5,000 in the bank. My son Mark was in college in Arizona and my daughter Tomi was living in Colorado, so I felt free to pursue a grand adventure. If I was going to go as far as India, I wanted to see other countries as well. I decided on a trip halfway around the world and back. After all, I seemed to have the money!

In February 1982, the first stop was Washington to read for my clients for a week before boarding a plane for Bombay. My friend Janene in Dallas had backed out. I was on my own on the Air India 747 flying at 40,000 feet, when I learned the woman beside me from Phoenix was also divorced with two children. Was it a sign?

Then, all of a sudden, I had a startling revelation!

Part of the revelation: while I was in India, Lee Strasberg, Susan's father, was going to die from a heart attack. I wondered how I might find out in a foreign country. Then, it seemed that my daughter Tomi, who planned a June wedding, would be married when I was in London (I would be out of the country for six weeks). That would mean I would be unable to attend Tomi's wedding. Besides that, I was going to meet a Master of the Wisdom, an immortal, without even knowing that I had met him.

All of this was perfectly clear as if occurred that very minute—direct knowledge—all I could do was wait and see.

Arriving in the middle of night at the Bombay (now Mumbai) Airport was surreal. The air was thick with smoke from dung fires. The streets filled with millions of homeless poor. Some streets reeked like an open sewer, which forced me to hold my breath to keep from gagging. Pattie wasn't in Kansas anymore—or anywhere near California. It was like being on another planet.

My Leo psychologist roommate, Fanya Carter, Ph.D., had decided which bed and dresser drawers were mine. Unfortunately, one suitcase had been taken off the plane by mistake in London, the one with my sandals and shoes. Bombay was hot and muggy. I had only leather boots.

That first morning on serious jet lag in the hotel dining room, an attractive blond man was watching me and smiling through breakfast. As it turned out, Aquarius Brian Bauerle resided in a royal palace in Bangkok. His cousin had married a princess of Thailand. Brian had his own suite in the palace and two servants, not bad for a boy from Iowa who had converted to Buddhism.

From the first moment, our relationship seemed synchronistic. Brian and I kept running into each other getting on or off elevators or walking into or out of rooms. The conference was spectacular, with keynote speakers each morning and evening. In the afternoon there were two mini-workshops. The dilemma: which one to choose, since authors of at least six excellent books were teaching workshops every day. It was as if I had died and gone to metaphysical heaven!

One workshop was with Jack Cornfield (Buddhist meditation); another with Michael Harner, author of *Way of the Shaman,* with far-out drumming. There were wonderful talks and wonderful teachers. My soul feasted on the information for years. People from every country were in attendance, nearly 1,000. Mother Teresa spoke, in addition to Buddhist, Yogi, Christian, Muslim, Jewish and Qabalist speakers, and scientists. Every subject was covered. I donated two summer outfits to Mother Teresa. I was speechless standing next to the tiny saint. Her message: "Love one another!"

There was a bald guy that captured my attention. He looked like a monk. At lunchtime there were banquets, vegan and non-vegan. We stuffed ourselves. Evenings, we were seldom hungry. A few times, Fanya and I went to the hotel bar and shared a quart of beer and ate salty munchies. No Indian women were in that bar, of course.

Later that week, Fanya dressed up for an Israeli Embassy soiree with music. Her wealthy Jewish father had made serious contributions to Israel. For that reason, Fanya was courted by Israeli embassies in every Indian city during our three weeks. I declined her invitation. That night the program was biofeedback with the Greens, who invented the method. However, after four days of lectures and workshops I was suffering from conference overload.

That evening the bald fellow joined our table. As it turned out, Gordon was not a monk. He was a businessman from Chicago. Years later, I ran into him again at the Esalen Institute in the Big Sur. However, on that night, Gordon invited me to go with him to attend darshan[1] with Babaji, the Divine Himalayan Yogi, somewhere in Bombay.

1   Sanskrit: "the viewing of an auspicious deity, person, or object."

"Who is he?" It had been a long week. My brain was nearly numb.

"He was Yogananda's guru's, guru's, guru! He reappeared in a cave in 1970 and now he's in Bombay with his disciples because of the conference. Some of those here are planning to spend time with him at his ashram in the North near the Himalayas."

I agreed to go. Many strange things had happened in India. To say the week was mind-boggling is an understatement. Why not skip biofeedback and see another Indian holy man? At the conference there were many holy men in loincloths with red ash on their foreheads under their wild, matted hair. From the look in their eyes, they were nowhere near this world.

Gordon hailed a cab that drove us through the crowded, smelly streets of Bombay. The backdoor handle came off in his hand. Near where we stopped, colorful Christmas lights were strung overhead near a building in considerable disrepair, the same as many buildings in Bombay. Mostly native Indians were standing in a long line. We were late. The holy man had already spoken to the gathering. The men were seated on the left, the women on the right, to the left of the guru.

Babaji was seated on a platform in the lotus position. Most attending darshan had brought flowers or gifts for the guru. I had nothing. He was young, attractive, with long, dark hair and dark, penetrating eyes. He smiled and nodded as he handed me a date. I ate the date and sat there alone questioning my sanity for being in India in the first place to sit there with some Indian guru in the second place. A constant mental argument continued between my left and right brain. At the conference, many spiritual disciplines and practices had been presented. Could any of them be right? Could all be right? How was that possible? *Why am I here? Am I crazy? What is this all about?* All this stuff churned through my head as I noted a bemused smile on the face of the handsome young guru. Then, Babaji stood and joined his followers behind him.

Before long, Gordon and I were in another taxi heading back to the hotel to get ready for yet another day of remarkable knowledge and wisdom from esteemed presenters: Karl Pribram, Fritjof Capra, Jerry Jampolsky, Stanislav Groff—the list was beyond amazing.

That night something odd happened. In my bed I started to shake uncontrollably. Was it the date? Something weird was going on. Had I contracted some terrible tropical disease? Finally, I fell asleep and was fine in the morning. I was, as yet, unaware of the power of *Shakti*, the sublime energy freely imparted by the guru. That date had evidently been a rather high dose!

The day after the conference there was a huge celebration at Swami Muktananda's ashram, attended by many conferees and the locals. Fanya and I were part of a tour of northern India and Nepal for two more weeks, so we attended the festival. Many monks with shaven heads in orange robes were standing in line to see Swami Muktananda. At one point, I could have sworn I saw Brian standing with the monks in an orange robe with his head shaven. In spite of this, Brian arrived dressed in white with his blond hair still intact. He had fasted all week. The fruit from his room was offered to the guru, Swami Muktananda. Brian had a reading in his room with its view of the Indian Ocean. In my opinion, it takes remarkable discipline to fast for an entire week! I was impressed, and remembered never seeing him at lunch.

Back to my "revelation" at 40,000 feet: Upon reaching London in two more weeks, I called Tomi in Colorado.

"I guess you know Lee died," Tomi said, briefly pausing before she added, "And I'm getting married on Wednesday."

My daughter then filled me in on the details. Lee Strasberg had died from a massive heart attack. I was stunned. Two parts of my revelation had come to pass. My daughter was getting married before June. So who the heck was the Master of Wisdom, the Immortal, I had met when I was unaware I had even met him?

Another three weeks were spent working in London. Then, two more weeks with clients in New York City, another two weeks in Boston that included an appearance on *People Are Talking* with Nancy Merrill. Finally, it was Dallas to stay with my Gemini friend Janene.

One night at dinner, I was talking about my trip to India and said, "And this one night I went to darshan with Gordon and met Babaji."

"No one meets Babaji!" Janene said in astonishment.

"They do too. I met him. And I think the date he gave me made me sick."

Janene showed me a Polaroid picture of Babaji's feet surrounded by flowers. I had no recollection of his feet, except that they were bare. Janene went on and on, "Do you any idea what a privilege it was for you to meet Babaji? It's like meeting Jesus Christ! No one meets Babaji!"

Well, some people evidently do meet Babaji. Because I met him at darshan in Bombay! Honest and truly!

Janene and I had several other discussions about Babaji and his purpose while I continued to do readings in Dallas, about how Babaji tended to spend time with Jesus Christ and some of the other Ascended Masters. Upon returning to California, I found Parmahansa Yogananda's *Autobiography of a Yogi*. Surely, Babaji was the "Master of the Wisdom" from my revelation on Air India. Since I had read the book many years earlier, I looked him up in the index.

Babaji was the guru of Lahiri Mahasaya, who was the guru of Sri Yukteswar, who was the guru of Parmahansa Yogananda, which made him Yogananda's guru's, guru's, guru. In one chapter it said that Babaji was in charge of all prophets on the planet. I am certainly a minor 'prophet' but I have been blessed to predict the future for thousands. I had actually been in the presence of an Immortal Master, Babaji, the Divine Himalayan Yogi, without knowing of his great and glorious achievements. Double wow!

In 1986, the periodical *Pathways* advertised a conference, Parliament of World Religions in Arlington, Virginia, at the Quality Inn. The parliament was sponsored by none other than Babaji, the Divine Himalayan Yogi. I called Janene and insisted that she attend with me. Over the past years, other books about the Mahavatar (Great Savior) had on occasion magically entered my life as other stories of the Master continued to reach me. For four years I had wondered if the man I met in India was the "Babaji." Others had assumed the name. However, at the parliament I purchased a book of photographs of *Babaji Mahavatar*—the same man I had met at darshan in 1982 in Bombay, India.

Miracles can happen to anyone in accordance with the admonition, "Seek and ye shall find" spoken by another avatar (savior, redeemer or deliverer, in accordance with Hindu tradition). Jesus of Nazareth was supposed to have studied in India and Tibet to prepare for his mission. There are records in ancient monasteries of Jesus having been there. Jesus is honored as a Master or prophet by Hindus, Yogis, Buddhists and Muslims. Christians and Jews are not as generous in honoring the teachers and avatars of other faiths. It is interesting that all the faiths in the world came into being within something like a 500-mile radius.

In 1989, when His Holiness the Dalai Lama was awarded the Nobel Prize, I attended the Harmonic Convergence Conference at which His Holiness was the main attraction in Newport Beach, California. It was wonderful, informative, and enlightening to hear the Dalai Lama dialogue with psychologists on important psychological, spiritual and karmic issues. I had a healing session with two monks. If you have the opportunity to be in the presence of a highly evolved being, do yourself a favor and make the effort.

In the 1980s, I read several books by Z'ev Ben Shimon Halevi, also known as Warren Kenton of London, England. It was interesting to study Kabbalah (Qabalah, many spellings) from a different perspective, since Ann had passed on and I had completed my BOTA studies. There were many correlations with additional information on the Sephiroth of the Tree of Life. In 1990, I attended two of Warren's workshops at the Omega Institute in Rhinebeck, New York. It was a pleasure to meet the Capricorn teacher. I also made some new friends.

Taurus Dr. Michael Hattwick from Virginia is also in another chapter. Years later, Michael taught Kabbalah classes in my Arlington home. I attended more Kabbalah workshops with Warren at Omega, as well as in the English countryside and several other cities in the U.S. In 1993, I took a Kabbalah trip through Spain. Kindred souls shared good times and the group practices were productive and powerful.

In 1990, I had an initiation from Pir Vilayat Inayat Khan into the Sufi Order of the West, which is discussed in the next chapter. Sufism is the mystical branch of Islam. I attended several workshops and meditation retreats with Pir Vilayat at Omega and at his ashram in upstate New York. His insights added to my storehouse of knowledge. In that Sufi order are people of every race and religious persuasion. As a master teacher, Pir Vilayat taught that the discipline is not as important as an opportunity to elevate awareness. His books are enlightening.

I studied with a Tibetan Buddhist lama for a short time, although I was unable to fully embrace Buddhism. The lama wanted his disciples to support him financially. The books of Tibetan lama Anagarika Govinda, *Foundations of Tibetan Buddhism* and the *Way of the White Clouds,* his autobiography, were an important aspect of my early development. Govinda was on the reading list of Clara Spring's Yoga ashram.

My spiritual path is more Western than Eastern in essence. During past lives I have walked nearly every path as a man or a woman. It is important to pick a Path, instead of hopping from spoke to spoke on the Wheel, although all spokes lead to the Hub or Center. Ramakrishna reached enlightenment on three Paths: Hindu, Christian, and Muslim. The Absolute has no preference on the Path to Enlightenment, Self-Realization. My connection to Babaji was strong because he embraces all paths to the Divine without making judgment. I believe in all Paths.

It has been my good fortune to be in the presence of many fine teachers and spiritual Masters. Their attainment and awareness has lifted me into a higher level of consciousness and understanding. When it comes to churches, cathedrals, temples or mosques, the intent of the worshippers creates an energy that heals and uplifts. Sacred edifices are dedicated to the work of the Divine. Those who enter, including monasteries and ashrams, do so for the purpose of worship or petitioning the Divine—with form or without form, as Babaji might say.

In India, where most are cremated after death, holy men and women are sometimes buried so their vibrations may continue to aid their disciples. Holy relics have the same effect on the devout. Belief is *key* in conversion or miracles. *Thy faith has made thee whole.*

For 21 days after his death, the flesh of Parmahansa Yogananda remained undefiled. However, because of California law regarding the burial of a corpse within a certain time, he was interred. Swami Yogananda predicted his own reincarnation. He said that one day he would attend his prior establishment and find the teachings had been altered beyond recognition. Such is the way of disciples and the disciples of disciples.

For this reason, an avatar (divine incarnate being) called a Christ or Ascended Master, is not known to establish a religion. The followers develop doctrine over time, colored by bias and the changing mores. Terrible wars and needless carnage have resulted from varying opinions or divisions within a single religion, with tragic results for the innocent. Unfortunately, such practices still exist.

Eventually, all karma shall be paid in full by every soul as every good and selfish thought, every compassionate and evil act, is recorded in the Book of Life.

21

KUNDALINI AND PLUTO'S POWER

The study of comparative religion, the paranormal, psychology and consciousness, plus meditation practices have been among my top priorities. From 1964, the study of astrology involved my chart and those of my family and friends well before thousands of charts of my clients became included.

In 1987, my first desktop computer and astrology software were purchased—an absolute godsend. Naturally clairvoyant, I was lazy about learning the math of astrology. Because of the brilliance and ingenuity of the technically and inventively gifted, such as fellow Scorpio Bill Gates (born the same day as Ann Davies, October 28), a computer with Microsoft Windows enabled me to view charts before printing them. Miracles do occur on planet Earth—rapidly in the electronic age! The spirit of free enterprise thrives in the Western World—a spirit well acquainted with the likes of Bill Gates and all the other computer wizards.

Even before my first computer increased my workload, the planets were often checked daily. Major planetary transits in natal charts have resulted in predictable patterns for astrologers for thousands of years. In my case, it was in 1969 when I first started to pay attention to progressed planets. That year, my second husband Bill died when my Progressed Sun squared my natal Saturn in my natal fifth house of children: Progressed Sun square Saturn is considered a "widow aspect," in addition to several other patterns. Even though Bill had remarried, he had once been my husband, and his loss devastated me because of my children. As my Progressed Sun conjoined my natal Venus in Sagittarius, each of my children inherited a considerable sum, which made our lives much easier. Suddenly, it seemed the ancients knew their stuff, which warranted a closer study of planetary progressions to determine and predict future events.

In May 1984, as I left California for my ultimate destination of the Washington, D.C. area, transiting Saturn in Scorpio was within a degree of my Scorpio Sun. Saturn transits are significant, with a difficult Saturn transit every seven years or even more often. The Saturn Return in a natal chart occurs every 28-30 years. Saturn also transits the natal Sun every 28-30 years. In my horoscope, Capricorn, ruled by the planet Saturn, governs my fourth house or home. Our California house had finally sold. Sadly, that house is now worth five times what we received and the same people live there—good house karma for them.

In September of 1985, I moved into my new home in Arlington, Virginia, with Saturn still in Scorpio but in later degrees. At the time, the recently demoted Pluto had also entered Scorpio on its slow approach to my Mercury, which squares my Leo moon. By that time, my life had dramatically changed, with major transformations constant. Shortly after moving into the house, the day after my new office was wired for a telephone, there was a strange thunderstorm in the area without any sign of rain.

A change of residence is always hectic, with a million things in immediate need of attention. In my newly wallpapered office there were curtains that needed to be hung on the two windows. A new client was arriving for a reading the next day. Then again, there was an ugly toilet seat in the upstairs bathroom. The new oak toilet seat matched the new oak washstand. The unsightly cover needed to be replaced, but the rusted bolts refused to budge. At the time, a major tug-of-war was going on in my head between the unsightly toilet seat and my office curtains. I stood in the doorway of my office staring at the bare windows when the toilet seat won. I entered the bathroom.

Then, all of a sudden, kneeling on the bathroom floor between the toilet and the tub, I heard what sounded like cannons being fired in the distance. Were they spirit cannons from the Civil War being fired in another century? My house was right off Lee Highway. Was I having a past life memory? There was no rain. It seemed strange to hear numerous claps of thunder coming closer and CLOSER—with no sign of rain.

BOOM! BOOM! BOOM! I heard as I applied the wrench to the stubborn bolt.

Then, all at once, there was a REALLY LOUD BOOM, and countless chunks of concrete and brick, mixed with tiny pieces of my brand-new flowered wallpaper, were blasted across the hall through the doorway and all around the bathroom as I cowered behind the toilet.

Suddenly, I smelled smoke.

Alarmed, I ran downstairs and out the door. My new neighbor across the street had just walked out of his house as I shouted, "I think my house is on fire!"

In an act of masculine bravery, he rushed over and ran into my house.

The roll of paper towels used to clean the windows I had left on the desk had caught fire. The lightning had struck the side of the house in the corner above my desk and had blown a hole in the inside wall! The lightning made an arc across the small room to the metal register near the door and ignited the roll of paper towels in the process. Luckily for me, I was not hanging curtains—or I might not be around to tell the tale.

In the far corner to the left of the window, the lightning had blown away the red brick and concrete block, and in the process, Jupiter's thunderbolts had fried my new telephone wires, melted my tape recorder, and blew out the 20-inch TV in my bedroom, in addition to the stereo plugged into a socket downstairs in the living room. The wiring in the wall, from upstairs to downstairs in the living room, had to be replaced.

The insurance man quickly arrived. The agent was amazed by the damage, considering my house was not the highest one on the block. There was more than $2,500 worth of damage caused by one lightning bolt on a bright, sunny September day! My new office had been *initiated* (cleansed) by fire! Welcome to the transit of puny, insignificant Pluto, Lord of the Underworld, cohort of Archangel Gabriel and co-ruler of Scorpio: the sign of death, rebirth and transformation!

The planet Mercury rules everything electrical and communications in general, all the items destroyed on that weird day. The moon rules the home. My moon is in Leo, a fire sign. Fortunately, the insurance paid for almost everything, except for the disruption and lost time caused by repairs and replacements. A helpful repairman finally replaced the ugly toilet seat.

As Pluto moved closer to my Sun and squared my Moon, I contracted viral pneumonia. Early in 1987, my fever reached as high as 103. I tossed and turned in my bed, burning up. The transformative power of Pluto was cleansing my body. A doctor prescribed an antibiotic, even though a virus needs to run its course, and blood oozed from the pores in my neck and chest. High doses of vitamin C and raw garlic (advice from a Greek taxi driver client from Baltimore) helped some, but the fever persisted.

Then, one night I had a dream.

In my dream, I was in a huge coliseum filling up with people, and my main concern was how I was going to feed them. A long black limousine pulled up, and in the backseat was young, smiling Cary Grant in a black tux. "I've come to take you home," Cary said.

And yet, all these people were tugging at me. Several times I tried to approach the limo to get in the backseat with Cary, but then I would stop and tell him to wait. Then I would go back to try to take care of more people. There never seemed to be enough to satisfy them.

The third time I approached the limo, I said to Cary, "I'm afraid you're going to have to go on without me. It seems I have more work to do here."

Cary smiled and waved. The limousine drove away.

I awoke from my dream with a start.

HOME?

Only months before, debonair Cary Grant, only glimpsed in person when he lived across the street from Susan Strasberg in the Malibu Colony, had died suddenly at age 82. Cary had died on his Uranus Return, the same as many celebrities.

Home was HOME—our BIG HOME IN THE SKY.

It seemed to me on that particular morning that I had made a decision to stay on earth to "feed the people" as best as I could, as the Master Jesus had once admonished. The fever was soon gone and my strength returned. The crisis had passed.

Who better than a smiling Cary Grant to escort me to the Other Side in his black tux in an elegant black limousine? I mean—if you've gotta go—it might as well be in style!

By the fall of 1987, the transformative power of Pluto was getting even closer to my Scorpio Sun. The slow transit of Pluto covers many years. During that time, I had periods of elevated awareness and heightened intuition. My meditations were profound. I walked around with a sense of "being in love" with no object for my affection. The love was universal and projected toward my clients. I often recommended inspirational books and workshops.

One evening, I attended an astrology lecture with my friend Judy Diamond before having dinner. Upon returning home, I played back the messages on my answering machine and one message was really disturbing. A man had used a device to distort his voice:

"Hello, Pattie McLaine, I'm going to kill you. I see you there in your little red brick house running around in your short red shorts, running upstairs to your computer, and I'm going to kill you. I'm going to kill that son of yours in the Air Force, too."

After I caught my breath, I called the police. An officer arrived in half an hour and I played the tape for him. The sinister aspect of Pluto, Lord of the Underworld, had surfaced.

"Have you given anyone a bad reading?" the office inquired.

He advised me to tell him about the threat. Mark had Top Secret Clearance at Carswell Air Force Base in Texas, perhaps a nuclear facility, which my son could "neither confirm nor deny." The policeman thought my son's commanding officer needed to be told even though there was little chance the psychotic would ever carry out his threats.

An evil prankster was causing me and my loved ones great anxiety. My suspicions involved a recent appliance repairman that had checked out my clothes dryer. As it turned out, it was not the dryer but a circuit breaker that needed to be replaced. There was no way for me to confirm my hunch. Since I lived alone, anxiety became my frequent companion.

The positive Plutonian aspects of heightened awareness had suddenly taken an ominous turn, with me trying to go about my life as normally as possible. The feelings of Cosmic Love persisted. The year before, I learned that an old love had divorced. Meditating on him, as perhaps in remote viewing, several things I picked up were confirmed later when we spoke. Regrettably, he had already remarried.

One afternoon in October, I was studying Tarot Key 3, The Empress, the Divine Mother, which involves love, abundance, creativity and imagination, and during my meditation, I briefly got in touch with my disappointment on learning of the Libra's remarriage. At the same time, I remembered actually *being love* in the Big Sur after my despair over Michael breaking off with me (we are all Love Incarnate). That emotional disappointment had, in fact, resulted in a major breakthrough—an unforgettable, undeniable, uplifting spiritual experience.

Suddenly, I was aware of the absence of a man in my life to love, and at that same time, I sensed a circular, clockwise movement of energy right behind my back and my heart. It was an unfamiliar yet distinct and subtle sensation of rotating motion. Next, I felt sick at my stomach, so I lay down until the nausea passed.

After a few moments, in a vaguely philosophical state, I went downstairs to cook my dinner. That week I had started taking a new supplement from my chiropractor that had improved my energy level. Perhaps it had also helped to alleviate the anxiety created by the malicious caller.

Later, eating supper and watching television—not centered and meditating—suddenly, a powerful, hot energy rushed from my solar plexus up to the top of my head and down both my arms and legs. Had the new supplements triggered something? The experience was followed by a mad dash to the bathroom, created in part by anxiety from the startling experience.

The next day, I went to the chiropractor and told him of my experience. He was metaphysically oriented and said that my experience was personal and had nothing to do with the supplements. A massage therapist checked me out and said, "Her triple-burner is really moving." Whatever that meant!

"You're probably having a spiritual experience that's affecting you physiologically. Everything is interconnected," the chiropractor explained.

For the next nine months, I had periodic diarrhea and strange experiences the medical community might have considered psychotic or hallucinatory, if not just plain weird. One doctor suggested lactose intolerance, which happened to be true. The diarrhea finally stopped.

That November people in my life started to die. First, my father from cancer; my friend Les from hepatitis C; another gay friend from AIDS; Ray Wood, the husband of my good friend Bobbie, from cancer; clients died and children of clients died. All of them with Pluto on my Sun—10 were gone in six months. In my chart, the Sun (Leo) rules my 11th House of friends. The Sun also indicates the father or an authority figure. The Lord of the Underworld was busy claiming souls that had been an important part of my life.

During my unusual experience, I read extensively about the Kundalini, or Serpent Power, which is coiled at the base of the spine. Unbeknownst to many, it is esoterically depicted in the caduceus of the medical profession associated with Asclepius, the Greek  god of healing or Rod of Hermes. On an esoteric level, the two serpents represent the solar and lunar currents (masculine and feminine energies) at rest in most individuals at the base of the spine. When aroused through spiritual practice or development, the energies rise up through the various chakras connected with the nerves in the spinal column (closely connected with the human endocrine system). The rise of the universal evolutionary energy through the various centers increases awareness, intelligence, creativity, and bestows gifts associated with the various spiritual centers, or chakras, in addition to ultimately bringing about Enlightenment or Cosmic Consciousness. The winged orb at the top of the caduceus represents wholeness (holiness), the ability of spirit to soar into higher realms after reaching the highest center, to reunite with the One, the Source or God. This state is also known as Self-Realization.

In books by Gopi Krishna, the kundalini is called "the evolutionary energy of the Universe." After reading of his unpleasant but remarkable experiences, I was glad that mine were not even close. In him, the solar current rose without the lunar current in tandem and caused considerable damage to his nervous system. Other authors knowledgeable on the kundalini include Arthur Avalon, Ramakrishna, Vivekananda, Brahmananda, the Yoga Sutras of Patanjali interpreted by several authors in the East and the West, the writings of Yogananda, and other books on Babaji.

I attended a conference on Kundalini in Pacific Grove, California, sponsored by the International Transpersonal Association, and importance was stressed on determining that symptoms had no basis in possible physical disorders. Some individuals experiencing the opening of the heart chakra thought they were having a heart attack. Nonetheless, the health of the heart needs to be determined. In Vivekananda's, *Raja Yoga*, he explains that when the third chakra (solar plexus, Jupiter center) is pierced by the kundalini, latent diseases are often released in the body so the individual may get rid of residual karma.

In 1989, my physical energy was suddenly and drastically challenged. After seeing several doctors in Washington and California, I was diagnosed with Epstein-Barr Virus and Chronic Fatigue Syndrome. Acupuncture treatments, which included tea tree oil, were administered in Santa Monica, California. That doctor stressed the need for exercise. Physical activity stimulates the immune system. I bought an Exercycle but at first I was so weak I could only manage five grueling minutes. A client with lupus said she had cured herself with gentle exercise.

That year, my Aquarius client-friend Valerie Barad insisted that I attend the Harmonic Convergence Conference in Newport Beach at which the Dalai Lama and his monks were the honored guests. Valerie planned to attend. She was aware of my struggle with my health, of how I had been forced to take several naps a day to be able to function. The monks were available for healing ceremonies. At Valerie's insistence, an appointment was scheduled. Valerie shared her hotel room with me and she also generously paid for many of my meals.

His Holiness the Dalai Lama was awarded the Nobel Prize that weekend, which was celebrated by all. The conference was amazing. It was a tremendous joy to be in the presence of a Bodhisattva. The chanting monks were also amazing in sounding three tones at once.

My healing session was with two Tibetan monks, one young and the other much older. Human bones were thrown as a reminder of the transitory state of human existence. The old monk read the answer to his throw of the bones from an ancient Tibetan divinatory text, which inspired little confidence in this particular psychic.

"Someone is trying to kill you," the young monk said interpreting the words of the old monk.

What?

My immediate response was to remember what Ann had taught: most psychic attacks are done by a person on him or herself because of fear and suspicion. A young woman at the Temple had done banishing rituals and she became sicker and sicker, thinner and thinner. Finally, it was determined that she had been banishing herself. Her doubts and fears of psychic attack had been unfounded. When she stopped the rituals, she was able to recover.

At my insistence, the old monk threw the bones again. The malicious caller had not been heard from for months. I knew the monk had meant psychic attack.

"Someone is trying to kill you," the young monk insisted. "Either a person is knowledgeable and knows what they are doing, or they have hired an evil priest to kill you. You must do nothing to retaliate or you will generate further bad karma. We will do what we can to help you."

Next, a colorful string necklace was placed around my neck. I was told not to remove the necklace even for bathing. An incense burner was ritually moved all around me as the two monks chanted in Tibetan. After that, I was given pills and a bottle of water from which to sip until the water was gone. I purchased the monks' chanting healing tape which I played during my morning meditation for months. My desire was to be healthy, regardless of how it might be accomplished. After all, I had once been healed by a long-dead Chinese doctor.

The next summer, I attended two Kabbalah Workshops at the Omega Institute with Capricorn Warren Kenton. That was where I met Taurus Dr. Michael Hattwick, an internist with a practice in Annandale, Virginia. Since Michael had read Warren's books and was interested in metaphysics, one day I joined him in the dining hall to tell him about my problems with the kundalini, Epstein-Barr and chronic fatigue. Because of what I had learned at the Kundalini Conference, there were things that needed to be checked out from a purely medical perspective. My heart was doing strange things: skipping beats or suddenly speeding up. I needed a sympathetic doctor who was conscious of the process of spiritual awakening.

That fall I had a complete physical with Dr. Hattwick, including an electrocardiogram and a heart monitor for 24 hours. There was a button to push every time my heart did something strange. In spite of the strange vibrations that often coursed through me, everything seemed to be normal. Nothing appeared to be physically wrong with me.

I heard of a spiritual healer, Bill Torvund from Minnesota, who had healed several Tibetan monks connected with the Dalai Lama. Bill had a past life as a Tibetan Lama. He planned to be in New York City, so I made arrangements with my friend, Janene Sneider, to use her apartment for our session. On the appointed day, I boarded a train to New York City.

On a massage table in Janene's apartment, Scorpio Bill performed psychic surgery on me for two long hours.

"Someone has done something to your etheric body in the area of the heart that is not likely to be detected by the tools of modern medicine," Bill said.

Whatever it was—he removed it. The process was interesting and exhausting. I still had on my faded string necklace from the monks. Riding the train back to Union Station in Washington, I had a great deal to think about.

The complete and total strangeness of the Pluto transit, including my kundalini experiences, involved too many incidents to include in this book. To name a few: finding light devas in my garden in the middle of the night, seeing a light palace in the corner of my living room after meditating, seeing Babaji in the Himalayas during one meditation in which I could have sworn I was there, finding a ring-pass-not in my front lawn (a mini-crop circle); running into a huge, shiny black spider the size of a large baseball glove at a Pir Vilayat meditation retreat, and finding a small, wiggling red-and-green snake on my front porch in Arlington. With fascination, I watched the tiny snake slither into my holly bush and decided not to ever again pull weeds without wearing gloves.

Large spiders, much smaller than the huge, shiny black one encountered in the Allegheny Mountains, showed up in my house with regularity. My Gemini friend, Lilavati Sharma, assured me that spiders were a positive omen from Lakshmi, Hindu Goddess of Wealth, Light, Wisdom and Fortune, wife of Lord Vishnu, the Master of and beyond the past, present and future. I would have preferred a white dove like the one encountered in California, albeit one day a hawk flew over my head with a writhing serpent clutched in its talons—another symbol of the kundalini and the sign of Scorpio rising to its highest level. The medical caduceus of serpents is topped by the wings of an eagle, king of the birds, higher symbol of Scorpio, and another symbol for the soaring kundalini that reaches the highest chakra to bring about Holiness (wholeness) and Illumination.

Late in 1990, I went to see a new chiropractor in Maryland who used radionics. "Your body shows signs of electromagnetic disturbance. Do you live near any of those huge electrical towers?"

I did not. However, there was an AT&T microwave tower a block away, and several more blocks down a high, transmitting radio tower. He said an ordinary person might not be affected by such frequencies, but someone with my sensitivities would be highly affected by the constant, disturbing frequencies sent out by these towers. He thought they might be responsible for the strange vibrations that coursed through me. At the time, I was also writing a book on the computer for long hours each day. He suggested that I move. It took me four years to sell that house.

Many gifted body workers helped me through that difficult time: massage therapists, cranial-sacral workers, acupuncturist, plus constant study and meditation helped me to deal with the unusual energies. I read many books on nutrition, vitamins, and herbs, something I had already done for years.

I made one trip to the ashram of Guru Mai in New York State, who had assumed the leadership of Swami Muktananda's devotees after his passing. It was not possible to make an appointment with the guru. She stopped and smiled at me once. Lilavati had insisted that I see her, although she was never my guru.

In 1991, on my New Moon Solar Return, I was initiated into the Sufi Order of the West by Pir Vilayat Inayat Khan in Washington, D.C. That night in my bed strong electrical currents streamed throughout my body. I began to shake but remained fearless. The energy was purifying and cleansing me for greater enlightenment. I had been dosed with Shakti by another spiritual master. God is God. There is only One.

The transformative Pluto energy had finally started to separate from its close orb with my Sun, so that life again assumed a measure of normalcy. My life will probably never be what most people think of as normal—as a persistent answer to my sincere, youthful prayer.

22

MY MAINE MISADVENTURE

In 1990, after completing my Kabbalah workshops with Warren at the Omega Institute, I visited Leo client-friend Kendra Conn in Cape Cod. In Boston, readings were given to my northeast clients at a charming bed-and-breakfast.

For years I had wanted to see the Maine coast. A Washington client, gossip columnist Karen Feld, who had a home near Portland, had extended an invitation. The initial plan was for Karen to accompany me farther north, but she had a dog and decided to invite others to her charming Victorian house on a lake. With the inclement weather, Karen stayed home. I headed north alone in my determination to see Bar Harbor and Acadia National Park. I had a book that listed New England inns and bed and breakfast establishments. My next stop was the Whitehall Inn in Camden, where Edna St. Vincent Millay once read her poetry on the porch.

As I started out, it was pouring rain. Farther north, the sun broke through the clouds and sunlight danced on the white-capped waters of the North Atlantic. All along the rugged Maine coast was a scattering of quaint lighthouses and charming Victorian towns. I felt as though I was going back in time and entering a gentler period removed from the bustle of Washington, New York City, and Boston. The towns north of Portland had the tall steeples of white frame churches, which reminded me of books such as *Little Women* by Louisa May Alcott and the film based on it, which starred June Allyson, Peter Lawford, Elizabeth Taylor and Margaret O'Brien. All of us were much older by that year, with handsome Peter Lawford already on the Other Side. In the 1970s, Peter had attended parties at the home of Gwen Davis and her husband, Don Mitchell. Don was on the Other Side by then, too.

All the towns in Maine had baskets of colorful flowers hanging from lampposts or overflowing from storefront boxes. Petunias of many colors bloomed in profusion. The picturesque, old-world allure of Maine was casting a magical spell over me. From Rockland on, the towns bordered the Penobscot Bay, with some islands visible off shore and others too far off to see.

On entering charming, picture postcard-perfect downtown Camden, chills suddenly ran up and down my spine and energy filled my head. All at once, it seemed that I was supposed to move to Camden and start a holistic center. There was a distinct sense of a calling not easy to describe or dismiss. At that moment, however, I hadn't the slightest idea how I was going to pull that off.

I spent two nights at the charming Whitehall Inn. I asked the bartender a ton of questions about Camden and the surrounding area. He didn't live there, but in a town miles away. The next day, I checked out the gift shops and art galleries. A two-hour sail on a 100-foot schooner on Penobscot Bay was fun. Dinner at the Waterfront Restaurant on Camden Harbor was tasty. Motor-driven yachts and sailboats, small and large, were anchored at the dock or out on the water. Camden definitely had me under its spell.

Later, in an Internet search, I saw that Camden was listed among the top 20 richest towns of its size in the United States. That sounded promising for a holistic center. The 1957 movie *Peyton Place* was made there, earning nine Oscar nominations and winning three.

The summer of 1990, I drove on to Bar Harbor, which is larger and more commercial than Camden. I spent time in another Victorian inn, where I was hustled by the ruggedly handsome owner. He wanted me to buy the house behind the inn for my center. This Pisces climbed rocks and rowed on a lake at dawn. He was in great shape. Puny me—I was at the end of my saga with chronic fatigue. Plus, he wasn't really my type.

I bought charming birdhouses for my children in Bar Harbor and browsed many of the shops. As I was having lunch outdoors, the vista before me seemed as unreal as the vista in Yellowstone National Park. Mother Nature was dazzling on the coast of Maine.

The next night I stayed at the Whitehall Inn in Camden again. The next day I checked out some real estate for a holistic center. The perfect property was seven acres of forest with a seven-bedroom, two-story Victorian house on a hill, with a fantastic view of Penobscot Bay. There were stables, a barn, and mountain trails. Camden is known as "where the mountains meet the sea." However, the property was on the market for $1.5 million. How could I raise that kind of money for a healing center? Business acumen was not one of my assets.

After that trip, my house in Arlington was placed on the market. The microwave tower was still across the street, the radio tower five blocks away, and no one was buying.

In 1991, my book, *The Wheel of Destiny–The Tarot Reveals Your Master Plan,* was published by Llewellyn Publications. I was their first author invited to sign books at Book Expo America in New York City. That summer, Tomi, her first husband James Brassard, and their four children: Oliver, Jonah, Lydia (July 15, 1983) and Shaina (September 11, 1983) and I rented a cabin on Lake Megunticook outside Camden. The rental included a motorboat, a canoe, and the bare-bones cabin with one bathroom for seven people. The loons called in the morning and evening. It was a peaceful, beautiful setting.

That August, Hurricane Bob forcefully blew into Maine, knocking out power to our cabin for two days. The toilet flushed with a pump. Water was carried from the lake to flush the toilet. For two days we roughed it with kerosene lamps and candles in the Maine wilderness. But we still had lobster in restaurants in Camden, Rockport and Lincolnville, where there was electricity. Acadia National Park was beautiful. Hurricane Bob had not curbed my enthusiasm for Camden.

After our vacation, I left my car with Tomi and her family. Then I flew off to London and later on to the Frankfurt Book Fair to promote my tarot book at my expense. In England, there were appearances on BBC radio and articles that featured me in *You* magazine of the *London Daily Mail,* and in *Empire* magazine after I returned to Virginia. In England, I also attended a Kabbalah Workshop with Warren Kenton near Stratford-upon-Avon. Later, the Gothic Image bus tour with Jamie George included sacred standing stone circles at Avebury in Wiltshire, in addition to Arthurian and Merlin sites in Glastonbury, Cornwall, and Scotland. The bus took us all the way to the Orkney Islands and Isle of Mull where Duart Castle from the 13th century is located, the ancestral home of the Clan MacLean, my father's lineage (not visited).

During the early 1990s, I called Brian in Singapore fairly often (the Brian from the conference in Bombay). He was enthusiastic about the development of a holistic center in Camden and talked about joining me. Meanwhile, Brian had become a Buddhist monk and sent me a picture of himself with his head shaved and him in an orange-yellow robe—to confirm my vision back in 1982 at Muktananda's Ashram. After moving from Thailand to Singapore, Brian had married a Chinese girl, but they had divorced. Their son, Torin, lived with Brian in Singapore.

Selling my Arlington house was not easy. I had started to have doubts about my move to Maine and looked at other houses in Northern Virginia. Astrologer Lynn Koiner said my chart was under aspects that involved education, but it didn't matter where that education took place.

I went to see a medium named Jim at the Arlington Metaphysical Chapel. He really surprised me when he said, "You know that healing center that spirit told you to open. That's your destiny. You have to do that." He had caught me completely off guard. I had never mentioned anything about a center.

"But I don't have the money," I explained.

"The money will come."

"I can't do it alone," I said feeling inadequate to the task.

"You won't be alone. You'll have lots of help."

He insisted that I move to Maine and start my "healing center." After I left him, I was both baffled and amused. After that reading, other psychics also said that the center would be a success with lots of help. But deep down, I had serious doubts.

In April 1994, while I was in Maryland attending a reincarnation seminar, my house in Arlington finally sold. And yet, I was still torn about my move to Camden. One day, during a telephone conversation with my daughter, Tomi said, "If you don't do it, Mother, you'll always wonder if you should have. You felt you had a calling."

Tomi was right. I would always wonder.

That summer, my belongings went into storage just as when our California house was sold. In 1984, I had traveled for six months in the United States and Europe (England, Scotland, Ireland, Switzerland, France, Italy, and Spain) doing readings and playing tourist. This time my trip was to Asia: Singapore and Hong Kong. Other than that, I had my passport, my laptop and tarot cards—will travel. Frequent flyer miles paid for my airline ticket.

My first stop was LAX to change planes. My Pisces friend, Ginny Loeffler, had brunch with me before the flight to Tokyo.

On that plane, I had this strong sense that I was going to run into Babaji again, even though he had left the body I had met in Bombay. I had heard he looked the same and lived in Nepal. There was a possibility of a return trip to India, since clients had recommended me to those in several Indian cities.

Waiting in the Tokyo airport for hours and hours, I had serious jet lag. On the next long flight to Singapore I lucked out with three seats, so stretched out and slept most of the way. The taxi pulled up to Brian's house after midnight, which was noon the previous day for me. The trip had taken 28 hours— and it was 12 hours later. I shall never understand how people on business trips do those flights and manage to function.

Brian gave me Torin's room, with a futon on the floor—a new experience for me. Several of Brian's friends booked readings. There were free readings for my host as my "thank-you." During the previous year, Brian had mentioned prominent friends of his becoming members of the Board of Directors for the Akasha Institute for Holistic Studies. One day, one of Brian's important friends called and I answered the telephone. The man had absolutely no knowledge of me or my center. That had me confused and suddenly uneasy.

Another of Brian's friends was Taurus Andrea. We hit it off. Andrea was then married with two daughters. She expressed sincere interest in my center. Perhaps others were actually going to help me out. That was encouraging.

Cancer Manize invited me to lecture on "Tarot and Consciousness" at the Theosophical Society in Singapore. Manize was also talking about starting a center in her native India. There was something about the woman that made me apprehensive and suspicious, something hard to dismiss or determine. Years later, my reservations proved right. Manize had been dishonest and taken money from people without fulfilling her promise to create a center in Bangalore. Several

Americans, including Andrea, donated large sums and ended up with nothing. It does not seem to be an easy matter to take legal actions against a person in India.

In Singapore, many question spreads (Celtic Crosses) were done for Brian, with surprisingly negative answers. He never told me the nature of his questions, but in reading after reading the cards were worrying with NO as the answer. Was he being warned not to be involved with the Akasha Institute? For an Aquarius, Brian was secretive. I learned his cousin, once married to a Thai princess, then had a sex shop business in Bangkok. I had heard about those shops from a friend with business in Asia. AIDS was rampant in the Asian sex trade. And, even though I believe that selling drugs and sex should be legal, I had no desire for my institute to be associated with those activities.

In Singapore, I made enough money from readings to fly to Bali, Indonesia, where more readings were done. One woman at my hotel was an American who worked in Dubai. I also contacted Nadia, a designer friend of Gwen's. Nadia took me to parties and told me about the Bali Spirit Hotel and Spa in Ubud. My hotel on the beach was surrounded by construction, with noisy jackhammers all day every day. The Bali Spirit Hotel in the mountains was in a peaceful, lush setting. My massage near the river was given under the coconut palms.

More Americans booked readings in Ubud. One young American had lived in Bali for years and belonged to a Yoga ashram. She invited me for a session with crystal chakra bowls where she was house-sitting. Perhaps not coincidentally, the owners of the house were in Switzerland for a month at the ashram of Mahavatar Babaji. Pictures of the Holy Man I had met in Bombay 12 years before were on the walls. Contact with Babaji was not on the physical plane on that trip.

In Singapore, friends of Brian's suggested that while on Bali, I should get in touch with a man named Moon Shadows (my pseudonym) who might donate money for my institute. In Ubud, I learned the man was a young American who lived with a Malaysian man in various houses around the island, one of them in Ubud. It never bothered me that he was gay, what bothered me was that he turned out to be a major drug dealer. I made no effort to contact him. Some suggested as donors for my institute were not even remote possibilities to my mind. I wondered which spirits had shown up when I had the session with the medium named Jim. Dead is not better. Not all spirit communication is genuine or reliable.

By the time I left Singapore, Brian was no longer on my team. He was planning a Buddhist Center in Colorado, or some state, and never bothered to tell me until rather late. After that, Brian pretty much dropped out of the picture after being my biggest supporter. The last I heard, he had returned to Iowa, married again and had another child—which I thought was in his cards—and his karma.

Back in Washington, D.C., I spent two weeks with my friend Judy Diamond where readings were given to clients before my departure for Maine. My car was finally packed, and yet, at the outset, I had an enormous sense of dread and trepidation that never lifted until I neared Camden. Then, suddenly, I felt better, as though maybe things would work out.

The first night was spent at the High Tide Inn owned by Sagittarius Jo Freilich. Her inn seemed like a perfect place for classes. That night, Jo and I had dinner at the Waterfront Restaurant on Camden Harbor and talked about all kinds of metaphysical subjects and experiences. Jo was a widow and had lost her young husband two years before. The inn had been their dream, but he was no longer there to help and share. I ended up renting the small house where she had lived with her husband. The two-bedroom house was on seven acres on Penobscot Bay three miles north of town off the highway. My adventure in the beautiful northeastern state of Maine had finally begun four years after my initial visit.

On Limerock Street in Camden was a three-story, 100-year old Victorian house with a "For Sale" sign out front. I was drawn to the dark gray house with white trim and rusty red shutters. I kept driving by and stopping out in front—and the big old house seemed to talk to me. The house had been turned into a duplex. The upper two stories were turned into one apartment, with the downstairs another. The property was on the market for $235,000—which was $5,000 more than what I had made on my Arlington house. However, that $235,000 price included a duplex. The house was on the corner of a smaller street and had an L-shaped duplex behind it that faced that street. This was the former "boat house" that had been converted into one and two-bedroom apartments, with both of them then rented.

Was it smart for me to buy the property with no money left over for my center? The center was my reason for being in Camden. Instead, there was a smaller, three-bedroom Victorian on Willow Street on the market for $89,500. I could afford that house and still have enough for catalogs and stationery. School classrooms might be used for summer classes.

Before the offer was made on the Willow Street house, I consulted a horary astrologer, Gilbert Navarro, in Maryland. He said, "It is okay to buy the house, but you may have boundary issues."

My offer was $5,000 under the asking price and the owner accepted. I could afford to keep the house if things didn't work out. Then, I would have a summer home in Camden—not a bad idea, I thought then. However, the kitchen had been added to the back of the house and was supported by posts. It was an adorable Victorian, gray with white trim. I planned to upgrade the kitchen and bathrooms. But first, I wanted a cement foundation to support the kitchen and keep the floor from rising and falling in the extreme Maine weather. Winters are long and cold. A contractor had quoted me $7,000 for a new cement foundation.

The day before the closing was scheduled I went to the house and found the neighbors in the corner house that faced the other street out in the yard staring at the house. They had seen the contractor and wanted to know what was going on.

"In a few days there will be some digging for a new cement foundation under the kitchen, but everything will be put back in place with new shrubs and perennials planted on that side of the house," I explained.

"But your kitchen wall is on our property line," the gruff man said. "You can't dig there."

"What do you mean?" I was stunned.

The man and woman both insisted that I would not be able to put a cement foundation around what was supposed to be 'my kitchen.'

I got in my car and soon arrived at the real estate office. "I can't buy a house with a wall on someone else's property. They told me I couldn't put in a cement foundation."

The deal was off. The reason: boundary issues.

Half of my $2,000 deposit was forfeit, because the lawyer in New Jersey who owned the house said I owed him for backing out the day before closing. What about the wall of the house being on someone else's property?

Welcome to the State of Maine—as an "away person." I was soon to learn that living in Maine was not only like living in a former time—but like living on another planet!

Driving by the house the next day, when I was supposed to own the property, there was a 6-foot, free-standing wooden fence two feet from the wall of the house—obvious boundary issues. And later, when I drove by on Halloween, the owner had painted that side of the gray Victorian a brilliant Halloween orange—perhaps as a raspberry to his grumpy neighbors that cost him the sale. Thankfully, I never lived there. Who would want those people for neighbors?

Meanwhile, a realtor had purchased the duplex behind the larger Victorian on Limerock Street. That meant the three-story house with the rusty red shutters could be purchased separately. I made an offer that was accepted. Then again, the realtor buying the duplex wanted to talk. One side of the duplex was only about 12 feet from the back of the house. The backyard was shared with a gravel driveway between the duplex and garage. Property lines zigzagged all over the place, which seemed to be the norm in Camden. The realtor wanted to purchase the larger portion of the backyard. Yet, the six-bedroom house was going to be a center. How could the larger portion of the backyard be sold? Where would students go to smoke cigarettes or chat under the tall pine trees?

When I refused to sell her the backyard, she backed out of her purchase! Suddenly, I had to buy the duplex too. For some strange reason, the rules had changed. Another business mortgage had to be secured at a higher interest rate. The house would be turned back into one residence, but I now owned two additional rental apartments—because of boundary issues. Gilbert's horary question had had long-term applications. The Maine issue: even though both properties were purchased for $170,000, a $65,000 savings, I had no money left to remodel—with both structures in need of considerable work to be useful as a holistic center.

The other Maine problem: I needed to advertise in national magazines to get enough clients to pay my bills. I no longer resided in a major metropolitan area in which I appeared on radio and television. Large numbers of satisfied clients no longer referred people for in-person readings. My initial telephone bills were $1,000 a month. Praise the Lord that telephone rules have since changed. When checks from strangers started to bounce, I opened a merchant's account to accept Visa, MasterCard, Discover and American Express. Another account had to be opened to book classes at the Akasha Institute for Holistic Studies. Then an 800 number was needed. The State of Maine had forced me not only to streamline my psychic business, but work six days a week to keep up, which was indeed a major challenge.

The local contractors were under the grandiose impression that some "rich woman from Virginia" had moved to Camden to open a holistic center. After all, gossip was that I had looked at a $1.5 million estate (during my delusional period encouraged by Brian in Singapore). Looking and buying are two different things entirely!

In those days, I was frequently on the telephone with my Gemini client-friend, Michael Crandus in Washington, to whine about my newfound woes. Michael had encouraged me about the center and agreed to be on the Board of Directors. He had business acumen in real estate. When I told him how the contractors had completed work without providing an estimate or contract, he said not to pay them. In Maine, the law requires a contract for work exceeding a cost of $1,500. An electrician had walked through the house and never gave me an estimate. He just went ahead with the work, including additional improvements never discussed, and then sent me a bill for $3,000.

The building contractor was told not to replace the windows in the big house at a cost of $8,000, since new windows depreciated the historic value of the original glass. One morning, I drove to the house on a hunch and found two windows removed, with workmen about to remove another. I had to argue with the contractor to get the windows put back. Many projects discussed were never written down and no contract was ever signed. He just went ahead and completed work without an estimate and handed me a bill for $14,000 after I had already paid him $10,000. Meanwhile, Visa and MasterCard checks were being written to painters, carpet layers, plumbers, building contractors, and an electrician, until my credit card debt exceeded $90,000, including printers for the Akasha Institute catalogs and stationery.

No doubt, I never should have pursued nonprofit status. A lawyer-client in Pennsylvania helped me with that. Letters were written to rich and famous clients for donations, but when my income taxes were paid in those years, I realized that someone had to really believe in something to make a large donation. I would have been better off with a private business with expenses written off rather than deducted as contributions. One year, my "$18,000 donation" to Akasha saved me only $1,500 in income taxes. There was no other choice but to work with clients six days a week. It took me four years to crawl out of that hole by cutting corners in every possible way.

In 1995, the first classes at Akasha Institute for Holistic Studies were held in the summer, the same season that the Open Center in New York City canceled all classes because of low enrollment. Interface in Boston had 30 percent attendance that year. Camden was charming and picturesque, but trains no longer ran there. Small commuter flights landed in Rockland. Camden was a three-hour drive north of Boston.

For two years, classes were held in my 12-room Victorian house and adjoining duplex. Two classes were held at the High Tide Inn. The faithful drove north from the Washington metropolitan area and other eastern cities: The largest registration for any class was 10 people. Some classes had four to seven students. Many workshops were canceled because of low enrollment. The nonprofit organization was fully nonprofit for everyone, except hopefully not for some of the students that attended those classes. Teachers received a room and meals, with each treated to dinner at the Waterfront. Teachers paid their own airfare and received a pittance for teaching. But they supported me, and for that I will be forever grateful.

Many months were spent driving up and down the state of Maine from town to town, distributing catalogs and stapling flyers to telephone poles from Portland to Bar Harbor. The Baptists in Camden tore down my flyers as fast I stapled them up, especially when the subject was past lives, shamanism, the Qabalah, or UFOs. Do they still burn witches in Maine's backwoods? Sometimes I wondered.

One summer, a man working on the Stephen King film, *Thinner*, rented my two- bedroom duplex with his wife. There were winter renters and summer weekly renters, which helped to pay the mortgages and property taxes. However, some tenants stole telephones and furnishings, or broke windows or wrote me bad checks. I shall never be a landlady again.

It was a thrill for me when Dr. Christiane Northrup agreed to teach at my center. It cost me $300 for a pap smear just to meet her and talk to her about it. My plan was to rent the Camden Opera House which seats 250 with presenters like Dr. Northrup or Deepak Chopra, Brian Weiss, or Jack Cornfield. All celebrity speakers were busy. I had little to offer, no money for airfare. And yet, every psychic consulted had insisted that help was on the way: a man and a woman. Where were they— no doubt hiding out somewhere on the Astral Plane?

In 1996, registration for Dr. Northrup's weekend workshop and Friday evening lecture was 30. The opera house was canceled. At the doctor's request, two rooms were rented at the Camden Harbour Inn for $150 a night per room, which meant $600 for two nights before taxes. She was unaware of how stretched I was or how small my operation was, perhaps.

The Wednesday before her announced lecture and workshop, her nurse called to check on registration.

"Dr. Northrup will need to be paid for 75 attendees," she said.

Only 30 had registered. Rent at an inn was going to cost me more than $600, and a hall needed to be rented. There was no other choice for me but to cancel my star performer when every cent and more would have gone to her. I was at the end of my tether, as they say.

In all honesty, I was pleased to learn that only 30 had attended Dr. Northrup's seminar at Interface in Boston. A woman who planned to be in Camden went to Boston instead. She said she was disappointed. With the number that showed up at my front door on Friday evening, and again the next morning, we would have probably had 60 in Camden—but not 75. With my confidence level so low after two years of deep disappointment, I was not up to taking the chance. Many women had driven miles to see the famous Maine obstetrician and gynecologist—and I had to turn them away. Their disappointment was not even close to mine in terms of cancellations and foolishness on my part for thinking I could pull off running a holistic center in Maine all by myself.

I am still grateful to my clients and friends who made the trip to Camden to attend or teach a workshop. Dale Graff (former director of Project Stargate, the U.S. government psychic spy program) taught a workshop on Dreams. Fredda Rizzo taught the Qabalistic Tree of Life, Andrea Swanson taught about Angels. Donald Ware spoke on UFOs.

In fact, around 40 people had gathered at the bookstore on the Friday evening that Don Ware was supposed to lecture on UFOs. As it turned out, his plane had mechanical problems and was diverted. Don arrived at midnight to teach his two-day workshop. There were seven students and I am sure there would have been more if he had lectured on Friday. Money had not been collected for that.

On Friday, when everyone in the bookstore was waiting for Don, I told a man about my woes in my attempt to establish the center in Camden. "Maybe if everything is so hard, you're not really supposed to do it. Have you thought of that?" he inquired.

At that moment, it seemed to me that my spirit guides had given me a strong message. I had tried very hard to believe in what the other psychics had said. And yet, I also remembered my dread in driving north. As Lucille Joy once said many years ago, "You're going to go to a lot of folk like me, but let it go in one ear and out the other, because you were born *knowing*. You know what's best for you."

For a number of years I resided in the same town as Dr. Benjamin Spock, the internationally known pediatrician. His *Baby and Child Care,* published in 1946, was a bible for young mothers. The popular peace activist passed away in 1998 while I was in Camden. Guitarist, singer, songwriter David Crosby of Crosby, Stills, Nash & Young of the Rock and Roll Hall of Fame, lives near the lake. It has been discussed on television that he fathered Melissa Etheridge's children, perhaps by donation. John Travolta has a house on Isleboro. Sometimes I saw him at Peter Ott's restaurant having dinner with friends.

Singer, songwriter Don "Bye, Bye, Miss American Pie" McLean lives in Camden. A few times I ran into Don at the post office. He would smile and say, "Hi." His wife, Patty McLean, is a photographer and I received many telephone calls from people who wanted pictures taken. Finally, her telephone number was kept near the phone: Patricia McLean, not Patricia McLaine. There has always been another Patty McLean (some spelling) somewhere near. It also happened at Alhambra High.

One good thing that came from the Akasha brochure being placed in a New York City bookstore: someone with Nonfiction Films picked one up. The call was to appear in a new video series for television: *Strictly Supernatural,* in the segment on *Tarot.* The show aired on the Discovery Channel and the Learning Channel. My airfare to New York was paid, and I stayed with Libra client-friend Janet Ruppel in Tribeca. When we had Sunday brunch, we saw Robert De Niro sitting at another table. The videos were sold and the segment aired repeatedly. I seemed unable to escape from my image as the Tarot Psychic—one ulterior motive for starting the Akasha Center for Holistic Studies in Camden, Maine, in the first place.

By 1997, there were no classes and I was traveling again as a psychic. I spent six months a year at the Park Center Apartments in Alexandria, Virginia. Looking back, I affectionately think of my time in Maine as my seven years in Purgatory. It was a joy to drive through the mountains during peak fall color, but no fun to dig my car out from the snow three times in one day. I enjoyed sitting in my library to watch large, white flakes flutter to the ground, but the black ice was scary. Fun times were spent with Sagittarius Jo, Taurus Dawn, and Leo Janet. As with every house owned to date, my money doubled, but with all that was spent on the institute I was barely breaking even.

Nonetheless, in May 2001, I left Camden with more money at my disposal than ever before and returned to Alexandria, Virginia. Perhaps another coincidence: the couple that bought my Camden property moved to Camden and Rockport, Maine, from Alexandria, Virginia.

Then again, by being forced to advertise in national magazines such as *Psychology Today,* more than a few new interesting clients entered my life from all over the world. Sometimes you simply have to follow your Destiny—wherever it might lead you.

23

PAST LIVES – PRESENT PATTERNS

From my perspective, we all keep running into each other lifetime after lifetime. Our role, location, set, genetic disposition, race, gender, economic standard, and costume may dramatically change, but the play goes on as another curtain rises on the Stage of Life. Not long after I first started giving readings, my first past life memories emerged.

In my Hatha Yoga classes with the remarkable Clara Spring, I learned to seriously meditate and to do Vedic chants in the manner of the ancient Yogis. In the beginning, I never realized that sounding *AUM* facilitated the opening of the third eye, the famous eye in the middle of the forehead connected to the pineal gland and higher aspects of consciousness and spiritual awakening.

My keen interests in mystical and spiritual subjects eventually enabled me to review other lifetimes during the history of our planet, and not only my lives, but those of many clients. For the most part, my previous life unfolded like a movie inside my head, usually in the portion of my brain directly behind my forehead or right on top. Generally, the review was in response to an intense need to know about a person or a difficult situation. My heart and soul were crying out for Light, a reason *why*, regarding a painful or unpleasant pattern, perhaps a strong emotional response to a situation or person, and in my sincere need—an answer was often forthcoming, though not always to my liking.

In accordance with my knowledge of Qabalistic (or Kabbalistic or Cabalistic) principles (since the greater part of my spiritual training this time has been in that discipline), I understand that a person is unable to access past life memories until he or she has achieved the soul growth necessary to view the bitter and the sweet with equal objectivity. In this way, the soul benefits not only from former glories and triumphs, but from past mistakes and indiscretions. During nearly every life, erroneous judgment, or even thoughtless, cruel, or willful acts create opportunities for growth during the present or a future life, with most issues better dealt with in the present.

It can take years, or lifetimes, for some to recognize glaring character imperfections to the point of being able to implement partial or total change. The only place a soul is able to transmute even one character flaw is in a physical body. Without the temptations and potential patterns of three-dimensional realities, there is little for the soul to overcome or attempt to rise above. On the inner or higher planes, the vices and ambitions associated with this world (three-dimensional reality) are temporarily on hold as the soul endeavors to chart its next course for another round in some planetary system where his or her talents and skills might be further refined and put to constructive or destructive use. While the soul is basically androgynous in nature, sexual appetite or preference is relegated to life in a physical body where reproduction and carnal engagement become possible.

All spiritual evolutionary systems, including the various religions on this planet, facilitate soul growth and development, some to a greater extent than others, depending on individual aspiration and intent. What most people need to learn is the expression of unconditional love that is not expressed as possession or any form of ownership. The Master of Compassion is also a Heart Master. The opening of the fourth, or heart chakra, enables an evolving soul to express love at a higher level and to live a compassionate, charitable and generous life. The opening of the fourth chakra also facilitates the opening of the other three higher spiritual centers, which lead to expanded awareness and the expression of superior talents and skills. The majority of those on this earth are governed by the lower three chakras: self-preservation, reproduction, and ego identification, with many unaware of their unity with all life, including the living planet on which we are blessed to exist.

Without an opening in the higher chakras, which involves the heart, throat and head centers, there is no ability to tune into past or future lifetimes, although some may have already developed these capacities during past lives and may be picking up from where they left off. My teacher, Ann Davies, taught that the soul recapitulates everything he or she has ever been or done once again the soul reincarnates. Many interests and tastes as children are conditioned by former life patterns. Recapitulation is required before a soul may embark upon a new mission and learn yet more.

Serious work on me and my character commenced with my first Saturn Return in my late twenties, with no turning back since. During the early years of my psychic work I was diligent in performing Hatha Yoga postures for 40 minutes, five days a week. After yoga, I sat cross-legged in meditation, since I was unable to do the full lotus of devout Buddhists and Yogis. Nonetheless, deep breathing exercises were used to center: breathing in to the count of four, holding my breath to the count of four, breathing out to four, and holding the breath out for four more counts—a common practice that quiets the mind.

While focused on the breath, one is not involved in mental calisthenics with the lower mind running from one subject to another. Breath is consciousness. Consciousness is breath. By practicing breath control, the mind and emotions come under control. When feelings of fear, anger, or distress arise, the breath is affected in a negative manner harmful to the health.

By controlling breath, there is control of emotions and feelings. In fact, the first key of the Tarot Major Arcana, Key 0, the Fool, depicts the Divine Breath or *Ruach*. When the soul leaves this earthly dimension the body no longer breathes.

During one surprising early meditation, a scene from the distant past vividly filled my mind. In my present life I was brought up on stories from the Bible by my devoutly religious Christian mother. During early Roman times I was also a devout Christian when members of my sect were being severely persecuted by the Pagan rulers of Rome.

For the "show" in the Coliseum on that fateful day, as a young woman dressed in a long white gown to represent a Vestal Virgin of the Pagan temples, I was led by guards into the arena to the sound of trumpets, accompanied by the deafening roar of the crowd. Two Roman soldiers took me to a wooden stake in the center where my hands were bound behind my back and my feet bound to the stake.

All the while, inside my chest my heart was wildly beating.

Trumpets again sounded as a Pagan priest entered the arena and ceremoniously placed a garland of flowers on my head.

All the while, I fervently though silently prayed to the One God and His Only Begotten Son Jesus Christ for my immediate release and salvation.

Once again, the trumpets sounded.

This time a gladiator entered the arena with two Roman guards on either side of him. A broadsword was placed on the ground several feet before him, and the guards hastily retreated. As the gladiator held the sword in his right hand, I noted the long, red scar on his muscular forearm. Plainly, he had engaged in many fierce fights. There were smaller scars on both his cheeks and on one side of his neck. As the warrior moved closer, his blue eyes registered compassion mixed with fear. He exhibited a fierce yet quiet strength as I wondered what crime had condemned him to his fate. Noting the jagged scar circling his left arm, I remembered him from secret meetings held deep within the ancient catacombs. My gladiator protector was also a member of the despised sect of Christians.

After another blast from the trumpets, five full grown lions were released into the arena—with the promise of imminent entertainment for those assembled. Loud cheers arose from the crowd, which sickened me. The Pagan Romans thirsted for my blood as wild beasts tore at and devoured my flesh and bones.

My brave protector stood before me in his valiant attempt to ward off the hungry beasts that were now circling the two of us. My heart raced and I earnestly prayed to my Lord and Savior Jesus Christ to hasten my end so I might join Him and Our Father and the Heavenly Host of martyrs.

The dance between the man and the five hungry beasts became irregular, uneven in terms of number, as a honey-eyed lioness moved toward me where I was tied at the stake. A lion and lioness were viciously attacking the gladiator, as in his futility he tried to fight them off from his ill-fated position on the ground.

Then, suddenly, an open-mouthed lioness lunged at my midsection, as my spirit instantly dollied up and out into the heavens as in some dramatic motion picture.

That past life memory confirmed for me that life is eternal—my soul can never be destroyed. The insight received on my walk in the sun after church at age 16 had been dramatically reinforced: I had always been and would always be. For there I was, in my living room in Sherman Oaks, alive and free of hungry lions.

Perhaps my memory is nothing more than another aspect of my overactive imagination. I am sure that imagination plays a vital role in past life recall, the same as in remembering things from earlier in the present life. There is no way for me to gain access to the ancient Roman archives to find the record of my previous existence or my sacrifice, since the year and my name were not recalled and probably never recorded. However, remembering a past life has a different feel to it from remembering a dream, which is even harder for some people.

Over the years, I have remembered fragments of 150 or more past lives as a woman or a man in different cultures. More female lives have been recalled, perhaps because of being a woman now. Dynamic male embodiments have been remembered. It would be impossible to describe all my prior incarnations in this chapter, so only a few will be recounted.

In my spiritual training, meditation is also used to solve problems by looking into difficult situations for insight to dissolve karma. By taking each husband into meditation at different times, my unrealistic expectations of each man became clear to me. I had never taken enough time to get to know Tom or Bill before they became my husbands. And yet, my daughter was born because of Tom, my son from Bill. I am grateful for my children and grandchildren.

In the early 1970s, I had a life reading from Aron Abrahamson, a medium who works in deep trance like Edgar Cayce to tune in to people's past lives. The reading was scheduled for a specific time with Aron in another state. He asked me to be quiet during the time, and at first, he likened me to an old kerosene lamp. Aron warned me to be careful of how much light I gave out to some, since not all were able to receive the light. He said I needed to use a shade to keep from blinding some people. He also said to keep my "wick trimmed," which made me smile!

Aron said that in a past life in Egypt I had been married to Tom when he was a merchant and we resided near the Nile. He said both my children were our sons at that time. It was interesting that Tom had chosen the name of Tomi for our daughter. During my pregnancy, I had a strong impression that I would have a son, but Tomi is a very feminine female.

In grammar school, both my children did reports on ancient Egypt. At age eight, Mark made a papier-mâché "mummy for his Mommy," red and green with "hieroglyphics," and a delicate face for my Christmas gift. That mummy is among my special treasures.

According to Aron, I had been married to Bill in ancient Greece and he was my wife at that time. I owned large tracts of land and herds of sheep and goats. At the time I was a prophet of Apollo and often traveled to the Temple of Apollo at the Oracle at Delphi. When I revisited Delphi in this life, the ruins no longer held their former luster, but those times were important to my growth. I have reconnected with more than a few of those from ancient Greece who are now my friends.

In the early 1970s, during a reading for an actress friend of Susan Strasberg's, I could see the woman's son in this life had once been her father. Realizing an offspring was once a parent or spouse happens often. Souls evolve in groups and change roles from time to time. In this instance, the woman's father had died when she was very young. It turned out that her son had actually been her father in her present life. He had returned more quickly than some.

In amazement, she said, "My mother always says that he looks like my father, acts like my father, he even talks and walks like my father. She said if she didn't know better, she'd say he *was* my father!"

And he was!

Her mother's husband had returned as her grandson. Her father was now her son. Life is stranger than fiction—and more interesting by far.

Early in my work in Sherman Oaks, one neighbor said that her three-year old daughter had once sat on her grandmother's lap and said, "When I grow up I'm going to be your mommy." There had never been any mention of reincarnation. She found it curious, but I thought the child might be right. Her grandmother could return one day as her child.

Many former husbands and lovers have shown up in this lifetime, which have sometimes been difficult lessons for my true Scorpio nature! At one Cayce meeting was a young man who had been my husband in India. He had been the caretaker of the Maharaja's elephants. We had five children in an arranged marriage. There was no passion and nothing left for resolution. We said goodbye and went our separate ways. No hard feelings. No worries.

In the late 1960s at the Philosophical Round Table in Los Angeles, I met an interesting, older, gray-haired gentleman. He reminded me of a professor but worked as a supervisor in a steel mill. That May, during the Scorpio Full Moon, which is the time of the Wesak Festival on the Inner Planes where the Masters gather, I had an extraordinary series of past life memories.

I had seen the man at the meetings on many Fridays. Sometimes we spoke. He was married, but his wife was rarely there. I had sensed a distinct past life connection without knowing where or when. On that Full Moon, driving home under the light of the Great Goddess, past life memories began to flood my mind.

In the beginning, I was in a murky brothel in some seaport in Malaysia waiting for my customer. In walked a sailor with a young, green tree python writhing around his neck. His hair was a short, curly, dark blond and he had a short, curly brown beard, not the white of his present life. The moment I saw the snake I shrieked and leapt from a window. He was bringing me what he thought was a gift, but I had a deathly fear of snakes. Bad choice on his part!

Finally, at home in my bed, other patterns from that lifetime vividly emerged. My mother had given birth to me in the brothel owned by a French madam. My father had supposedly been an English sailor, but how can any prostitute know which man had sired her child? My mother had been madly in love with the English sailor. He had promised to return and take her away, but he never did. Devastated, my mother had leaped off a cliff onto the rocks and died. I was raised in the brothel and lived a short, sordid and miserable life.

In my bed, during that Scorpio Full Moon, in a sense of deep desperation I wanted to know the reason for my deathly fear of the small, nonpoisonous snake. What had triggered my fear?

All at once, the walls of my bedroom disappeared. I was in a dark rain forest, perhaps in the Amazon, with a damp, musty smell. I was a small, dark-skinned, native woman making my way back to the village near the river when I came upon an enormous anaconda 30 feet long! The great snake opened wide its mouth and swallowed my head, while wrapping itself around and around my small, slender body, contracting tighter with my every breath.

In my bed, in my darkened room, I was fighting for my breath. I could sense the huge serpent tightening around me as my soul cried out for the reason why. Why was I forced to suffer such an unusual, horrible death alone in the dark, dense jungle?

Suddenly, I was traveling back, back, back in time and found myself in what appeared to be ancient Mesopotamia (modern Iraq). In that culture, I was a striking snake priestess with long, dark hair with a curvaceous body. Should anyone disobey my command or go against my wishes, they were tossed into a huge pit filled with slithering, hissing, deadly snakes: cobras, vipers, asps and adders—the more venomous the better. My offenders generally died from numerous bites. I ruled my snake cult was a slithery, power-hungry hand in an entirely manipulative manner. My ego was—shall we say— somewhat out of control? If a lover rejected me, he was quickly disposed of by one of my obedient though lethal serpentine pets. Perhaps that was why it was my karma to be reborn to a prostitute and forced to die a painful, horrible death from syphilis at a young age in Malaysia.

In reviewing my past life in Mesopotamia, I was horrified by the extent of my evil and ruthless behavior. How could sweet, innocent me have ever been so wicked? In that life I eventually died from the self-inflicted bite of an adder to avoid a more terrible death at the hands of a malevolent high priest. Live and learn! But must it always be so difficult? For a long time I never spoke of that life—triggered by the May Full Moon in Scorpio.

Before becoming serious about metaphysics, I lived next door to Aquarius Diane Johnson (later Theyken) in Glendale during my marriage to Bill Jacobs. Diane was the same age as Bill, 15 years my senior. But Diane and I really hit it off. Her older daughter, Sue, often babysat young Tomi and Mark.

The most interesting thing about Diane: she remembered her past lives while she was a child in Colorado and she was born long before television was invented (1922). At four, Diane told her parents about dancing as a concubine for the pharaoh in ancient Egypt. No books about ancient Egypt were in the house. Later, Diane remembered being a slaveholder on a Southern plantation prior to the Civil War. She still loathed Abraham Lincoln, which seemed odd for a woman born in Colorado in 1922.

Diane had grown up in the same town as Morey Bernstein, author of *The Search for Bridey Murphy,* published in 1952. That book is about a Colorado woman's past life memories of being an Irish woman in Cork, Ireland, in the 1800s. Her memories emerged during hypnosis. Diane's memories of other lives and times took place before that book was written. Because of her vivid memories of her past lives, Diane's parents joined the Unity Church, in which such beliefs are accepted and embraced. Diane introduced me to numerology, which I used in my early readings.

In fact, in the 1970s I added an "e" to my last name, because Patricia McLaine became a 17/8 name and my birth path in numerology is 8. The "e" helped me with mystical power and money! Dramatist Play Service started publishing my play, *Love is Contagious*, under Patricia McLaine instead of Patricia McLain by the late 1970s. Diane and I remained friends until her passing in 1999. I am sure she is doing fine on the Other Side, but I still miss her sparkle and wit.

In 1992, on a Kabbalah trip in Spain, I had a strong sense that I had been there before. In 1984, I had lectured on tarot and astrology on the Spanish island of Ibiza at a conference sponsored by my good Scorpio friend astrologer Jeanne Avery. That year I had returned to Madrid to stay with Sarah and Adolpho Pfeiffer and do readings in their lovely home.

In 1993, as the bus with our Kabbalah group drove through the Spanish countryside, I kept looking for a sign or a feeling. Nothing happened until the bus started to approach Toledo, a quaint medieval town on a hill. All of a sudden, the hair on the back of my neck and both arms rose up and chills ran through me. I knew I was getting close to my former Spanish home.

In a Catholic cathedral in Toledo, Spain, once a Jewish synagogue, I had an extraordinary experience. Over and over inside my head this Jewish prayer was repeated: *Blessings upon your head and upon the heads of your children and upon your children's children unto the third and fourth generation ...* I felt I had been there before.

When our group reached the town's square, the guide said, "This is where the heretics were burned at the stake," and the hair on my neck and arms rose again. That was where I had been burned at the stake because of tarot cards and practicing Kabbalistic magic. And yet, there I was again to experience yet another day.

In my heart, I knew that many in my Kabbalah group and other friends as well had been with me in the Essene community in Qumran at the same time. We had walked where Jesus walked. Jesus was a member of our group and was married with a family (wife and children), the same as other men in our sect. I sensed that Dr. Michael Hattwick had been a scribe in Qumran, a grandfatherly type or uncle with a long, gray beard. As a child I had sat upon a stack of sheepskins to watch him where he was seated on a high stool writing on scrolls of parchment. Many oil lamps burned on a ledge near the ceiling to light the room. I have had many past lives with that Michael in various roles in different countries.

In Crete, Michael was my father. He carved tombstones and sculpted. During the conquests of Alexander the Great, he was my brother and a fellow soldier as we helped our leader conquer the then known world. Toward the end of that life, we marched into Egypt where young Alexander was buried. Others from my present life were with me in ancient Macedonia. In ancient Rome, Michael was a doctor and also my husband in an arranged marriage. We developed a close friendship. He was a philosopher and scholar at that time.

In the Scotland of Queen Mary, we were cousins of the ill-fated queen and of each other. His name was David, mine was Lorna. Our mothers planned our union from the day of my birth in the Highlands. David was five years older. That life is perhaps the most vivid I have ever remembered, although others are clear in fragments. Several friends were with me in

Scotland, some as my children. David and I had eight children. Two died, including a stillborn daughter and a two-year old son from meningitis. It was a colorful time. I was a devout Catholic. My husband had embraced the convenient new religion of King Henry VIII, the Anglican Church of England. David was something of a philanderer, nothing like his present self. Many men in my life have been named Michael, which is the name of my favorite Archangel.

The first time I saw Michael Crandus, I *knew* he was someone from one of my past lives. His former persona flashed before me: he wore a black cape and black top hat, not the summer business suit of that afternoon. He was just as tall (6 feet 3 inches), or taller, with dark hair. His energy was familiar as we had lunch with Janet Ruppel at Washington Harbor. Michael called me for an appointment later that day. That was the beginning of a meaningful friendship.

Our most recent past life together was in Prague, when he was a count with a great fortune, and I was married to a womanizing, gambling fool. My silly husband (I'm still unsure of his present identity) was after a wealthy woman, and idiotic enough to challenge her husband to a duel with pistols. My husband died two days later from his wounds, leaving me with his gambling debts. Suddenly, my two children and I were penniless.

Who should come to my rescue but the dashing count! He had always been fond of me as a gambling acquaintance of my husband's. On the other hand, Michael was in an arranged marriage with a woman he could hardly tolerate. She had yet to produce an heir for his vast fortune. He thought his wife was barren. I had children and was still of childbearing age, so he set me up comfortably as his mistress. During the ensuing years, he grew fond of my two children, providing them with fine educations and making sure my daughter married well. I never conceived his child.

The sad truth: The Count was sterile because of a childhood illness. Ours was not a great passion but the love between us was strong. We were good friends, perhaps because of our former life together in Qumran. In the Essene community, Michael and I were married and had three children. Ours was a loving, devoted marriage, with no negative karma for resolution. Perhaps that was why we reconnected in Prague, even though we had no children that time.

During this lifetime, I predicted his marriage to Melissa and in her reading saw their future three children. Triplets were not what I had in mind. And yet, they had triplets, two adorable sons and a pretty daughter. Good job!

In the early 1990s, I read Dr. Brian Weiss's book, *Many Lives Many Masters,* which was one reason for attending a reincarnation seminar in Baltimore with my friend Judy. Brian was one of the keynote speakers. When Dr. Weiss appeared on stage, I instantly picked up Scorpio and Capricorn. The doctor has a dry sense of humor and plenty of charm. I approached him about coming to Camden to do a workshop for the Akasha Institute for Holistic Studies. His reputation would certainly have boosted attendance, in addition to his knowledge on a subject of ongoing public interest. Brian was much too busy to oblige me.

Our mutual friend, another Scorpio, astrologer Jeanne Avery, had put Brian in touch with her editor at Simon & Schuster where his first book was published. One of Jeanne's clients, a friend of Dr. Weiss, had told her that the head of the psychiatric department at Mt. Sinai Hospital in Miami had written a book on reincarnation. Jeanne and Brian met in person near the time her book, *Astrology and Your Past Lives,* was released. Jeanne featured me in *The Rising Sign* and *Astrological Aspects,* two of her six interesting books on astrology.

Since then, Dr. Brian Weiss has been recognized the world over for his work in past life regression. At the conference in

1992, I learned that Brian's birthday is the day after mine in a different year, with the Sun, Moon, Mercury and Venus in the same signs. Brian has Capricorn rising; mine is Libra. My intuition was correct by picking up Scorpio and Capricorn for Dr. Weiss. There was affinity between us. We were kindred souls. I knew we had shared at least one past life.

At another seminar in Baltimore to learn past life regression, I was pulled to Dr. Weiss. I had a strong desire to know about our connection. Therefore, when Brian led the group regression, he was the one who appeared to take me into my past life. My name was Sarah, a common name. Brian was my husband in, perhaps, the land of Canaan. We had three children, twin sons and a daughter. Upon being taken to the end of that life, I died peacefully in my bed at an advanced age.

In another session on the same day, I was with Brian again, this time in Babylon. I was unsure of our relationship, except romance seemed to be part of it. Perhaps I was his concubine when he was a high priest.

The Monday after the seminar I awoke with a start. Brian's former name popped into my head: *Bedeiah*. It was as though my spirit guides led me to my Unity *Metaphysical Bible Dictionary* to look up the name. Bedeiah: servant of Jehovah. The scripture read: "an Israelite who had a foreign wife after the return to Judea from the Babylonian captivity" (Ezra 10:35). For me, it was a form of confirmation. I could not go back to check the records.

Since Dr. Brian Weiss is a happily married man with a lovely family, I had no desire to do more than to learn of our past life connection. I attended another lecture of Brian's in Boston, and he later presented workshops in conjunction with medium James Van Praagh on a cruise through the Greek Islands in the year 2000. Later that summer, Brian had a reading. Dr. Weiss has continued with his good work throughout the world.

Many writers create stories based upon past lives without consciously remembering the persons or events. The stories are elaborated through imagination, or by tuning in to the Akashic Record without being aware of the process. I have had many past life connections with those in my Kabbalah, or Qabalah group, regardless of the spelling—the word means *being receptive to divine influence*, which is advisable for all of us.

A point that needs to be made: some clients tended to become so caught up in the grandeur of another life and time that they forgot to live their present life. There is also the possibility that we live all of our lives at the same time in the Eternal Now—a difficult concept to grasp. In the final analysis, the life you are living is the only one that you can do anything about, unless you happen to be a time traveler, which is a fascinating thought. Perhaps, in reality, we are all time travelers!

Several theories of reincarnation exist that tend to confuse the matter. In a book on experiments with DMT and the pineal gland, one Buddhist sect theorizes the soul reincarnates within 49 days. That means 49 days after conception a soul attaches to a new embryo developing in a womb in accordance with personal karma. Parents may be chosen in terms of familiarity, karma and genetic disposition in accordance with Destiny. Another Buddhist group claims that the soul reincarnates within 48 hours, which means only two days out of this dimension. Quick review! I sincerely hope not, but neither do I have the last word on the matter.

In my Qabalistic training, we were taught that the soul remains out of the body twice as long as it stays in a body. If you lived to 70 that means you are unlikely to reincarnate for 140 years. Vacation time! That sounds wonderful to me. It can be so hectic on this planet.

Masters supposedly remain out of the body for 500–1,000 years, smart it seems to me, considering the relative chaos of planetary life and the reluctance of many to raise their consciousness. Spiritual evolution can be a very slow process, similar to the evolution of matter. Clairvoyant Rudolph Steiner said that mortals live only eight or nine lives on the earth. The concepts vary greatly. The Hindus claim we live 500,000 lives in human form.

What about the dearly departed who show up at séances to contact mediums to speak with their loved ones still here or move the thingy around on the Ouija board? And what about the souls stuck between planes because of suicide or from being especially evil? Those involved in metaphysics never accept Dante's hell. Go to war—hell on earth! Be in a major volcanic eruption, catastrophic earthquake, or devastating tsunami—equal hell! Go through a divorce—another kind of hell! But then, heaven is here on Earth on some days, some weeks, or for some years, although usually briefly. Fall in love and find yourself in heaven—or hell—as the case may be. Agony or ecstasy is a matter of focus, of conscious or unconscious creation. You are a co-creator with the Infinite! You only need to refine the process to achieve greater success from your efforts.

Do no harm is excellent Buddhist advice. Generating negative karma is never advisable, for everyone will ultimately pay the price in accordance with the principles of Universal Law.

Basically, a great many creative drama students are living on the Earth creating roles for themselves and others in the Divine Play, either in a simple or glorious fashion, in order to add to the constantly turning pages of planetary history. Why not create a positive, interesting, inspirational story for yourself?

Each soul is the sum total of every life and every thought and act up until the present moment. Everything we have done in the past is responsible for creating our present personality with all of its quirks and admirable traits. Our past lives have produced our present patterns in fact.

I have lived and I have died so many times, the same as every other soul on this planet. I have loved and I have lost—loved and won—with the patterns constantly changing. I have been lifted up and shot down, literally; as a Blackfoot brave, I was shot in the back with an arrow by the member of another warring tribe—and that was the end of that! I have reached the mountaintops of attainment and been cast down into the valleys of despair, only to reawaken to another day and another opportunity to learn and continue on the great adventure.

In due time, the veils between the planes of existence will disappear, or at least be more easily penetrated, so that souls may learn their lessons quicker and develop with greater expediency .

May love, joy, wisdom, excellent health and heightened awareness be your constant experience on your continuous journey, lifetime after lifetime, throughout our magnificent Universe!

THE END FOR NOW!

AUTHOR'S BIO

Patricia McLaine is an internationally known psychic, tarot reader, astrologer and writer. Her worldwide clientele includes the celebrated in the fields of entertainment, politics and business, in addition to those from every walk of life. She has written several books, appeared on television and radio shows, and been featured in newspaper and magazine articles, in addition to being presented in the Time-Life Books series, *Mysteries of the Unknown,* in the volume *Psychic Powers* as one of the "psychic elite." Her show on Blog Talk Radio, "Exploring the Paranormal with Pattie," may be heard or downloaded at www.blogtalkradio.com or on her website: www.patriciamclaine.com.

Patricia McLaine
December 1992

Pattie resides in Alexandria, Virginia.

Proof

7000929R0